THE HOUSE OF TIME

BY

DAVID BRINNING

*To my chickee
friends
Carol & Bob
Thanks so much*

This book is dedicated
to My Mother and Father,
to Amy
and
to You.

With Special Thanks to
Amy Gingras

Chapter 1

The Stage

If at death
We find memories alone
And see with clarity
The effects of all our actions,
Would not the pain we caused
Become our own hell
And all the acts of love
Be surely heaven?

"I returned to find him no longer alive," he said and drifted back from a dream so real he must have lived it time and again. With the corpse of a friend, he was alone again, alone on an island shrinking smaller in the tide, soon to disappear beneath waves. Cold, the curtain of twilight drew night from the east, erasing colors from vision, leaving only a sketch and the sound of waves washing through kelp, crashing to rock, the drops spattering near him.

"My head," he said to himself as he gently probed his brow with cold fingers, senses returning, but his hands were too numb to make fists. He forced a breath. "I must have hit my head." Searching his thoughts for pieces that came together as an answer, his mind could no better understand than his eyes could focus on the lighthouse across the sea, flashing in the clouds. All he knew was that his friend was dead and the boat, thudding and scraping, thrashed on rocks like an empty barrel.

He tried to stand, but fell back dizzied. Each breath he took chilled him further and the clothes, those wet clothes, sucked life from him. He must do something or be taken. "His coat! I must get his coat." Crawling on knees to his gone friend, he tore at the buttons of the jacket, pulled it from the body and wrapped it around himself, not bothering with the sleeves. The sounds of the sea became muffled as he huddled to the rocks to escape most of the wind.

The island was covered in darkness and the only noise above the wind was the sound of the buoys marking the rocks, one a clanging bell and one a horn, moaning randomly through the evening waves. The boat knocked against the rocks and, again, a crash and a wave swept over. The current streamed so fast that the island seemed to leap through the troughs of waves as if it were moving forward. A wake trailed swirling.

Am I to die here? Too tired to stay awake, he knew he must. As the wash of mortality flooded his mind, he saw the image of his fleshless skull. Teeth clenched, he pulled himself closer to the rocks and shuddered, chilled to where he could not warm himself, cold more overwhelming than fear. Darkness grew deeper, the air stilled, and he could not help but be engulfed in the dream once more.

There in his visions, a morning unleashed before him as a dog weaved through his knees and out the screen door to join his two boys at play in the yard. He called a farewell to his wife and children and took two stairs in one bound. Late and with a long ride ahead, he made swiftly down the clam shell path, past the gate and onto the stones that wound down the hill toward the town and main harbor. The clock on town hall chimed like a ship's clock, striking two bells to tell he was late. Two boys greeted him as they puffed up the hill to the house.

"Good morning, per-fessor," one prodded.

"Morning Robby…Malcolm. You boys well today?"

"Better than you, per-fessor!" laughed the jester.

"You're going to Stage Island today, Doctor?" the other called as the distance grew between them.

"I thought so," he yelled and turned to walk backwards. "Want to come?"

The boys weren't listening anyway, talking amongst themselves in heavy breath as they plodded up the hill, one exaggerating the steepness of the road by pushing his knees with the palms of his hands. He turned back around and stopped short by a fence to meet the earthen face of an older woman whose head appeared suddenly from chores in the garden. Through the years, her face had frozen stern, even though she was actually smiling.

"Good morning, ma'am", he said and slowed out of courtesy.

"Good morning, Doctor Wyman," she said as she posed with one hand holding a shovel on her hip and wiped her brow with the other sleeve. With a deep breath and quick exhale, she asked, "Did I hear young Malcolm say Stage Island?"

"Yes, ma'am. I'm going out there to—"

A man's voice called from the porch. "Be careful out there, Professor!" the man warned. "The rocks around that island are quite fond of taking boats for their own," the man said and then fell into a wheezing cough. As Dave moved along the fence, he met the eyes of the man, a cheery salt with his face shining in the morning, his coughing fit now over.

"Morning."

"Ayuh, fine one," he rasped, sucking on a cold pipe. "Approach her from the north-east. You'll see the rocks better that way."

"Thank you," Dave said, wondering if the man was kidding, "but I don't think we'll be going ashore...Good day." Before he could move along, the man stopped him.

"Oh, Professor," he said, dragging out the last of the word with a rising inflection. "Professaah...anything special you want a see out theyaah? It's just a pile o' rocks."

"I know, but it's a great place to dive."

The man nodded slowly, silent. Dave went. The road was lined with other small houses whose gardens spilled over fences, filling the air with a sweet life its own. Cobblestones led to the village, though a path broke off to the left and meandered down a steep hillside. The harbor appeared like a photograph pulled up slowly from an envelope of high grass.

The scent of flowers was replaced by salt and fish, borne on a freshening breeze, and the sun glistened on cat's paws as it bathed those already working among the boats. His pace quickened down the hill, his knees nearly buckling from the added burden of the slope, and soon he was waving to Thomas to bring the boat to the dock. A chill bit him as he stood in the early-morning shade of the fish house and squinted over the inlet towards the sea. Thomas released the Elizabeth from her mooring and she neared with the drone of lumbering diesels. The silence broke as he boarded, the engines ever present.

"Morning, Tom. Are you ready?" he asked in a raised voice, already knowing the answer since the man at the helm glared at him with one eyebrow raised. Elizabeth slipped by the dock in one motion and roared toward the shimmering slice in the beach.

Then something was wrong. Swimming to consciousness, freezing, shivering, rubbing his arms to warm himself, a ship's horn breached the rhythm of silence. A light swept past, a light from a searching boat.

"They're searching for us!" he yelled, forgetting.

He pushed to his feet and stumbled over the rocks, toward the sound of an engine. Again, the horn called. Where is it? Where is the boat? The light shined and blinded him.

Someone yelled, "There! See him? It's Dave Wyman."

"Keep the light on him!" another voice called out. He heard men talking. One said something about keeping the boat where it was and holding the lamp, but Dave couldn't see out as the spotlight made him wince. "Stay there, Dave!" one of them yelled over a loudspeaker. "We'll come and get you!"

A young man came in a small boat, the lamp from the larger boat lighting his way as he rowed through the rocks and onto the island. He slipped to one knee getting out of the boat, grimacing in pain for a moment as Dave approached.

"What the hell, Dave? Where's Thomas?" he cried over the waves.

Dave pointed to the other side of the mound where in the distance the Elizabeth rocked in waves crashing over her sides. "I think he's dead," he whispered in the wind. The man stared expressionless.

"Hold the boat," he said and started away. Dave took half a step and fell hard to the ground. Waves came over the rocks, washed the boat sideways and pulled it away. The man ran to it and took a line tied to the bow, then came back to Dave. He looked at him with a small flashlight, seeing a man almost unconscious, then glanced around the rocks, nowhere to anchor.

"Hold this, Dave," he said to no response. "Dave! Dave, wake up!" he shouted, pushing at him with the rope in his hand. Still no response. The danger set into his mind as another wave took the boat and tugged at the line. He had no radio and looked out to the boat with its light shining on him and held his hands out to the sides, palms up. He thought for a moment.

"I'm gonna tie the rope to your arm, Dave. Don't let go of it," he said, knowing he was talking to himself.

The next thing Dave Wyman remembered was struggling to get himself into a boat with a stranger who he was sure he knew. The man rowed them through the rocks and waves, past the wreck of the Elizabeth, out toward deep water. The spotlight silhouetted the rower as they approached the larger boat waiting. Then the water sucked out from below and they were atop a rock with a wave breaking down on them. They nearly swamped, but the rower pulled hard away from the rock as the sea filled around again. Dave fumbled in an effort to bail, but they were alongside the other boat before any water had been cast over the side. Dave clambered over the gunwale and flopped to the deck. He looked up to see the silhouette of what seemed to be the chief of police.

"One hell of a sight-seeing trip you took today, Doctor Wyman," the chief said. "A guy in an airplane radioed just before dark and said he saw a boat on the rocks here...Jesus, you're in bad shape. I'll get you a blanket!"

The other man stepped onto the boat and tied the dingy line to a stern cleat, calling out, "Thomas Soverge is dead!"

The chief paled and said, "Are you sure? We should go back."

"He's dead, all right. I couldn't lift him by myself. He'll make it through the night where he is. That's more than I can say for us if we go back ashore. It's easier on the way in, but you can't see a damn thing comin' back. The light blinds you. Let's go. I brought soup, Dave. I'll get you some. Just sit here. We'll be home soon."

The chief returned to the helm as Dave Wyman struggled to sit up and wrap himself in blankets as the propellers engaged, pushing them from the island. The man who was familiar to Dave, his name still forgotten, handed him a steaming mug. The liquid was hard to contain for the waves and spilled over his hands, burning the numbness. The nameless man went to the wheel and talked to the chief. Dave couldn't hear what they said as he spilled the soup, but he thought, How did he know Thomas was dead?

The engines yawned to life and the boat plowed into darkness, toward a beacon by the harbor. The warmth of soup flowed into Dave and fear began to leave his body, overwhelmed by exhaustion.

"Coast Guard Portland, Coast Guard Portland, this is Harbor Patrol Wianno on Channel One Six, over," said the chief into a microphone, slowly, as if an exclamation point followed most of the words. The other man steered the boat through unseen waves. Dave watched with his eyes half open and chin to his chest, his nutant head shifting with the seas.

"Vessel calling Coast Guard Portland, switch to Channel Two Two, over."

The chief switched the radio and called back, "Coast Guard Portland, Harbor Patrol Wianno, over."

"Harbor Patrol Wianno, Coast Guard Portland, go ahead, over."

"Coast Guard Portland, this is Chief Prence from Wianno. We've just picked up a man from a wreck on Stage Island. We are headed back to Wianno. Apparently, another man is dead and his body remains on Stage Island. Repeat, a man is dead and his body remains on Stage Island. Male, Caucasian, mid-forties, over."

"Harbor Patrol Wianno, Coast Guard Portland, that's a Charley. We will dispatch to Stage Island, over."

7

"Roger. I'll call you when I get to the harbor on Wianno. Harbor Patrol Wianno out."

The chief came to Dave and asked what happened.

"I returned to find him no longer alive," he said, and drifted.

The chief looked at him with a flashlight and asked, "Did you hit your head, Professor?" There came no answer. "I'll get a doctor to come down to the pier. You just sit tight. I'll get some more blankets." He made his way back to the helm and radio and told the other man to keep Dave warm.

Awake, Dave was in bed. A dream, he thought, for an early-morning confusion made him feel like he awoke into a dream. The lamp seemed upside down in the sunrise and gulls laughed outside, but the pain he felt as he sat forward forced him back to the pillow with a wince. His wife came to the room, kissed his forehead and told him not to speak. He whispered for her to say what she knew.

"Honey, you were in a wreck. You hit your head on something. You have a concussion. Do you remember?"

He nodded painfully. "Sort of."

"Do you remember about Thomas?"

Slowly, he recounted, "He's dead."

"Yes," she sobbed, burying her head into his chest and hugging him. "I'm so sorry." She sniffed. He tried to hug back, but the pain was too much. They lay there for a while, both crying for a lost friend, and then she sat up, composed, and wiped her face with her wrists. "Honey, the police want to talk to you. They said that they would come this morning. Do you remember anything?" He could only shake his head.

"I'll bring you some tea and toast. Do you want anything else?"

He shook his head once again.

Through the pane beside his bed, Davis Wyman followed a flock of starlings as they approached, darting back and forth like schooling fish, flashing black, then silver, then black again. In unison, they landed on a tree, then they took to wing and landed by a puddle to drink. Their heads dipped to the water and rose to the sky, the fluid flowing down their desperate throats. Each skittish bird turned its head and looked around before taking another drink. At once, they all flew again, flittered in a silver circle through the air, then back to the tree, then on wing, the puddle, the tree, the puddle and so on until the puddle was nearly gone. Then they flew away, leaving the island.

The sky was dim, but the sun broke through the clouds every now and again. The room brightened each time and as soon as he no longer needed to squint, the light faded and he had to wait for his eyes to readjust. He closed his eyes for what seemed a while until he heard a car approach.

An unmarked police car is as obvious as one with lights flashing on top of it, he thought as one approached. Perhaps it's the fact that it looks like a cop car, perhaps it's the headlights, or maybe it's the look of the person driving. Dave noticed them because of his driving record. He used to drive like James Dean. Nevertheless, such a car came up the hill and into the driveway and he was stricken with a feeling of flight, a feeling never before had in his body. Perhaps he was simply anxious.

Two men climbed from the car and stepped to the front door. His wife greeted them as he watched from the window by his bed. He heard them speak, but could not discern the words. Then the three of them clogged up the wooden stairs, Dave's wife first to announce them.

"The—" she said, cutting herself off when she knew it was obvious what she was going to say.

"Send them in," Dave said.

The men entered the room with hats in hand. His wife opened the window, then left after asking if anyone wanted coffee or something to drink. Dave recognized one of the men as the local police, Chief Jim Prence. He did not know the other man, but his matching socks told that he was not from the island. So did his jacket and tie.

"Good morning, Dave," said Chief Prence. "How are you feeling?"

"I can't think of a witty response, Chief, so I'll just say fine," he answered with a half smile.

The chief cracked a sad smile back. "Dave, I can't tell you how sorry everyone is about Thomas. We know you were friends." Dave looked away for a moment. "This is Sergeant Kipridge. He's with the state police."

"Hello, Doctor Wyman," the sergeant said with a nod.

The chief continued, "There seems to be a small problem, Dave. Can we talk?"

"What sort of a problem? Thomas is dead. That's not a small problem," Dave said, realizing he was being short with them. "Please," he said, "excuse me. Please sit down."

Sergeant Kipridge took a seat on the windowsill, but Chief Prence, after looking around to see only a rocking chair, remained standing by the door. The sunlight again crept from behind the clouds and in through the window like a spotlight on the bed, keeping the faces of these visitors cloaked in shadow while Dave's eyes adjusted.

The chief started slowly. "The problem is...that we...we haven't found his body." Silence clutched the room for a moment, with no one knowing what to say and none having the urge to speak. "There's more," he continued. "But first, are you sure he was dead? You were in bad shape when we brought you in."

"I'm pretty sure. I can't say I'm positive, but… Who was the kid who rowed me out to the boat? He was sure, wasn't he?" He paused. "What more is there?"

"That was one of my officers, actually the assistant harbormaster. He agrees that Thomas was dead, but—"

"But what," Dave flared.

"He insists that Thomas had a gunshot wound."

Dave's cheeks fell and crumpled in disbelief and Sergeant Kipridge stood up. "We're not making any accusations, Doctor Wyman," he said. "We just want to find out what happened. We've been out to Stage Island and found nothing. Was there anyone else with you yesterday? Anyone at all?"

Dave could only answer no, but bits of his memory were jostled. He became apparently confused. *A gunshot wound?*

"I'd like to swab your hand for traces of gunpowder, if I may."

"What? What are my rights, here? No, I don't think so."

"Doctor Wyman, I have a warrant," Sergeant Kipridge said as he pulled papers from his jacket. "You could make it easy. We can do this here or down at the station."

"You have got to be kidding me!" Dave said as he looked at the warrant. He felt blood rush to his head and echo his heartbeat. The look of incredulity on his face didn't change much from the pain. He put a hand to his head. "Based on someone's opinion in the dark? He's just a kid!"

"That kid risked his life to save yours!" snapped the chief.

"He is still just a kid!" Dave said, and the chief stopped short of saying more, his expression agreeing. Dave continued, imploring to be left alone, "He's a kid who is wrong. How many head wounds has he ever seen in his life? Minor cuts on your head bleed badly. He's mistaken. Thomas was my friend. Why would I shoot him?"

After a brief pause, the sergeant said calmly "That's all good and well, sir. However, that kid is a government official. I could arrest you on obstruction charges, I believe, but that's not what I want. This is what I want to do. Now, if I can get it done, we'll be leaving."

Dave extended his right arm and the sergeant swabbed it with some sort of wipe with cool solvent. He placed the swab in a bag and took out another and swabbed the under-side of his arm.

"Now, the other arm, please."

With a sigh, Dave complied.

"I also want to take a photo of your head wound, just for the record." He took a camera from his bag and snapped a photograph, the flash blinding Dave momentarily as the sun had.

"Well," the sergeant continued, "I don't want to take anymore of your time today. The doctor said you have a pretty bad concussion. Relax. Amnesia rarely lasts more than a day or so. Just rest up, and if you do remember anything, please call me or Chief Prence." He handed Dave a card with the state police insignia emblazoned on it.

"One more thing, Doctor Wyman," he insisted. "The boat you were on, the Elizabeth. We haven't found her yet. Do you recall what happened to the boat? The Chief here says she was on the rocks last night."

"Maybe Thomas took her. I wouldn't put it past him if he were still alive. If I were left on that island alone, I would've swam out to that boat and tried to do something…"

"She was a wooden boat, though. Was she breaking up?"

Dave shrugged and shook his head and stared past the men as they filed down the stairs. They said goodbye to his wife, Aimee, and he heard every word through the open window. The men walked off the porch and spoke as though Dave couldn't hear them, but every word was clear. He remembered the times of childhood when adults spoke of him and others as though they were not there, like they would not understand. Adults said things with authority, disregarding the fact that a child isn't stupid, but merely irresponsible. People said things about others in front of Dave and the other kids, thinking they were too young to know the meaning, but they would go to another room and talk about it. As such, these men talked about Dave, about this case, in his front yard as they meandered to their car. Dave heard the sergeant say the head wound looked like a pistol whip and that he'd wait a day or two before he believed an amnesia story involving a dead man.

Another day started on the edge of the world. The sky, once black, was now warming. The clear air was gray, as if covered by clouds, and Dave walked toward the harbor, the day growing older and birds fussing over whatever it is that excites them so in the morning. Approaching the main wharf, he saw no one, but as he stepped under the porch roof, someone turned to him, only turning away when he knew Dave was no one he knew. A small outboard sputtered past, its wake creaking the dock below the pier, and the ferry stood idle, its engines pulsing quietly, belching cool water through the exhaust in a random rhythm.

Across the calm water, a flame passed to a point on the horizon as the sun breached the sea. The low clouds were first to come ablaze, but the flame quickly crossed the bay and caught the tip of the lighthouse. It burned down the tower to the house and beach grass and passed along the dunes, the grass waving in wind and sun-soaked flame. Soon the boats floating on the falling tide burst into glowing embers of the new day. Dave leaned on the rail and watched the day flow into the harbor on the waves beyond the breakwater. On the hill above, windows flared in the heat. The fish house blazed beside him.

"Beautiful morning, isn't it?" asked the man standing nearby, sucking on a cigarette, the ash near his fingers. He flicked the butt over the rail and Dave watched it fall and sizzle in the brine, looking up to find the fire quenched and the gates to the ferry opening. The man was gone, too, having walked down the wharf to assist with the lines. A few early risers approached and a small girl whined to her mother about their plans. "I wish my day was so simple," Dave said silently.

He paced down the pier and called to a dockhand laying a hawser in a flat circle on the deck.

"Good morning, sir. How are you?" said the worker.

"I'm good, except for one problem."

"What's that, sir?"

"I've left my money up at my house and I'm afraid you'll leave before I get back. I'm going to the bank on the mainland, can I pay you on my way back here?"

"Sure, whatever. You look honest." He laughed. "Whatever that is."

Dave smiled. He was going ashore. With the others, he boarded and waited for the ferry to leave. It took enough time for the ferry to untie that he could have made it home and back, but he didn't want to wake anyone there at the house. He passed the time standing on deck watching the calm water rise and fall, not in waves, just randomly bobbing, higher and lower against the pier. A gull floated by, aglide on the crisp morning air, his beak as yellow as his eye, which spied Dave for any food he might offer.

The mate asked him to move away from the docking line so they could leave, and soon the ship backed from the pier, where no one seemed to notice the horn blaring. The ferry wheeled around and made way towards the ocean. They rounded the last buoy, the waves built to a spray, and Dave saw his house alone on the hillside; he envisioned his family waking to find him not there, the note on the table. From this vantage, memories came back to him.

It was to have been a small day, he remembered. A cold morning in June, the family away, he built a fire and settled with a book into one of the old, winged rockers by the wood stove. The popping fire scented the room while rain tapped on wrinkled windows too old to keep wind from moaning through them. A door upstairs rattled as gusts filled the house and he dozed in the warmth cast from the fire, every now and again bolting awake as though he had forgotten to breathe. Then something brushed by him and he opened his eyes and she was there, no farther than his hand, yet not.

Her eyes seemed an urgent whisper. "Don't worry, don't be afraid," she said as the wind crushed down on the house and sucked the air back through the windows.

"I'm not afraid," he breathed out, even though he was. She stood there, smiling slightly, and said nothing for the longest time. She just stared into him and he into her. She took his hand, yet he felt nothing. She seemed to speak, but then the door opened and closed and she disappeared. It was as if he had just woken from a dream in which his eyes never closed. His wife came to him and asked if he was all right. He told her "yes" and of his strange dream, but dismissed it as only a dream. She and the kids had left what seemed like moments ago and yet the whole day had passed. The fire had long since burned out.

Weeks went by before he had a moment to himself in the house. He told no one else of his encounter with the woman, though he longed for her like a lover never kissed. His chance would come, he prayed, when his wife took the kids to visit with her parents high in the woods of the mainland. He sat by the fire for hours waiting for her to appear, but she never did. He even called for her, not knowing what to call her, and he cursed when she refused to show. Then he cursed himself a fool.

On the day that everyone was to return, a storm built and the ferries were canceled. His wife called to say that they were all right and that they would stay with friends in Portland. Shortly after they hung up, the power flickered and failed for about ten minutes.

With nothing left to do, he placed more logs among the embers and they crackled to flame. The dog howled on the porch to be let in and headed straight for the wood stove while Dave fought to latch the screen door again. He returned to the floor by the fire and stroked the dog's hair as it dried and he listened to the fire and the storm and the sea. He felt cool wind pass through the closed windows and wash over him as he moved to the chair, only to find her sitting across from him.

The moment stretched eternal as she spoke in windswept song. Lyrical fragments overlapped his thoughts with stories of places she'd been, people she'd met or known, books read in different languages. Stories came in bits. He tried to ask questions, but couldn't breathe a word. She said something funny and he thought he laughed aloud, but noticed that their faces never changed from a smile, conversing the night without speaking. Her stories flowed without effort or motion or sound.

It seemed to dawn on them both at once that something was wrong, though nothing in the world could be wrong. So what if he was seeing ghosts. This one is quite charming, actually. But something truly was wrong, and that is why this revenant was there.

"I came here in…" she said, but the fragment was lost. Words became images flashing. He saw a boat. He did not want to see anything more. It was dark, tumbling, the waves. He saw Stage Island.

The ferry let loose her horn and brought Dave back from his thoughts to watch the boat spin around and back to the pier. The small group of tourists waiting to board had no idea that beneath their feet ran a large pipe that takes sewage from the city and deposits it only a hundred yards into the harbor. As Dave wound through the streets past steaming manholes, he imagined the sewer below and seemed to follow it to his destination.

Sewers beneath the city, any city, become more acrid in the summer, yet the odor seemed concentrated on this corner, which is odd for the streets carry signs with the most respectable names. Still, though, the odor was piled up about the place like compost. At that corner, where the streets converge at an angle, stood a triangular building that came to a point, one wide enough for a single window, and stretched back such that standing at that end provided a perspective where the building seemed larger than it truly was.

On the ground floor was a popular cafe with outdoor seating. It must have been the address, the legend, and perhaps a favorable wind that kept it popular, but the people were content to sit there on a breezeless day and soak up whatever atmosphere was available in the contrasting sapid odors from the kitchen and that from the tunnels below. His prejudice must be noted, however, for in that building, at the top of a staircase winding up the middle of the fat end, sat the office of his attorney, a friend who gladly took his money for advice he rarely needed.

His attorney sighed, having listened to the story of ghosts just told by Davis Wyman, and now he wished that he wasn't Dave's closest adviser. "So, you went out there, to…uh…find something?" he said.

"I suppose," Dave answered. In the moment before anyone spoke again, there in the corner office of the triangular building, Dave watched the shadow of a pinnacle trace across the carpet and heard every sound from the open windows.

"Did you?" the lawyer asked.

Dave almost had to ask what he meant, but answered, "I don't remember."

"Was Thomas involved in it?"

"I think so," he said, hoping he not said more than he wanted to say.

"You think so. Well, Dave, you can't keep the amnesia thing up for too long, especially if Thomas' body turns up with a bullet in it." He sat back with the smugness that only a lawyer would show. "The police are—"

"I know, I know," Dave said. "I know about that, but what advice can you give me for now?"

"Dave, I've known you for years. You are not the type of person to just up and kill a friend. You're much too smart and you don't get angry. The chances are that the kid is wrong. He's young and not even a cop. The assistant harbormaster never gets to see a crime scene. He knew Thomas and was freaked out. It was dark. He was scared. You've got a head wound; Thomas might have, also. There can be a lot of blood with even a small cut on your head. In the dark, they can look pretty gruesome.

"You've got until they find his body. If there is a gunshot wound, you will be arrested. You're going to have to talk, but only to me. Certainly, don't say anything about ghosts. Jesus, if you need to mount a defense against something and your first story on the record has ghosts in it, they're going to put you away somewhere. Don't tell anything to anyone, especially the police, without telling me first." He paused for a moment, like he was running a check on his systems because he felt somewhat inclined to believe. "Did she tell you her name?"

"No," Dave said, shaking his head, incredulous at his own words.

"Well, don't go talking about this. If you're really serious, go to the library and look for a missing person if it helps you, but don't talk to anyone about it. I'm serious, Dave. And remember, they're small-town people. They tend to blow things out of proportion in a situation like this. There's no reason in the world for this to be anything but a tragic accident. You're no killer, Dave. So keep that in mind and just be cool." He paused for a while, then continued with a look of concern, "Have you seen a real doctor, yet?"

Not much more enlightened than that morning, Dave followed the sewer line past panhandlers on his way to the boat that would take him back to a place where no one begged for change. He boarded the ferry hoping to find himself on a quiet trip back to the island and climbed to the observation deck to watch the cars embark. Two buses waited for the signal as cars loaded onto the side lanes. Then one bus inched onto the boat and he could feel the load shift the hull, rocking it slowly backward, then forward, and then side to side as the bus came to a stop in the center lane with just the back window still showing below his feet. More cars loaded, then the second bus crept on board, again shifting the boat and stopping as close to the first bus as it possibly could, the air brakes creaking and squeaking, then blowing out a loud hiss before the engine went silent.

Soon the door opened and out stepped a fat man in outlandish attire: light blue plaid shorts and a shirt that clashed even though it was the same type of cloth. His hat clashed even more. The jovial man jiggled with roaring laughter as from the bus came running forty children. From the first bus, Dave could hear another forty and soon they were scrambling all over the deck, shrieking, pushing, playing without toys. Seven girls chased one cowering boy, calling, "He's going out with me!" "No, he's going out with *me!*"

The horn sounded just before they left the pier and all hell broke loose. The kids screamed even louder and the ship's flag wrapped around a wire that caused it to beat against the wind. The boat made it down river to the sea and started to pitch and roll in the waves. Some fool had set his car alarm—where is it going on a ferry?—and the motion detector felt the ocean and started the siren wailing three tones: one like a fire engine, one like a European police car, and one like some of the video games being played inside the main cabin. The alarm could not be shut off because one of the buses blocked the door, so the sound stayed with them, as well as the children and the beating flag, for the rest of the trip.

Dave searched through all the decks to find a secluded place, but there was none. Everywhere he went there were children screaming. All those little faces with minds and lives still to be found had no idea how hard they made it for Dave to find his life, changed in an instant and he did not know how.

Standing by the starboard rail, children bumping into him as they ran in circles around the cabin, Dave's eyes stared at a point far to sea where a dark knife blade stood tall on a horizon that melded into the sky with no discernible edge. A sail. He watched closely, blocking all else from his mind, his eyes fixed on the ship as it pounded gently closer. She sailed nearer, very slowly, as the sun glimmered on the waves and prepared to set.

Dave forced the sounds out and waited for the sailboat to pass. Eventually, she came close enough to see one man at the helm, all alone with his silent ship. The boat passed through the channel of sunlight and the man waved.

"It's Thomas!" Dave cried and walked quickly toward the stern, around the life rafts, and tried to focus on the man's face as he braced to pass through the wake of the ferry. It could not be Thomas, he thought. I have been staring too long at the daylight. His head sank into his hands and he closed his eyes, dozing until the sea sprayed his face.

Chapter 2

Another Story

Years later, another story took place on the island. Early in the spring and high on a dune, a house stood and its windows flared with the reflection of the sun as it sank into the sea and its light slowly followed. Inside the house, a woman, not small but feeling so, rummaged through a closet for a blanket that she thought she'd put away for the year.

It had snowed in May before, thought Ursa Taylor before accidentally kicking the dresser while walking to the bedroom with a down comforter spilling from her arms. The pain followed moments after the fact. She placed down her bundle of blanket and sat on the edge of the bed, hearing Mozart's Jupiter flowing soft then loud from the radio. She turned to watch the flakes fall and rise in the last of the light outside the house.

She rose and spread the blanket over the bed, methodically smoothing the cover to the sheets, and thought of the cold night to come and then of the last time she saw snow so late in the year. She paused a while until she remembered her husband when he was young, still alive. What did he do that day, that time it snowed, when we got the boats ready for the summer and it snowed as we set the sails?

"It's so odd that it would snow now," she said aloud, then her eye caught a shell that had somehow made its way to the porch outside the bedroom. Funny what the wind will do, she thought. Or a bird. Maybe a bird dropped it there.

She sat again, the pain from her foot still present, and thought what she'd been thinking all day, how she's still young enough to move about freely, that the injury she suffered during the winter had hobbled her just for a while. She told herself to stop thinking about death. Maybe she should move away. She'd been here for most of her life and, while it was no different than other places and so full come summer, the winters were just bitter, hard. Her son knew it long ago, and if he had found a ship he liked, he never would have stayed the past winter, but he did and Ursa wasn't sure if he'd ever come back now that he'd lined up a good post in a few weeks. And her friends—especially with that roughest of winters —it seemed all they spoke of was death or the nursing home they'd selected and been insured for should they need it suddenly.

I've got to get away from it, she thought, this talk of death, and she pushed herself up and straightened herself and rearranged the things on her dresser that she'd knocked aside with the comforter when she tripped. She looked at herself in the mirror. She was still young at sixty-five and pretty well off for a woman her age, her doctor assured her. It was just a hairline fracture, a broken leg, fortunately not a hip, and her muscles were still strong. Sure it would take a bit longer to heal at that age, but nothing needed replacement. She needn't worry.

It threw her into a spin, though, the pain and the torment of living so alone as the snow kept piling higher, keeping her trapped with crutches for much of the winter. And now it snowed still, even though spring had shown its promise of another summer. She was glad her son was around to bring food and check up on her, but he was leaving soon.

He told her exactly why over the course of the winter. It wasn't because he hated it so much, but his wife couldn't bear it and his children would need a school soon, a real school, not someplace where kids grew up knowing nothing but the sea. The sea was nowhere in the future. They'd over-fished it and now kids found it easier to smoke dope and stare at the TV where freaks did whatever they could to attract their attention, in the meantime distracting them so they could pick their pocket or steal a piece of their soul.

She smiled at that thought, seeing in her son's words some of her own from years past, but she knew what he meant. The island's schools were only good for the early grades. Then kids grew up in a world of dejection as their parents fought over money because there was little to be made here, especially in winter when boats rarely went out, and all that was left to do then was get on each other's nerves. Or drink. That was what many folks did in her day. Now it wasn't much different, she supposed.

Still, there was summer and people swarmed here to bask on the beach or simply strive to do nothing at all. Then they'd go and take their money with them, and those who remained would joke about winter and make like it wasn't so bad. And it wasn't until a few days past the New Year when the harbor froze again and left you feeling trapped unless you took off for warmer or more exciting places. The feeling of springtime was even more special if you'd stayed for the winter, and that feeling would stretch through the fall and lull you into staying the winter again. She was sure of it. That's what kept her here all these years.

She smiled at herself in the mirror as she thought back to the days when her hair was long and brown-turned-golden by days in the sun. She was a child on the beach again, running with a bucket to show Daddy the crab she had caught with her own bare hands and he was proud of her. Not because she was brave enough to pluck a crab from the sea, as she thought at the time, but because she was so excited and happy all of the time. She loved her father so and he loved her, taking time every chance to tell her with a hug. And that love grew stronger every day so that when he was old and tired, he'd tell her again and she'd say she knew and to rest, and she cared for him until the moment he was finally silent and they turned off the machines that kept him alive.

The mirror showed that the sun had taken its toll on her skin by the time she reached sixty, but she didn't care. She wouldn't trade those days in the sun for a fresh face now. Her father taught her to sail when she was too young to remember anything else and those days went by so fast and never came quickly enough. They'd sail all day long, even going past the same places two or three times in an afternoon just to stay out on the water. When she got older, they started to race and that was how she met her husband.

Even though she was too young to know it, she'd met more than just someone to race with, but they raced together each weekend. They'd win and lose, each chiding the other for the loss and claiming the victory, but it was merely flirtatious banter and they were too young to know it. Then, as they grew and school made their summers grow shorter, they started to date and to see each other back on the mainland at college. The distance between schools was just enough to keep them away and wanting to be closer.

After graduation, he came to the island to fish, but he knew that wasn't going to be all that he did with himself. She worked tables and knew that wasn't all for her, either, but the island was home now, so much more so than any place on the mainland they'd ever been, and the happiness they had with each other made them never want to leave it. They conversed over hours of candles and beach fires and one day he brought her a small box and said she was all that there was for him. There was no other but she, and of course she said yes, for there was no one but him, either.

The days became whirlwinds and there was hardly time for each other. She took a job at the bank and worked her way from teller to assistant manager, but that wasn't what she really wanted, so she used her degree and became a teacher as well. That gave her a job at the bank in the summer when they needed her most and she taught the young kids all winter long. She would still wait on tables now and again just to keep busy and help save for a house of their own.

He studied the sea and took courses and exams, becoming first a charter boat captain—the youngest one on the island still to this day—then moving on to bigger boats and to ships until he became captain of a tugboat by the time their son was born. He was only gone a week at a time as the boy grew to a toddler. Then came the big jobs: first mate on a freighter and then on to captain.

His time away wasn't as hard on her as she thought it would be and their son knew nothing else, so it wasn't a burden to him. At least, they couldn't tell, and he grew up to be a fine man. And when her husband came home, it was as though nothing had changed. Meals and chores became part of their dreams. They'd laugh together and sail together in the summer, both of them showing their boy how to sail and to fish and to eat what they grew in the garden. Then he'd be away again for a while, but never so long that he couldn't make up for the time gone. When he was home, the three of them rarely saw anyone else.

Once, when their son was about ten, her husband's ship was bound for a port near the island and he brought her as close as he could. He called from the radiophone the day before and said they would be by around ten in the morning. She brought their son to the porch to watch the ship as she passed—all six hundred feet of her—and the crew fired green practice flares and blasted the horn. She saw the look in the boy's eyes and knew he was his father's son. She took him to the mainland to visit the ship and that was the day they were sure of their boy's future.

In that time, they hardly noticed the change in the island itself. While people had flocked there in the summers, for the most part they'd leave everything behind. Then a part of the island silently left. Those who had first come to the island owned all that there was and left it to their children. Most of them stayed or returned for the summer, but only a farmer needs so much land and no one really farmed on the island anymore. So the land became the best kind of investment—bought for a song, passed on for a dance and sold to the highest bidder as the place became a haven.

As word spread of the solitude, the immaculate views and the abundance of land, people started to subdivide their property. The ownership of the island left without so much as a word or a care until the first big development came. Then the papers predicted the end of heaven. More houses would go up and they'd be rented and more people would come and fall in love with the place and the cycle would go on. The term "wash ashore" became a way to describe those who'd come for a week and stay the rest of their lives. Resentment built up between the newcomers and those who had been there forever.

People not only washed onto the shores, they also washed away. As the population grew, so did some people's grudges. Residents migrated away to live somewhere with other things to offer: better schools, better jobs, warmer climates, cheaper housing, no swarms of people in the summer. People left just to leave, yet more people came than moved away.

Now her son was leaving and she wasn't sure what to do next. She could easily sell the house and make enough money that she could move almost anywhere, but she wanted to stay for as long as she could. She didn't need the money. She was afraid of being alone, though. She had friends, but it wouldn't be the same without her son and the grandchildren. It just wouldn't be the same at all without the family to remind her of the life that she had—a life so nearly perfect that she longed for it to stay just a while longer.

The mirror showed a face near tears. My, she thought to herself, you've never been this way before. Surely there is something you can do. There must be someway to change, to make life new again. You're not so old that you can't carry on and do something more.

She sat on the bed once again, the pain in her leg more a bother than a pain, but still she couldn't do all that she wanted. With her son gone, she was afraid she might not even be able to carry things from the store or work the garden, yet she knew she had to do something just to keep herself going. She tried to think of the things that she had done in the past, things that didn't require her to walk so much, and she again heard the music coming from the radio and she smiled once more in the mirror.

After a moment, Ursa pushed herself up to her feet, stretched her leg and stepped to the stairway and down to the kitchen where she telephoned a friend just to talk. She told her she needed to do something with herself. They spoke for a while, Ursa not wanting to take back a gift, though it was really just a loan, and her friend agreed to return her piano since it was just a decoration in her house anyway.

After she hung up, Ursa sat at the table and looked at a notepad that she bought earlier in the afternoon. She might be able to get help without having to pay for it, she thought, and then scribbled a note:

> *Older woman desires a live-in person. Her home is clean and warm. She requires no personal care but perhaps help with supper, grocery shopping and some gardening. The live-in person could have a job. House is not far from the center of town.*

She finished the note with the last four digits of her son's phone number. From any phone on the island you could reach another by dialing only the last four digits of the number. Pay phones placed the call for free. Ursa saw herself posting the note on the town notice board in the morning and closed her tired eyes, the ticks of the clock lulling her asleep. When she snapped back awake, she looked up to notice that the clock in the other room had come unwound, the pendulum stopped, and that nothing had been written on the notepad.

Chapter 3

The House of Time

Thomas Soverge was dead, that fact near certain, but when he lived it was in a house and a group of small buildings sitting atop a dune-cliff overlooking the surf. The sand of the dune rose high to the house, approaching the windows of the rear, and swirled around front to drift on the porch. One side was lined by a snow fence that fell this way and that, victim to the unsettling sand. It kept nothing in nor out since the grains slipped easily through it and the fence slowly snaked as the dune shifted through weeks and years.

The house, though pickled by time and exposure, had fought off the elements through the careful attention of its owner. A fresh shingle showed here and there, and green shutters painted only the previous year were already peeling and swung outward to the start of the Indian summer.

Getting to this home was no easy chore. A road skinnied through a long, sandy nook, eventually coming to a place where vehicles were left behind. From there, it was a walking effort, yet the view improved with each step. A footpath led up the dune through beach grass and scrub, and then between a bush and the first building. The path steepened to the house and, once there, one stepped straight from the sand to the porch, the stairway long ago swallowed.

The grit, whipped to the air, had etched itself on the trim, the shingles, the glass and the door. The latch lifted with a clack and the door fell open, pushed from below by the sand drift, now an integral part of the hallway floor. Inside, the house warmed in setting sunlight falling through two large windows looking out to the sea, the air perfumed by a fire from another night. A poster of Van Gogh's Irises wilted from the wall.

The house was filled with tiny rooms, each a separate world with a different purpose and style. To the right of the entranceway, the kitchen was sparse and unused; the burden of carrying sacks up from the road made food here a luxury. Yet, something had come to life in the garbage can and the odor was quite foul. A short hallway led to the main room, which was dark but for swathes of light beaming in through the windows, painting the walls a new shade and highlighting parts of the treasures brought back from abroad, tokens of time taken elsewhere, and everywhere the sand.

Thomas was a man who often left the island in winter. He worked hard all summer so he could travel when things went cold. He went everywhere he could imagine and collected all he could afford, sometimes coming back to the island with barely enough money to pay for the ferry, and on every shelf-space was some part of his life story.

The house had belonged to Mr. Thomas Soverge, Sr., a prominent man of stature and wit, father of the recently deceased. His son lacked those traits, but was no less content living in his shadow. A housewright and a fisherman and a builder of boats, the man still to be buried, indeed, yet to be found, was both well read and knowing, though he rarely spoke out when facts went challenged. He kept the house neat, though the sand could never really be swept from corners or any trinket of memorabilia.

Many photographs chronicled the times of the family, but one in particular captured attention like no other. It was of Elizabeth, a child whose charm led lips to laughter and souls to dance. The image framed her standing side to a window, light passing through a quilted curtain and parting her dark curls and wan face in a crescent. She had her thumb to her mouth, a smile of shy adoration and her mother's white sweater wrapped round her shoulders. The picture had only one chance to be taken for the young girl soon after leapt to her father with an ecstatic shriek of childhood happiness.

Elizabeth was Thomas' daughter, whom he loved and missed more each day since she drowned in the waves behind the house, pulled from the beach by a riptide that was clearly visible to any adult. After that day, he began to drink his life away. He lived each day as if they were pulled from a matchbook, lit one by one and watched till they burned his finger. A bad year later, his wife left him with his memories, his problems and sorrow, left him to this island. He missed her, though not nearly as much as Elizabeth, his pain poetic, timeless.

To make that day all the more horrible, he tried, he had the opportunity, the chance, to save her. He was to watch her and she sneaked away for but a moment, one of those moments you long for the rest of your days to have again and do differently. As he began to search for her, he heard her cry and leapt over and down the dune as she swept seaward, dove to the waves and swam fast, arriving in time only to feel the life leave her and accompany her body in the riptide as the shoreline fell from view.

The chief of police blew dust from the picture of Elizabeth, put it back on the table and glanced over the window sill, until then unaware of a man standing on the dune, facing out over the ocean, smoking and barely holding a bottle between his thumb and first fingers. He drank from a glass, slowly, more like breathing, holding in the same hand a smoldering handroll, which he toked in time with the wind. The chief moved through the side door with enough sound to be noticed and met the eyes of Eddie Vanson, who turned and walked toward the policeman as he inhaled deeply from a joint.

"You going to arrest me for this?" he asked.

"I don't think so, Eddie," he said with a slow shake of his head.

The two men forced a smile and shook hands. "A few years ago," Eddie said with hesitation, "when Thomas stopped drinking so much…he bought this brandy…It's damn good brandy…He said, 'When one of us dies, the other will stand here at sunset and drink this entire bottle.' I guess maybe he knew what the feeling was like. Would you like some?" He gestured with the bottle.

"I can't turn down a dead man's poison," the chief pursed his lips and forced a sideways smile, hoping to cheer him.

The two men went back into the house through the side door, respectfully tapping the sand from their shoes outside. Eddie stepped softly to the kitchen and fetched a glass from the cupboard. He was as familiar with the place as any best friend would be. The two had grown up together, the island way. The chief knew that losing Thomas was a severe blow to Eddie, but no one else could know just how hard it really hit him.

These men chatted, awkwardly at first, as would any men who were at opposite ends of a spectrum, but as the liquor closed the generations, the conversation flowed honest and warm. They talked of the times of trouble, the day years ago when the elder had confiscated the kid's mini-bike, and of losing friends and fathers.

Their fathers had fallen together, victims of the sea whose sounds never leave you, no matter where on the island you stand. The chief was old enough to see the humanity in it, to realize his own mortality, but Eddie refused to believe that his father was dead. There was no body to prove it, so he thought that the man had just gone away for a while and would come back. His father had simply run off from him and his mother as she said he would in their arguments. Eddie, twenty years younger than the chief, lost more than a man that day. He lost the guidance of an elder, and survived alone with his mother, who took to the island habits: drinking through days and summer nights with this man or another.

The older man was much older the day his father died, nearly old enough to expect it, though one never can. He aged a great deal in one moment with the realization that he now was an elder of the island, that younger men would look to him for guidance and he could no longer look up to his father for answers.

He held an untold promise to mind after the son of his father's mate, the boy's teary face carved so deep in his thoughts that he always saw it, even to this day, even when he stared straight at him. He gave Eddie money when he realized that the boy's mother had spent unwisely the small sums given her. His wife cooked for Eddie, too, making sure that he ate a good meal as often as possible. But on a day that both wished never passed, when Eddie was a young man and the chief a man with a point to prove, the two met at a crossing of thoughts and Eddie was arrested with a harvest of marijuana. He was not meant to go to jail, but he did, and from thereafter they knew that neither was right and that a mistake had been made.

Eddie said he learned nothing in the joint except how to bench press while keeping an eye out so no one got close enough to jag you with a make-shift shiv. They weren't really knives, simply sharp pointed sticks made of plastic, or wood, or a spoon handle...a toothbrush...anything.

When he was convicted, he was let out on bail until sentencing. He went to see Chief Prence at his office. Prence had tried to use his influence to get the court's lenience and told Eddie to come as soon as he got back to the island. The chief, then a lieutenant, waited anxiously to expiate in whatever way he could. He thought all he could do now, in addition to trying to get the DA to ask for a minimum sentence, was to prepare Eddie for jail. He told him:

"I'm sorry this happened. I'd blame the state cops if I were to blame anyone but myself. I should have told you to knock it off, but there's nothin' I can do anymore. I'm workin' on the DA. I want him to ask for only a few months. Whatever the sentence, and I know you're goin' to jail, but whatever the sentence, I'll visit you before they take you away. I've asked guys I know, men who are prison guards, what you should do and they told me that you should shave your head."

Eddie was astonished. "What?"

"I know, it sounds weird, Eddie, but they told me you should shave your head and not take a shower for a week. You'll appear really sick, crazy. And that'll keep guys away from you. You know what I mean. And the first guy that messes with you, no matter how big he is, you screw him up. You fight him with everything you got. Fight crazy, even if you're gonna lose. And after that, chances are nobody's gonna mess with you. You understand?"

He did understand, yet the judge was not about to let someone with twenty pounds of locally-grown grass get off with a light sentence and he gave Eddie three and two-thirds years. Where he came up with two-thirds nobody knew, but Eddie showed up on time, un-bathed for five days and head shaven. He was harassed when he got there. Big, ugly men yelled about his ass as he walked to his cell and the fear inside him swelled until he nearly stopped breathing. He walked around looking at no one, even when they puckered their lips and called him names generally reserved for lovers. He knew it was coming, the fight, but he never knew when.

But the time came. A man with a round head and stone jaw caught him off-guard. Eddie looked sideways and saw the man approaching slowly, shoulders six inches higher and ten inches wider than his own. Eddie slowed down as he put on his socks and shoes, facing the wall and trying to think while adrenaline pulsed in his veins. The big man sensed his fear and moved closer, more quickly, self-assured. There would be no resistance. He pushed Eddie's shoulder and Eddie wheeled around and slapped his face with a shoe, which did little but surprise the man for long enough to give Eddie time to kick out the left knee of his attacker. When the man screamed and fell to the ground, Eddie pounced on him and beat him senseless and bloody.

When the guards came and hauled him off to solitary, Eddie did not give up until out of sight of the other prisoners, and then he stopped acting and told the men leading him away that he would not fight them. He would never fight them. He wanted only to prove himself to the others and they let him go, knowing exactly what he had just done, and he walked on his own to solitary confinement. When the door closed behind him, for a sentence of two days alone, he sat down and cried with excitement because he'd just won the most important battle of his life, and from then on few came near him.

As he sat on his own for those days, not his only days in solitary, he swore he would never cut his hair again and he rarely did. It grew back, black against his dark skin, and he let it grow into long curls by not brushing it, and then kept it back in a braid. He grew a thick mustache and goatee, and before getting out of prison, he had another inmate tattoo a light-blue teardrop below his left eye, a symbol of his mother passing away while he was jailed. Add to this the fact that he lifted weights at every free moment, every free moment in jail, and he gained a look that parted crowds on city streets.

He rarely spoke to the chief after that. Not that Prence wanted it that way. It was amazing how they could seem to avoid each other on such a small island. Had it not been for this mess of official business for the chief, they still wouldn't have crossed paths. Sometimes they'd pass on the road going in opposite directions and the chief would wave, but Eddie would just stare on ahead. The chief still saw those teary eyes of the child he never should have let go.

But now they sat together in silence, sipping brandy, Eddie in his buzz of local-grown pot, well ahead of the chief on the road to a bender. Without words they watched the sun glow in the clouds and, as did the aroma of brandy, the story of their fathers' demise filled their heads.

35

Two captains met on the bow of a large ferry as cars and passengers debarked. The small talk quickly changed to the conditions of the sea. One captain told the other, "It's pretty heavy out there, blowing up to forty."

"Should we cancel?"

"No, you'll make it."

"All right, then I'll see you tomorrow."

"Right-oh, good night."

The captains parted with the chief's father, Captain Egerton Prence, taking the watch, leery of the temerity innate to the previous captain that often seemed tainted by part ownership of the ferry. As he climbed the stairs from the vehicle deck, he was called by a deck hand who approached with a passenger straggling behind him and spoke in as low a voice as the engines would allow.

"Captain," he said. "This guy's with Letitia Marsh, the singer. She's in that bus with some others. He wants to know if they can stay on the bus."

"Well, I'm not sure. It's gonna be pretty rough."

"Please, Captain, we don't want people..." said the man, his arms outstretched.

"All right, but don't be surprised if we call you on deck."

"Thanks, Captain."

Now the captain turned and continued upward and along the main deck to the bar door. The bartender greeted him and asked if he wanted coffee, which he did, and filled a large cup, black, and wrapped it in paper napkins. She tore a mouth hole from a lid and placed it over the cup, handed him the warm liquid with a smile. He thanked her, turned with a mien of dignity and sipped the cup down from the top to keep it from spilling as he walked. He pushed open the door and moved up another level to the wheelhouse, where he found the young helmsman staring over the bridge, sipping coffee and listening to the weather report.

The young man turned. "Evening, Captain, how are you?"

"Fine, thanks, and you?"

"Good."

"Keeping a close watch on her?"

"Not too close," shied the pilot.

"Turn this crap off," said the captain, flicking off the radio. "They're wrong."

"How do you know?"

"They're always wrong. Besides, I heard it in the office and all they said was it's going to rain."

"It is raining."

"I know."

"I heard the whole thing. You're right, they are wrong. It's going to be a rough crossing, isn't it?"

"Captain Thompson says the seas are four to six feet."

"That's big."

"Any bigger and we won't be leaving. So, you know where the tide is?"

"It's full up."

"And what does that mean?"

"It means that it will be running across us the whole way, especially at the race."

"And with this wind?"

"It'll be running harder."

"Indeed, but how hard? How much different is your course going to be?"

"Five degrees?"

"You're asking me? Well, a little more than five, maybe six or seven, but we'll see, won't we?"

"We will."

The door opened and Edward Vanson, Sr., stepped to the bridge. "Helmsman," he bellowed with a smile. "What's the course correction?"

"Six, maybe seven degrees," he answered nervously, wondering if the first mate was kidding or serious.

"Very good. Very good. The captain's been quizzing you already, eh?"

"Don't fool with him, Ed. This is going to be the roughest passage of the season. A lot to learn today." The captain turned to his chair at the back of the wheelhouse and placed his cup in the holder. Then they all joined in unison as the captain repeated himself, slowly: "A-lot-to-learn."

"Yeah, I know," said Ed Vanson. "Like you always say, everyday there's a lot to learn."

"I'm right, aren't I?"

"You're always right." Then he said behind his hand to the helmsman, "The captain is always right."

"That's right," said the pilot, finally picking up on the lightness of the conversation and welcoming himself into it.

"Anyway, Cap, we're almost loaded. What's with the bus?"

"A Letitia so and so, popular with your generation, I believe," the captain nodded from his chair to the helmsman.

"Really? She's on board? Cool."

"Do you think it's wise to let them ride in the bus?"

"I don't see why not. Important people don't want crowds all the time. Maybe they'll puke all over the bus. Besides, if it gets too rough, we'll send young Johnny here down for an autograph."

"Yeah. The funny thing is that the driver is already drinking at the bar," Vanson said as the call came over the radio that they were lifting the ramp from the boat. The captain acknowledged and shortly the boat was free from the pier. The horn was sounded for a full five count.

"OK, Johnny," said the captain, "the wind's holding us on pretty good. Helm half to port, all back one quarter." The engines engaged and the ferry creaked back along the piles, away from the ramp, which the dock master set back down to rest. "Thruster to port, starboard engine three quarters astern. Helm to one quarter. Good. Both engines half back. That's enough thruster. That's it. Now port to neutral. Slowly. All right, we're clear. Helm to starboard one half, starboard idle aback. Port forward one quarter. Good, bring her around and take us out at three quarters. Not bad, eh Mr. Vanson? Every passage an adventure." The captain returned to his chair and his coffee. "Your maneuvers are great, young man, you just need confidence around the pier. It takes time. You don't want to embarrass yourself by crashing the pier. You'd never live it down." The three laughed together, one of them nervously.

"Rumor has it, Captain," gloated Mr. Vanson, "that you crashed the pier once."

"That's right," the captain said and sipped some coffee. "And I still haven't lived it down. I look at that dent every time I board the ship."

The ferry slipped away from the pier, out past the rocky point and lighthouse, and turned through the cut out to the open sea, the waves already causing her to roll side to side. The coffee cups swung in gabled holders as spray began to wash the deck. Ed

Vanson sat in the other chair at the back of the wheelhouse and the helmsman braced himself between the bench and the helm. The captain stared to the west where the sky was brightest.

"It looks like the course will be about twenty-four degrees," the captain ordered.

"Aye, two four."

"It's going to get steep in an hour, once we get around the cape. Don't worry, though. We've been through it before, haven't we Mr. Vanson?"

"Not me. This is the roughest I've ever been through," he smiled.

"I meant me and this ship," said the captain with a laugh, trying to calm the nerves of the young helmsman. He gave a stern look to Ed Vanson, as if to tell him to agree with everything said.

"Is there any chance we'll have to turn back?" asked the helmsman.

"I don't think so. It's rough, but she can take it," the captain responded as the hull slowed in a wave and spray flooded down the windshield.

Seas reached a steady eight feet when they were halfway through the trip. Night closed the door behind them. Visibility was less than half a mile and bursts of rain took turns with splattering sea to wash over the windows. The wipers barely kept the windshield clean, so the captain occasionally opened a viewing hole to see, but the river of spray was so intense that he mainly kept it closed, relying on his senses as their enclosure moved forward. Over the intercom, the bartender told the first mate that people were getting seasick. The captain looked at one of the radar screens and found that the course was a bit off from the next buoy. Silently he watched the compass over the helmsman's shoulder. The young man was holding the correct course but the wind was gusting stronger than before.

"Johnny, you've held the course well, but we seem to be slipping more than we figured. You'd better bring her to eighteen degrees. We're coming up on the ledges and we're a little low.

"Roger, one eight."

"Roger? It's aye," the captain said with a smile, trying to keep the young man calm with a pat on the back.

"Sorry."

"The weather has changed. It seems that the wind has veered around on us. All right, we're about three-quarters of a mile from the buoy. Better bring her to fifteen. The tide's really running. Mr. Vanson, do you see it?"

"Not yet. Johnny, keep your eyes on your course. We'll look for the marker. Do you suppose its light isn't working?"

"Nah, it's just thick out there. I'm switching the radar to eighth mile range."

"Wait, there it is. Better head up to ten degrees."

"That's right, Johnny, ten degrees," confirmed the captain. The ship was heading almost straight into the seas, pitching fore and aft and making only half its normal speed through the tide, moving barely at all over the ground. The captain opened a window to the lee side of the ship and looked out at the water and the buoy.

"Man, it's really running. Let's give her a little more juice 'til we get past this." The captain staggered to the helm and eased both throttles forward a little and the engine tone changed. The number ten buoy passed close off the starboard side.

"Come starboard five degrees."

"Aye, bringing her starboard five degrees to one five."

"Did you even see the other buoy, Ed?"

"No, but I didn't look for it."

"The next one is coming soon," said the captain, looking up to the radar screen.

"There it is," called the helmsman.

"All right, hold the course." The helmsman looked back to the compass. The number eight buoy passed off the starboard side and there was open water between it and the next buoys, a few miles off to starboard.

"Bring her to twenty degrees, Johnny."

"Aye, Captain, two zero."

Again, the captain watched over the helmsman's shoulder, making sure that he held close to the proper course. The captain did not let apprentice helmsman rely too much on the electronics, but he occasionally looked up at the radar to make sure that they were moving in the right direction. In about ten minutes, they closed in on the next marker, the first of a series through a pair of reefs. They passed the buoy and came starboard five degrees. The next buoy passed and they adjusted back to port. The captain looked up again, only to find both radar screens blank.

"Mr. Vanson, what's up with this thing?"

Vanson stood and put his hand to the short-range radar, though both it and the long-range radar screens were blank. "I don't know. It's got power, but—"

"What's the matter?" asked the helmsman.

"No time for questions. Watch your course close," the captain snapped.

"The power is flicking off and resetting the thing. It doesn't have enough time to warm up before the power cuts out again," said Vanson with a little excitement in his voice. "It's the same for all the electronics."

"Damn it," said the captain as he struggled to the helm. "Check the breaker box, Ed. See if one's come loose. If you can't fix it, get Phil up here. Don't worry, Johnny. A lot to learn."

"I'll call him anyway," said Vanson, stepping to the intercom and calling for the chief engineer. After a brief conversation, Ed moved to the rear of the electronics cabinet and removed the back panel, all the time fighting the sea as the ship pitched and rolled. "Phil says he'll check things below and come up if he doesn't fix it." He dropped the panel cover at the back of the wheelhouse, startling the helmsman, and began fidgeting with the wires.

The captain paid no attention to what Ed was doing and watched through the wipers snapping back and forth. "OK, Johnny, we're doing fine. We're both going to watch the course and look for the next mark, OK? It'll be up ahead, just off the port."

"OK, Captain," the helmsman answered with a quiver. "There it is!"

"Good. Stay close to it. This next heading is critical. Hold her close at two six."

"Aye, Captain, two six."

The chief engineer tumbled into the wheelhouse, barely keeping his footing. "Jesus," he said, "pretty rough, eh, Cap?"

"Don't interrupt, Phil. Just fix it."

The engineer looked at the screens and then moved to the back of the electronics cabinet. He talked with Ed Vanson in a soft voice and then went to the starboard side of the bridge and opened another cabinet.

"Mr. Vanson," called the captain. The first mate stepped to the helm. The captain ordered, "You better go get Miss what's-her-name on deck." Then he lowered his voice. "All hands to stations. Quietly!" It turned out to be an order to die, to be seen never again.

The captain returned to the helm and checked his watch again. "Johnny, we've been two minutes at two six, ten knots slipping slightly to starboard." Vanson turned to the starboard door, but the engineer was blocking it, so he exited through the port instead. "Christ, Ed," the captain called as the door closed. "Crap! Johnny, in weather like this, never, ever, do that. Only go out on the lee side of the ship!"

Vanson fought his way down the wheelhouse stairs to the main deck, which the sea flowed along and fell back to itself through the scuppers. He held the rail and moved toward the stern, stopping next to the life rafts, checking that nothing kept them from deployment. A line was wrapped around one of them and he reached out to free it. The ship nearly stopped as a large wave hit and flooded the deck. Vanson was knocked off balance and the wave took him over the side, back to the sea with it. He popped to the surface with a gasp and swam for the side of the boat, scratching at the steel as it slipped by him. There was nothing to grab onto and the boat left him in the wake, with no one yet aware of his loss.

He called out, thinking he saw someone on deck who surely must have seen him, and called out again, only to have his scream muffled by a mouthful of water. He, with no other choice, waited for the ship to turn into the wind.

It takes a while for someone to get to the wheelhouse, he thought. Then the captain has to be sure of what he's doing before turning her. But the ship disappeared into the rain and the sound of her engines followed.

At first he laughed aloud and said, "Now what do we do?" But the cold water, with the bite of a snake whose venom takes minutes to kill, slipped through his raincoat and drained into his boots. He felt the depth below as the tide pulled him along. "What do we do, now, Dear God?"

The tide! Use the tide! Swim with it and get to the marker. It's not that far! He waved his arms to get his legs trailing behind him. The boots dragged in the current and the jacket made it impossible to swim, but he did swim. He knew the channel marker was only half a mile or less and the current, moving fast, would carry him almost straight to it. If he could only get there, he might live long enough to be rescued.

He could hear it, the horn on the marker groaning low in the waves. *Where is it? Which direction?* The sound carried everywhere, making it hard to tell the direction of its source, but he knew it was still down stream.

There it is, he reassured himself as he crested a wave, but he was lost again in a trough. The marker howled closer. *There it is! There it is!* he shouted in his mind, spitting out seawater as he tried to breathe. *Come on, Ed. Swim damn you. Swim! It's right there. Not ten feet, boy. Come on!*

The number eight buoy loomed ahead. He was sweeping onto it fast. *You've got it, man. You've got it!* He reached up with his right hand and grabbed onto one of the large rings of steel used to haul the buoy out for repairs. The buoy bobbed and swayed in the sea. He was tired, but his strength was focused on his one hand holding the last of his life. The water flowed around the buoy faster than the rest of the current, making it harder to hold on than anything he had ever had to hold onto. The buoy turned and he dragged downstream behind it.

It is the end, his numb mind told him. The water flowed too fast around the buoy and the clothes that he wore, the boots, dragged him away. He knew not to let go, but his hands were too cold to hang on.

The buoy lifted up in a wave and he felt his fingers slipping, but then the wave passed and the buoy lowered down long enough for him to get both hands on the ring and bring a foot up. His boot slipped and he kicked again, screaming to let all his energy go. But it was no use. He could not get onto it. He hung there for a few moments longer, then with a whimper he succumbed and let his fingers slip, happier now just to die without struggle.

He had scraped his side on the barnacles and the salt water stung. In the wind, salt crusted on his eyelids, but washed away with every wave. He was almost warm from swimming before, so he tried to swim more.

There's another buoy, he said to himself. His hand hurt and he looked at it in the darkness. Two fingernails had ripped off, one dangled and the other was gone completely. He held his hand under the water to quench the pain throbbing at the rate of his heart. He began to feel the last seconds of his life count down the minutes it would take for him to die. His feet ached of cold. His head felt like he had eaten too much ice cream. He was asleep, yet awake.

He inhaled water and returned to consciousness. *It's the ship! Is it? Another ship?* He thought he heard engines, thought he saw it, but no one saw him. He let out a scream—the best he could—but again a mouthful of water. It was a gargling scream, like when his mother made him gargle with salt water when he was a boy with a sore throat. He remembered her and remembered how, when he was well, they went to see a film, a cartoon, and after that they went to meet his father. He saw his wife with her deep eyes and her dark, black hair, the same as the hair of his son.

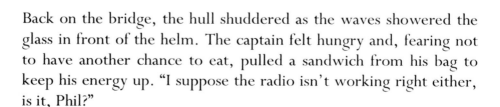

Back on the bridge, the hull shuddered as the waves showered the glass in front of the helm. The captain felt hungry and, fearing not to have another chance to eat, pulled a sandwich from his bag to keep his energy up. "I suppose the radio isn't working right either, is it, Phil?"

"Probably not."

"Well, check it out now. If it is, let the base know what's going on. Johnny, we're close to the rip now. Let's take it up five degrees to port."

"Right, Cap. Coming port five degrees to two one."

The two stood side by side and watched over the bow for the next buoy. Suddenly, the sea moved in a different direction. They had made it to the race and the lee of the island. The tide flowed hard over the rocky bottom, strong enough to pull the ship with it.

"We're too low," barked the captain. "Hard a-port, port engine back one quarter, starboard engine... I'll get it, hold the helm hard over." The ship groaned and leaned to starboard, the hull shuddering with the engines. The buoy appeared off the port and they were well below it. The engineer paled, pointing to the buoy and bracing for the impact with the rocks it marked as the ship turned hard and then harder. The bow barely cleared the buoy, which cast a wake in the current and banged along the steel of the ship, tolling through the hold.

"Bring her amidships. Pray we don't catch its chain!" The men sighed together as the captain put both throttles back to cruising position. That danger had passed.

"We're not out of it yet. Bring her to one five."

"Aye, one five."

"Nice work, Cap," said the engineer.

"Forget the electronics, Phil. Help us look for the next marker."

The engineer took a place by the helm and the three located the next buoy. The seas were calmer and the harbor light appeared through the weather.

"Good job, Captain," said the helmsman.

"I wasn't alone, Johnny," assured the captain, placing his hand on Johnny's shoulder and shaking him a little. "But make notes when we land. The Coast Guard might want to hear about this."

"Captain," paused the youngest on the bridge, "can you take her to the dock?"

"Sure thing," smiled the captain. "I hope we can dock her."

It was not until well after the ferry was unloaded that Ed Vanson was found missing. Despite the assurances of everyone else, the captain knew his mate was dead, that there was no way he would be found. That night a mist rose from the thunderous surf and climbed over the dunes, falling into the valley to settle on the town as fog, but clear above the stars shown through brightly as the townspeople gathered for prayer.

The captain went against the orders of his doctor and took a few drinks. Years of seaman drinking had taken a toll on his heart, swelling it until he had a spell. The doctor told him his next drink might kill him. It was a conscious decision. Folks said that he passed in his sleep, but no one knew how awake he really was.

Eddie struck a match and touched it to the wick of a large candle by the windows, the flame flickering bright as the sun slipped behind it. If you did not know what to give Thomas, you could always buy candles. The bottle was poured again.

"So what?" Eddie said. "Everyone's gotta die sometime. Hell, people are dying all day long. What difference does it make?"

"It still hurts," said the chief. "You learn a lot from it, I guess, but it still hurts. Especially when they're young. You don't expect it."

Eddie took a long sip and let out a gasping sigh. "Shit's not made to drink fast," he said, then paused. The sun cast red on the walls and through the windows back out to the sea.

"Eddie," said the chief, "did Thomas say anything to you? Was anything going on between him and Dave Wyman?"

"No. Nothing special. He said they were doing some diving. Went out to Stage Island to get some lobsters and look at the wrecks."

"Thomas used to have a thing for his wife, didn't he?"

"That was years ago, Chief. It was just a summer thing, before Thomas got married."

"Did it start up again?"

"Nah. He talked about it a little, but he never let on that anything was happenin'. He said it was kind of weird."

"What's that?"

"Just hangin' around with a guy who married his old lover, but he wasn't angry, or anything. There's nothing more than friendship there, if anything."

"Yeah, but he's dead."

"You think something is up, Chief?"

"Don't know, can't say. The troopers were over this morning."

"The troopers, huh," said Eddie, leaning forward and pulling a boat key from his pocket. "Gotta have a lot of respect for those guys."

The boat key was chained to a plastic float shaped like a buoy with a cylindrical base and a cone top. Eddie twisted the hollow float in half at the seam. The inside was waterproof and meant to hold a boat registration card, but from it Eddie spilled out some aromatic green buds and started breaking them apart.

"So that's where you keep it," scoffed the chief. "You learn something new everyday."

"Don't abuse the knowledge, Chief," said Eddie as he twisted another joint, laid it on the table and scraped the rest of the pot back into the float.

The chief looked at him sideways and said nothing, except, "You're gonna kill yourself with that stuff."

"Yeah, like booze ain't a drug," he said and sipped from his glass. It was not what he said but the way he said it. Like *booze* ain't a drug. The truth of that became so clear as the chief sipped his brandy and felt its sweet sting burn down his throat and float some sorrow.

"You're right, Eddie. Booze killed my father. Cocaine is one thing, but pot, hell it grows here. You smoke it like tobacco. Only not as often. And it's not processed like cocaine."

"All drugs should be legal."

"I can't agree with that. You do LSD all your life, what are you gonna be to society later on? A burden."

"Yeah. OK. But pot is—"

"The line has to be drawn somewhere."

"Draw it for yourself." His tone became hostile. "I don't do heroin. I don't do coke. I don't smoke cigarettes. I drink and smoke pot every now and then." Eddie put the joint in his mouth and lit it, taking a few short pokes, then one long, smooth drag and held it.

The chief sipped from his glass and stared out the window. He did not come here to fight with Eddie. He didn't even expect Eddie to be here. His chance, he thought, this could be his chance to strike some chord with Eddie and bring him back. He thought of his father and how he almost hated his father when he was young. Everything his father did was wrong, it seemed. Then he got older and realized that his father could be his friend, indeed that he was all along. He could treat him as almost anyone else. That is where he wanted to be with Eddie. The arrest, that stupid cop from the mainland, that's what separated these two men. Eddie never got the chance to get over a young boy's dislike of his...Prence was sort of his father. That stupid cop. Things could have been handled so differently. Prence knew they only needed to bring the boys in, scare them a little. No arrest was necessary. The people on the island could have handled it. They should have been given a chance.

"Let me have some of that," the chief said, waving his hand at the wrist. Eddie passed the joint to him with a look of curiosity. The chief at one time smoked cigarettes and thought the smoke was no different, but it expanded in his lungs and he coughed once and then twice. Eddie smiled.

"I'm gonna quit this stuff soon," Eddie said, taking back the joint.

"We should both quit, Eddie. I mean, quit everything. It's gonna kill us."

The men talked on and before long the bottle went dry and the time to part had come. The sun was hours down and darkness hid the path from the house. The chief left alone, Eddie remaining behind, and stammered away from the buildings. When he had come to the house, each step was short, slipping back in the sand one half. Now each step moved quite faster, not only gaining the half step, but equaling a run as he plunged down the dune to his car.

Chapter 4

Rebecca

The cemetery at Cobb Hill was actually dug from the sides of the hill and surrounded at the base by a wall of large stones, each skillfully cut and placed. Time covered them with lichen, ivy or moss. The wall was a circle at the base of the hill, maybe a quarter of a mile around, and leaned slightly outward, holding back the burgeoning necropolis. Along the wall, in varied distances, crypts were tunneled straight into the hill with only the archway pushing out through the grass. More crypts were dug from the hill up above and all the archways formed heaps and mounds rising up to the flagpole atop the crest.

Among the small mounds, so many headstones were gathered together, how could one believe that all these people were down there? Some stones were gray slate, some of those with the names worn away, and some barely anything at all. Many stones had fallen or leaned in await, and some stood like they may stand there forever, the names living on in a dark lichen that resided only in the carves of the imported marble.

A stairway cut the base-wall and then stopped. A few more stairways of much smaller stones continued here and there, but they weren't to be walked on by any but the oldest visitors. They were scattered about and wended up the hill around the cryptic mounds.

Rebecca closed her sketchbook and thought how she might like to be buried there, with the view over town hall and the bay. Then she turned to walk back to town and thought how silly it seemed to mark a grave with a headstone. Just look at those worn slates, she thought. How long until the name wears off? How much longer until the stone tumbles? Even the imported stones will fall someday.

Why be buried anywhere; have a hole filled in around your box? It keeps your corpse from being eaten, at least by mammals, and gives you a place to put a stone. It keeps you with the others, the ones that you love, but they are not there. What if there was someone that you hated all your life and he is now buried beside you? A headstone is simply a way for the living to remember you, to carry on without you, yet know where you are and that you were tended for in the end. Rebecca supposed it was up to them to do as they will.

She recalled what her grandmother said not long before: "Spirits perpetuate through the remembrance of our ancestors, the recognition of our families and friends, and celebration of the new."

"Forget it," Rebecca said aloud to herself as she lifted the receiver from a pay phone, dropped coins down its slot, and dialed the island exchange followed by the four digits printed on the note she found pinned to a bulletin board. The line rang three times and a machine answered.

"Damn," she said to the machine that picked up once again, but then a man answered and told her to wait a minute. Rebecca assured herself that he hadn't heard her. The machine beeped and then the man said, "Hello."

"Hi." Rebecca hesitated. "I'm calling about the live-in person. Is that still available?"

"You're the first person to call."

"Great."

"How old are you?"

"I'm twenty-one," she lied.

"That's pretty young. Do you have any experience helping the elderly?"

"Not really, but the note says just shopping and cooking."

"Can you cook?"

"A little."

"What do you do for work?"

"Uh, well, I'm an artist. An art student."

"A student. Well, I don't know, it might work out. I don't think she wants someone who's gonna be partying all the time. You'll be the only one there. You can have a guest or two, you know, but we're looking for someone responsible."

"I never throw parties. I'll go to them, but I don't intend to have any."

"When can I meet you?"

"Anytime today. I'm leaving tonight."

"Where are you?"

"I'm outside a place called the Dog Tavern."

"Can we meet in about twenty minutes?"

"Sure."

"OK, I'll meet you at the Dog in twenty minutes."

"Great. See you then."

"What's your name?"

"Rebecca."

"OK, Rebecca. Just tell the bartender that you're waiting for Mike Taylor and he'll point you out to me when I get there…"

Rebecca hung up and sort of jumped with excitement, but looked around to make sure no one saw her. With time to kill, she wandered to the pier and walked past some men talking by a large boat. One of them said to the other, "I'll bet you're glad to see us go."

"Well, you guys are OK, but there's no need for an icebreaker anymore this year, thank God."

"Hopefully she won't break down so much next time."

"You all fixed up now?"

"Yeah, she should make it back."

"So, we'll see you next year then."

"Unless I get a new job."

"All right, then. Have a good trip back. See you next winter." The two men shook hands, one went onto the boat and the other walked back to shore and said hello to Rebecca as he passed her. She studied the icebreaker with the eyes of an artist for a few moments and then walked back to the Dog Tavern. She headed inside, sat at the bar and told the bartender that she was waiting for a guy named Mike Taylor.

"Can I get you anything?" he asked.

"Just some tea, please."

"Comin' up."

The room was empty, but some people were playing pool in a back room. Rebecca heard the break shot and decided to see who was there. She walked through the room to the doorway and watched as an unnerving man walked around the table chalking his cue. She watched him carefully as if his attitude and appearance told a story all about him. He had the long beard of a lobsterman and such intensity in his unblinking eyes that this game was clearly the most important thing in his life. He looked at the balls remaining on the pool table, studying the break for what seemed to be the better selection, solids or stripes. Stripes were much better. Just sink the ten ball and the rest will carry, he told himself. He signaled for the ten ball cross side, off one bumper into the pocket beside him, lined it up, and shot gently. The ball dropped straight in the side pocket, but not the pocket he called.

"Nice shot!" an onlooker shouted. The man took that to mean it was all right to continue and he did, sinking a few more shots. Rebecca saw the whole thing. She knew he cheated and turned back to the bar, where a small kettle of water steamed next to a cup and a tea bag. She called the bartender and asked for an application.

"Ever work in a restaurant?" he said.

"I've been at the Rusty Nail for over a year now."

"The Nail. I know the owner. If you've worked there for a year, then I assume you can cocktail. Do you want that or lunch and dinner hours?"

"Probably just cocktailing. I want my days off."

"When can you start?"

"I'm not sure. I don't even know if I'm coming here or not."

"Well," he said, now more hesitant. "Give me a call when you know for sure. My name is Will; I'm the manager. What's your name?"

"Rebecca."

"OK, I hope to hear from you," he said and went to the kitchen and returned with an application.

Rebecca looked over the application and decided not to fill it out just yet. She opened her sketchbook and started shading the scene she just outlined. A few minutes later, the doors to the tavern opened and an elderly woman stepped carefully over the threshold. She made her way to the bar and called for the bartender.

"Hi, Mrs. Taylor. How's the leg?"

"Just fine, William, and you?"

"No complaints. Can I get you some tea?"

"Yes, please. My son tells me that a young woman is waiting here. Is that her?"

"You've got great intuition, Mrs. Taylor," the barman quipped, knowing full well that there was only one young woman sitting alone in the place. Ursa Taylor moved along the bar, and Rebecca, having heard the conversation, stood up and cut the distance between them more quickly.

"Hi. I'm Rebecca. I called about the live-in person."

"Hello, Rebecca. My name is Ursa Taylor. My son called and said that you'd be waiting here. I left his number on the note because I didn't want just anyone calling me, but when he said a young girl called, I didn't feel the need to worry. So, are you living on the island?"

"No, I just came here today and saw the note this morning. I've been thinking that I'd like to live here for the summer."

At first, the conversation chopped along. Neither was comfortable with an interview.

"This is the first time I've rented out a room," Ursa said shyly. "My son tells me you're an art student."

"Well, sort of. I suppose every artist is always a student. I've taken some classes, but I'm not sure which way to go, right now."

"Do you plan to work here?"

"I guess. I really haven't thought too much about it. I just came for the day, saw your note and figured it might be worth doing, just to get away for a while...just to think."

"I see. Well, what do you do on the mainland for work?"

"I'm a waitress, at the Rusty Nail in Portland. Have you heard of it?"

"Yes. I don't think it's my kind of place. Maybe I'm just too old."

"It's not my kind of place, either," Rebecca smiled with a slight blush. "But the money's good."

"To be frank, I am concerned about having a young girl staying with me. I know that it won't be easy to find someone perfect, but I don't want to be...you know, boys and parties. You could have guests—"

"I won't have any guests. No one comes to my house now and I'll respect your privacy. I don't have a boyfriend. We just broke up. That's another reason I want to get away. I think I'm through with guys for a while."

"Oh?"

"Yeah, he kind of tries to manipulate me."

"Well, that's not good. The next time he tries to manipulate you, tell him to manipulate himself."

Rebecca's eyebrows lifted with mild astonishment and she tried not to smile.

"Oh, my," said Ursa, and she blushed, "did I just say that?" The two laughed together. Just then a horn sounded. The icebreaker pulled away from the pier and headed for open sea and the women struck to friendship like a match to flame.

Ursa glanced at Rebecca's sketchbook and asked, "Is that Cobb Hill?"

"Yes, you could tell."

"That's beautiful. How long have you been working on it?"

"About an hour."

"Really! That's wonderful. My son said you were an art student, but you're already an artist."

"Thanks. It's a little dreary, but I only brought a few pencils."

"Well, a graveyard is dreary, but my, it is a beautiful sketch. You know, I'll be the last person buried there. No one else alive has a plot there. Anyway, how long will you be here?"

"I'm leaving on the next ferry, ma'am."

"Please, call me Ursa. Would you like to see the place? It's just up the hill a ways."

"Sure."

They got up to go as two men walked to the bar. One was the cheating pool player.

"Ah, Daniel" said Ursa. "You're just the man I wanted to see."

"Uh oh, I'm not in trouble am I?"

"No, not today. I was wondering if you might be able to find someone else and help me move a piano into the house. It's a small piano, but we'll need a truck like yours."

"Sure, ma'am. Same one you gave Mrs. Davis?"

"That's right. Michael would help me, but he's going away with the Merchant Marines."

"I heard he got on a good ship. That's great! When do you want the piano moved?"

"Whenever it is convenient for you. There's no rush. It's been at the Davis' place for a few years now, no need to hurry," she said, tacitly believing that by thinking it through there'd be less chance of damaging it.

"How about next Saturday?"

She paused for a moment at the seeming urgency of it, and then agreed. "That'll be fine. In the morning?"

"How does ten o'clock sound?"

"Fine, I'll see you then."

"Well, Mrs. Taylor, how about me and Steve here go get it and bring it around to your place? You just tell Mrs. Davis that we'll be over around ten."

"Are you sure you won't need my help?"

"No, ma'am. I'm sure." He smiled through his beard.

59

"Very well, then. I'll call her and let her know."

"OK, we'll see you Saturday."

As the two women left, Steve said, "Nice of you to offer my help. Saturday morning at ten, I'll be needin' the hair of the dog that tore my face off."

"Relax. When's the last time you did somethin' nice for an old lady?"

"Is she gonna pay us?"

"Maybe. She'll at least give us lunch."

"Who's the babe?"

"I don't know. Her son has no girls. Maybe her sister's granddaughter, or somethin'."

"Kind o' cute. Wonder if she's gonna be around for a while."

"Whatever. Buy me that beer I just won, would ya?"

Outside, the two ladies made towards an old station wagon, Rebecca slowing her pace to match the older woman's limp.

"You play the piano, Ursa?"

"Well, I used to. I gave it up a few years ago and let my friend borrow my piano. It was taking up too much space, I thought. But she doesn't use it. When I broke my leg this winter, I got to figuring I'd better take up something more suiting my age."

"How did you break your leg?"

"Skiing."

"Skiing?"

"Well, don't seem so surprised. I'm not as old as I look. This island does something to a woman."

"I...I don't know what I thought. I guess I thought you were old because of your limp."

"Well, thank goodness. At least the doctor says I'll get over that. Don't mind Abbey," Ursa said as she opened the door of an older Ford wagon with fake wood sides. Rebecca didn't know what she meant until a black dog clambered to her feet and began shaking from side to side with her tail slapping on the back seat. Rebecca opened the passenger door and the dog began a welcoming groan and divided her time between the two women.

"She's a Labrador all over, including the tail. Aren't you, Abbey?" Ursa said, trying to distract the dog from Rebecca. "You have to have to watch out for that tail. Abbey whacks things off the table. Otherwise, she's very friendly."

Whack, whack, whack went the tail.

"Oh, hello, Abbey," Rebecca said. "Aren't you a sweetie," she said as the dog licked her face repeatedly. Ursa started the car, drove from the lot and headed up a hill. The dog turned her attention to the open window.

"This is a cool old car, Ursa."

"Well, it doesn't get much use. I generally walk everywhere I go, or ride a bike. Sometimes it's weeks before I even get to the other side of the island."

"You're serious?"

"Well, yes. There's sometimes nothing to do, so I drive over to the other side. Everything I need is right around here."

"Wow, I think I'd go crazy."

"Well, maybe I am getting old. So you weren't here last night?"

"No. I had to work."

"It snowed here. Did it snow on the mainland?"

"No. But this place is a little further north and out in the ocean."

"Maybe it's a good sign. Maybe it won't be so busy this summer."

"Does it get very crowded?"

"You've never been here before? My dear, it gets so crowded that you'll never want to leave the house. Lord knows why so many bring their cars. There's nowhere to go you can't walk to. Do you have a bicycle?"

"Yes."

"Well, if you decide to stay here, be sure to bring it. Even in the rain I love to ride around the island. It'll get you everywhere you need to go in the summer."

"Great. I need to live in a place like that. I just want to get away from the city."

The car traveled down the main road and before long turned left, onto a road that seemed to be one lane but was actually two, the sand swelling around it and choking it thin. There was no line down the middle and the road split the valley of two dunes. Phone poles climbed the dune alongside the road that suddenly stopped. At the end were a bicycle rack and two homes, one on the left that sat atop the dune and one on the right, with only part of its roof visible. The women got out and the dog jumped to the front seat and out the driver's side door.

"Slow down, Abbey," Ursa said. "You practically knocked me off my feet!" The dog, looking back over her shoulder to make sure the two ladies followed, started up a path to the right that cut through a thick patch of Bearberry covering the dune that they climbed to get to the house.

The Bearberry, an evergreen plant closely related to azalea and rhododendron, had small leaves shaped like little tongues. Its long, thin vines spread wildly, but grew only to about eight inches high. Yet this field stood tall with it, rising some forty degrees from the base, the dune covered thick with bearberry and a few corkscrew pines growing at the same angle and kept equally short in this environment of wind and sand.

The path made one switchback about halfway up the hill. As they approached the turn, Rebecca saw that the soil was sand with just enough loam to sustain the Bearberry, which not only held the loam there, but actually helped produce it by dying and decaying in place, thereby sustaining itself. The entire area was covered with Bearberry and when the wind blew sand through its leaves, the little tongues spoke in soft whispers.

The jawbone of a whale, stained yellow by lichen, stood on end, arching over the path. As the summit approached, a roof appeared over the sand and grew into a squat house with low pitched roofs and short dormers. Looking down on the ocean and town and the harbor and bay, the house was held firmly on the ridge of the island's highest dune by four corners of stones stacked into columns, also yellowed with lichen. It was small, like all the old houses, with real shutters and a porch wrapping all the way around it. On one side, closest the road and closest the sea, the porch spilled out round, like a bandstand.

"Ursa!" said Rebecca as the dune flattened. "The porch alone is worth staying here for."

"Yes. I love that porch. My husband built it for me with his own hands. He jokingly asked me if I wanted a widow's walk and I said, 'I'd rather have a porch so I can have people over to keep me company while you are away,' and did he ever build a porch. I love to sit out there and have company in the summer."

"Was he a seaman?"

"Yes. Captain of a large steamer."

As they neared the porch, Rebecca noticed a porcelain cat, but the cat opened its eyes and stared at her.

"I thought the cat was stone!"

"That's Foamy. I hope you don't mind cats."

"No, I love animals."

"She stays out most of the summer, anyway. She practically feeds herself all summer long. Come, let me show you the house and then we can sit out here if you want."

The tour lasted only a few minutes, but the conversation went on for more than an hour, with the older woman feeling younger and the girl feeling very happy to have made friends with Ursa. The two knew that they got along swimmingly and agreed that Rebecca would come back on the weekend with her things. When Ursa dropped her off at the ferry, the two had some parting thoughts.

"Well, Rebecca, I've had a marvelous conversation. I look forward to having you in my home. It's so odd that you were the first person to call."

"I know. I'm glad, though. I really enjoyed talking to you. And it's so pretty here. I think it will work out for both of us."

"Are you sure the room isn't too small?"

"It's perfect, just so long as you don't have any mothballs."

"Mothballs?"

"Yeah. You don't use them, do you?"

"No."

"That's good. I knew it. You're too young to use mothballs, Ursa."

"Why, thank you. I guess." They both smiled wider than they had been for the last hour and the dog kept beating her tail against the back seat.

"Well, I'd better get on the ferry. I'll be back on Saturday and I'll call you. OK?"

"That's fine, dear. Nice talking with you and I'll see you soon. Bye bye."

"Bye, Ursa," Rebecca called as she turned and walked to the ferry dock. She got almost to the ticket booth before looking at the clock on town hall. She still had some time, she thought, so she went back to the Dog Tavern to fill out the application.

"You're back," said the bartender.

"Yes. I'm going to fill out the application you gave me."

"Made up your mind to come for the summer, have you?"

"Yes."

"And you've never spent a summer here before?"

"No."

"Well, let me tell you, you're gonna have a lot of fun. This island is tremendous in the summer and I try to make it the best for everyone who works here. I'll give you some prime shifts, but you've gotta take some bad ones, too, so everybody makes money and gets time off. I take it you're gonna be stayin' with Mrs. Taylor."

"That's right. She's renting me a room in her house."

"She's a good woman. I figure, if she's gonna let you stay in her house and you've worked at the Rusty Nail, then you're probably OK to work here. The application is a formality. When can you start?"

"I could start next weekend. I've still got some shifts at the Nail and I don't want to just walk out without notice. They're mid-week shifts, though, and I'm coming back next weekend. When do you want me to start?"

"It's good to hear someone say they don't want to pull a no show. Are you going to be working all summer? Cause if you're not, then please don't start here. There's plenty of girls want to waitress here. It's good money in the summer."

"I'll be here for the entire summer. Maybe longer."

"I can't promise that I can keep you for too long after the season. Things sort of dry up here after the summer, but we'll see."

"That'll be fine. I can probably always go back to the Nail if I have to."

"OK," Will said. "Consider yourself hired." He reached out his hand and they shook on the deal. "It's still early in the year, but you can come in for training next Saturday night. Why don't you come in for the five o'clock shift? That means be here no later than quarter to five. We'll train you for both dinners and cocktails. Shouldn't be too busy."

"All right," Rebecca said. "I'll see you at four thirty on Saturday. And thanks a lot."

Will knocked on the bar and walked away. Rebecca finished the application as quickly as possible and was thrilled as she walked out the door. She had to rush for the ferry, but now it was a new life.

Chapter 5

The Dog

The Dog was a restaurant and a place to take drink. It sat beside the ferry pier, whose white painted piles glowed through the darkness of the wharf. Dave walked down the pier to the shore, past a ship's cradle and an old, rusty windlass and up to the first door of the Dog. The doorknob turned as well as the day it was first used. Inside was a foyer decorated with a ship's telegraph, a wheel, and a bare-breasted figurehead. The second doors, French doors, had a latch that kept them closed to the cold.

Inside, the air was thick with pea soup, spiced rice and a garlic sauce. There were many tables, each different and known to the staff by name. Their chairs were all different, too, with a look and comfort of their own, perhaps a placard on the back telling whom the chair commemorates or was given by. In fact, no two things were alike in the tavern, except for the menus, glasses and flatware. Each barstool was as unique as the ceiling fans and lanterns, everything collected over the years.

By the hostess desk there was a barograph—a barometer that slowly scribbled the air pressure on a cylinder of graph paper. It had chronicled some of the storms that passed the island, and the best ones were posted on the wall beside it, clearly labeled. It didn't show very much of a change in the past forty-eight hours, though, and Dave looked up from it to see the hostess.

"Hi, Dave." She smiled. "Would you like a table?"

"Uh, no thanks. I'm just checking out this thing."

Dave was acquainted with her well enough to know her name, chat briefly, but knew nothing of her life beyond what had transpired at the Dog, barely knew anything about her except that she'd been there for many years. Her face looked more concerned now and she asked him how he was doing. She'd heard about the accident and tears welled in her eyes. She hadn't heard anything more than Thomas had died in some sort of accident out on Stage Island, couldn't imagine what they were doing there, though she'd never been herself. She'd just heard stories about it now that Thomas was dead. Just a trip to the mainland hospital, he lied. Everything's fine with me, but I just can't believe it. I don't really know exactly what happened; we were just there and then…Dave shook his head and walked away.

He took a place at the long bar, which had a few customers sitting at the other end, and waited for the bartender to notice him. The bar itself was sliced from an elm tree that fell in a storm years ago. The walls were covered with pictures, charts, and mirrors, and a fish, once a record, posed over the mantle. Above an ancient brass register hung a bell that was rung once in a while, for a good tip or bursts of enthusiasm, and the shock would silence everything in the room for a moment.

Gas lamps dropped from the ceiling and each table had a storm lantern. All told, there were about a hundred oil lamps flickering in the room, but each haloed flame reflected in the windows and the mirrors, and back and forth between those, and so on forever— thousands of apparitions dancing in the air.

"Hi, Dave. Can I get you something?" asked the barman.

"Hi, Will. A beer, please."

The bartender spun a mug on his finger and placed it below the open tap.

"Heard about you and Thomas. I guess everybody has. Can't tell ya how sorry I am, Dave. I can't believe it. I went fishing with Thomas just a couple o' weeks ago. Saturday. Hard to imagine being there one minute and not the next. What happened?"

"I'm not sure. I got a concussion and it's still not clear."

"Should you be drinking?" he asked, hesitating before placing the mug on the bar.

"No, but it'll sure make me feel better."

"It's on me, Dave," he said, knocking three times on the elm tree bar.

"Thanks, Willie."

The place was as old as the island, at least it was to the residents. It was the very first establishment, having gone from a general store to something like a bar and then becoming a restaurant with a bar. Whatever it was, it had always been the center of town. There were photographs of almost every fisherman or seaman who lived on the island since cameras were invented. Record fish were weighed, and some cooked, here. It expanded under a small tent in the summer to keep down the lines of patrons. By the door, there was a mug shot of the man who once frequented the place and was wanted for stealing money from some of the townspeople. The poster was stuck to the wall by a voodoo doll with a dart through its head.

Dave walked to the window and watched the ferry lights slip back from the pier. The lights formed a tall triangle and reflected in the mirror behind him and then on the windowpane, and the image pulled apart in refracted streams of red, white, and shallow sea green, leaving behind the lamp flames and their reflections.

By one of the windows there was a large model of a sailing ship. Through the glass case, Dave studied her lines and sheets and halyards, the meticulous detail of a model that could only take years to complete.

"Do you like her?" asked an old man sitting over a few tables.

"I always have. She's beautiful."

"Want to buy one?"

"Are you a dealer?"

"I build them. Built that one twenty years ago."

"How long does it take you?"

"Oh, I don't know. I pick 'em up and work for a while, then put it down and come back a few days, maybe a week later. Sometimes a month. I've got a few up at the house that I started years ago and never got around to finishing."

"I'd love to see them. How much do you sell them for?"

"Depends. That one would sell for a few thousand, maybe more since it's kind of old."

"Wow."

"I have some that I sell for a couple hundred."

"You've been doing them for twenty years?"

"No, I've built models forever. My grandfather, God rest him, he's the one who got me started. My dad, too. You should see some of the one's those two built. I've got a few of 'em still."

"I'd love to see them."

"That one's an old pirate ship that used to come here centuries ago. People said it was a ghost ship because she'd come in when the time was right, when there were no other ships around, and then leave before another one came into harbor. The myth has it that she could sense the presence of other boats and she'd tell the captain when the coast was clear and when to leave. Truth is, the captain kept good lookouts posted.

"There's a long story behind her, actually. She was a slave ship and she encountered another ship that was going down. When she came alongside, the crew of the sinking ship jumped on board and cast off everyone in the lifeboats, everyone but the slaves, that is. The captain set them all free. They made for a port far north and the captain gave each man a choice as he did at every port: anyone who wanted to go ashore could go and anyone who wanted to stay could stay. Half of the slaves he freed stayed on to be crew and he gave them an equal share. Every crew member got one share of the booty, the captain got two shares; standard rules. The captain knew the importance of a reputation—good lookouts made her a ghost ship, good seamen made her a legend. And if you never killed anybody, your reputation was such that the crew of a ship would gladly give up without a fight. The crew didn't own the cargo. Why fight for someone else's property?"

"I'll bet you know a lot of stories about this island."

"Sure do. I've lived here all my life, like the rest of my family. There's nothin' else to do in the winter but sit around and tell stories."

"Ever hear of a young woman, a girl, being killed, murdered, on the island?"

"Nah, can't say I ever heard that one. There was a killing here once, but it wasn't a girl."

"You mean back before the Civil War, right?"

"Yeah, you heard that story?"

"Yes, a while ago."

A pause interrupted them. Dave knew the question was coming. He'd tried to prepare for it all day—the inevitable. He still hadn't found an answer. Though he didn't know this man very well, they had met earlier in the year and said hello on a regular basis. He's a local who's been on the island so long that he could tell you how long everyone else has been there. The man asked it: "What happened the other day? You're the guy who was with Thomas, right?"

"Yes," was the answer Dave gave, then another pause while the man studied him as he waited for an answer to the same question everyone else in the bar wanted to know, for they were all listening. Dave could feel it. "And we've met before, in the beginning of the summer," he said.

"That's right. I remember. So what the hell happened?"

"I'm not sure. A boating accident. I hit my head and can't remember anything more than being rescued."

He scoffed. "A boating accident!" Then reluctantly, after another pause: "It'll come back to you."

Dave looked to the clock, trying to get away from the questions. "I'm sure. Well, it's after nine thirty. I better get going. I'd love to see your collection," Dave said, edging to the door.

"Stop by the house anytime. I got nothing better to do than show 'em."

"Thanks, I look forward to it. Goodbye."

"Bye, now. Take care of your head."

Dave opened the foyer doors and took a breath, a sigh really. Everyone knew about what happened, everyone but him, exactly. He closed his jacket and stepped outside to find the weather in a flurry. It was cold again, getting colder, and he pulled the jacket collar up to keep the wind from his ears, but it just filled around his head with a seashell whisper and into his mind slipped thoughts of another time.

Chapter 6

Delivery

In the back of a blue beater truck rode an upright piano that was tied with six ropes. It bounced a bit, swaying side to side, and struck a note on the larger potholes and bumps. Inside its simple yet elegant case, the piano moved much more, though the strings were hammered only now and again. Behind the truck followed Ursa with a worried look on her face. When the turn to her road was finally in view, she let out a relaxed hum.

The truck drove to the end of the road and turned around with gears grinding, backing up as close as possible to the dune below Ursa's house. The piano quaked and settled as Dan unlashed the ropes and took off the cushioning.

"I think we'll leave it in the truck, Mrs. Taylor," he said. "If we bury the anchor high enough on the other dune, we can pick it right out of the bed. Save us from lifting it twice."

The two men, Dan and Steve, climbed the hill to Ursa's house and Dan went to the porch. He ducked underneath and pulled out two crossed boards with a rope tied to the middle. Then he took out two long boards crossed close to one end, but hinged like scissors.

"Get a shovel from the shed and there's a long rope in there, too." Steve went to the shed and returned with the rope, but it was so long and heavy that he couldn't carry both it and the shovel.

"Give me that and take this down to the truck."

"Aye, Captain," joked Steve, and he dumped the rope on the ground, picked up the crossed boards and dropped out of sight down the dune.

Dan lifted the rope with ease and carried it to a pole near one end of the house. He tied one end to the pole and then moved away, casting rope behind him in loops, stopping every few feet to undo tangles as he carried the line down the dune. He stopped, returned to the shed for the forgotten shovel, and then finished laying out the rope, walking past the truck and up into the opposite dune.

"Dig here," he said to Steve. "In a cross pattern so the anchor fits in. According to the manual, this drill should take less than five minutes."

Steve dug the hole and Dan dropped the X-shaped anchor into it, leaving its rope trailing out. Then they filled the hole. The heavy rope was tied to the anchor line and the two long boards were stood up vertically, the hinge at the top, the boards scissored apart to provide legs and a crotch at the top. They ran the rope through the crotch.

"Hold it just like this," said Dan. "I have to go back up the dune and crank it taught. Make sure it stays at this angle." He walked toward his truck and raised his voice a little to say, "It's just like they did it hundreds of years ago! Right, Mrs. Taylor?"

"I'm not that old, Daniel," said Ursa who noticed a taxi had turned onto the road. The taxi stopped near her and she smiled because Rebecca had arrived.

"You should have called me, Rebecca," she said as she opened the car door. "I would have come to get you."

"I tried, but there was no answer, so I figured you were busy. It's not that expensive, though."

The driver said with a smile, "A man has to make a livin'. How are you today, Mrs. Taylor?"

"Just fine and you?" she said to a man she had known forever.

"I'll make it," he said.

Rebecca paid the driver and he lifted her packs and bicycle from the trunk. It was cool, but she and Dan were both sweating.

"Daniel," called Ursa, "this is Rebecca, my tenant for the summer."

Dan looked at her before saying anything and she looked away, knowing what he was thinking, what most guys thought when they met her.

"I didn't know you had tenants, Mrs. Taylor," he said. "Can I help you carry some of that to the house?"

They made their way to the house and Ursa talked about the piano, how excited she was, how nervous that it might fall and how she hoped Rebecca could tolerate her practicing. Dan placed the bags on the porch and went back to work while the women stepped inside.

Dan used a come-along to pull the heavy rope so taught it would sound a note if you struck it with a hammer. He waved to Steve, who came up the hill as fast as it could be done. Dan put a pulley on the taught rope and told Steve to walk it down to the truck as he fed out a line attached to the pulley. Then Dan went down to the truck and they worked on attaching the piano.

The women came out to watch as the piano made its way up the dune, the two men heaving on the line in unison. The piano trembled each time the rope was pulled. When the piano reached the top, Dan tied the line to the bumper of his truck and the two men climbed the dune again. The piano was eased to the ground and the men paused to catch their breath. Ursa went to the kitchen to get the iced tea she had brewed and the men talked with Rebecca.

"Now that you've seen how it's done, do you want to ride in the breeches buoy?" Dan asked her.

"The what?"

"That's what this is," he said and disappeared into the shed, reappearing with a thing that looked like a life ring with pants. "It's a breeches buoy. They used to rescue people from ships that went aground. No need for them anymore, with helicopters and all. But Captain Taylor knew he'd need it for something, so he kept it. Works pretty well rescuing a piano. Do you want to try it?"

"I don't know. Is it safe?"

"Probably not," said Steve. "It looks pretty old."

"I think I'll pass. Besides, I want to go into town and do some drawing before I have to go to work."

"Where are you working?" asked Dan.

"At the Dog Tavern."

"Uh oh, the Dog. We'll see you in there later, I'm sure," said Steve.

"I hope it won't be too busy on my first night."

"It's a Saturday, but there won't be that many people."

"It won't get busy until middle of June," Steve added, hoping to get the attention of the new girl.

Ursa pushed backwards through the screen door with a tray of glasses and a pitcher. "Here's some tea," she said in her voice that often sounded like a laugh. "You boys must be thirsty after all that."

"Thanks, Mrs. Taylor," said Steve, who took the glass that was handed to him and poured half of it down his throat.

"None for me, Ursa, thanks. I want to go do some drawing."

"So soon? You are dedicated."

Rebecca thought to herself, *Hardly*. She simply wanted to get away from these guys, from everybody, actually. She came to the island to get away from people and she wasn't going to start with these. The one guy cheats at pool and the other kept looking at her whenever she turned her eyes away. She hated guys like that, but to her that was pretty much all of them.

"I just don't want to waste any time here," she said and picked up her backpack.

"Hey! Time is all we have here," said Steve.

Rebecca forced a smile. "I probably won't be home until late, Ursa. My shift lasts until closing."

"OK, dear. Enjoy yourself."

She did not answer. All she wanted was to be away from everyone, to be free from everything, at least for the rest of the daylight. She had only a few hours before work. It would be dark by seven or so, anyway. She passed the bike rack at the bottom of the dune and decided to walk rather than take her bicycle. Down the road to the left she walked rather quickly until she realized there was no need to escape anymore. She was alone with the grains of sand and the winter-scorched trees just budding.

It was about a mile to town and Rebecca made it there faster than she thought she would, even though she slowed her pace to a saunter. The clock on town hall stood in the sky, held high in a steeple. Its black hands against a white face moved and it chimed. The sound was lighter than one would expect from such a clock and she did not know why it struck just once at twelve thirty.

As she stared up at the clock while walking, she felt a little off balance and looked down at the road. Just then the blue pickup truck slammed on its brakes and came to a loud, skidding stop feet behind her. Dan leaned out the window and asked, "Want a ride?"

Great, she thought, how am I going to get rid of these guys?

"No thanks," she said. "I'm just going to the town hall. Thanks anyway."

"All right," Dan said as he revved the truck beside her. "You're sure?"

"Yeah. Thanks, though."

"We'll see you tonight at the Dog," called the passenger as Dan floored the truck and it skidded away in some sand. A third guy in the back lifted a hand to wave without waving and kept a deadpan stare as they turned a corner.

Just great, she thought. I'll probably see those guys every night. "I hope I didn't make a mistake," she whispered to herself, "coming here. Everyone can't be like them."

She got to the town hall and walked around it. It was a square building with three stories and a tower toward the front. Next to the building was the graveyard. She sat on the steps and sketched for some time, but then she got an idea for a better picture and walked inside the hall. She went to the door that was open. Inside, two women were talking, but not about town matters, more like gossip. After standing at the desk for a few minutes, Rebecca was not sure if she should clear her throat to get their attention. Surely, they knew she was there, but the two women went on chatting and did not look her way.

"Excuse me," she said after enough time had elapsed to ensure that she wasn't the one being rude.

A woman who was standing with her back to a file cabinet stopped talking, turned her head and peered over her half-rimmed glasses. She said nothing for a while, as if assuming that Rebecca would continue, but then asked in a whining voice, "Can I help you?"

"Um, I was just wondering if it's possible to get into the clock tower. I'd like to do a drawing from there."

"People are not allowed to go up there," came her flat response.

"Really? There can't be that much of a demand."

"Tourists come in here all the time and demand everything. It would be impossible to accommodate all of them."

"So, I cannot go up there?" It was the tone in the woman's voice that got to Rebecca. The woman had an air of superiority and had to exercise whatever authority she could.

"How many times do I have to say 'No'?" she nearly yelled.

"Once kindly would have been enough," Rebecca said under her breath as she turned to walk out and bumped into a uniformed man.

"I'm sorry," he said with his arms raised out to catch her if she fell. "Is there a problem here?" he asked in an authoritative tone.

"No problem, officer. Just maybe...forget it."

"The girl wants to go up in the clock tower and won't take no for an answer," the woman called from behind the counter.

"What do you want to go up there for?" he asked.

"I don't anymore. Good bye," Rebecca said and walked out the door.

The woman said, "She thinks she's an artist and wants to draw a picture."

Rebecca heard her from the hall as she walked into the sunlight outdoors and stopped on the stairs. She spoke to herself in her mind: What a bitch. She sits in there doing little all day, I can tell. They sit in there and talk and get nothing done and cost the taxpayers money and they can't even be friendly about it. Tourists! How dare she call me a tourist. If she shows up at the Dog, I'll spit in her soup. I hate people like that. That whiny voice, ahh. The rules and regulations apply even here. Then she thought again, Maybe I should have tried a different approach.

She felt a tap on her shoulder and turned around to see the cop she bumped into looking down at her from one step above. "What'd you want to go up there for, Miss? A drawing?"

"Forget it, it doesn't matter."

"OK, but I'll let you up there if you want. Shouldn't make any difference less you fool with somethin'."

Her spirit was lifted. "Really?"

"Yeah. That woman's a tough one. All she does is complain. Maybe if she had an appreciation for art she'd be easier to work with, or somethin'." He had a slight accent.

"Don't get me started." Rebecca smiled.

"Come on. Let's walk around back so she doesn't see. If you get caught, my name is Jim Prence. I'm the chief of police. Just tell them I said it was OK."

"Thanks. I really appreciate it. I don't even know if there's a good view, but I'd like to see."

"You here for the summer?" he said as they walked.

"Yeah. I'm working at the Dog Tavern and I'm doing a study."

"A study?"

"Drawings and paintings. It's so pretty here. I'm sure I'll find more than enough to paint."

"That you will. Even if you're here all summer, you might not find enough time to see all the spots. It can be bigger than it looks."

They walked in the back door. The hallway was so dark that Rebecca couldn't see ahead of her and she fumbled for the wall. She walked slowly ahead, but bumped into the man. Her chest hit his elbow, one breast yielding before she stopped.

"We'd better give it a moment for our eyes to adjust. The light is out. I've been up there before, but if I can't see anything, I know you can't. Can you see yet?"

"A little."

"OK, come on. There's a stair right here," he said and kicked the stair lightly. "And the railing is on the left."

She was nervous. He's a cop, she thought. He won't do anything. They got to the second floor and he pushed through the doorway. It was light again and she wanted to kick herself because there were many people in the building and there was no way she was in danger. She was thinking of those other guys. Now she was being silly, she thought. Those other guys have just got her creeped out. They climbed another stairway and came to a door. The door was stuck, but he pulled it open and stepped back.

"After you," he said. "Watch your head."

Rebecca ducked a little and went up the steep, creaking stairway. The stairs were wooden and the room smelled of a parched attic. A pigeon warbled. The man followed, closing the door behind him, but she was not afraid anymore. When they got to the top, it was dim and light skewed through the dusty air. The clock ticked, its pendulum swaying in the musty heat. There were two long windows on either side of the clock face and she went to open one, but he stopped her.

"Be careful," he said and pointed to the floor, which was littered with bird dung. She stepped over a mound and opened the window.

"Will that do?" he asked.

"Yes! It's perfect. Just what I imagined."

"Good. It's kinda neat up here—sort of the 'attic of the town'. I gotta go, though. What's your name?"

"Rebecca."

"Well, Rebecca, it's nice to meet you. I'll probably see you around."

"I hope so. Thanks a lot," she said as he turned to walk down the stairs.

"Don't get stuck up here. If you do, kick the top of the door. That's where it sticks. And cover your ears when it chimes. It can be pretty loud."

"Why does it chime once at twelve thirty?" she asked.

"It chimes like a ship's clock. Do you know how they work?"

"Not really."

"Well, let's see if I can get this right. A ship's crew works in four-hour shifts. The first one starts at twelve. The bell sounds once for every half-hour that passes, so you get one bell at twelve-thirty, two bells at one o'clock, three at one-thirty and so on until the shift ends at four o'clock, which has eight bells. Then it starts over again at four thirty with one bell. Does that make sense?"

"Yeah. That's pretty neat. I didn't know that."

"Well," he continued. "You know how you hear about someone yelling 'three bells and all is well'? That's what it's all about."

"Huh," Rebecca said with a nod of approval and new knowledge.

"This island kind of runs by that clock, you know, with almost everyone working the sea. You can hear it almost everywhere, even out on the water in some places. The sound just carries and everyone keeps time by it. We get complaints if the clock is wrong. Of course, we get complaints about the noise, too, but it would take an act from above to turn the clock off as far as the people who run the town are concerned. That's why the lady downstairs didn't want you up here. She's lived here all her life and doesn't like strangers too much."

"I should have been friendlier," Rebecca said.

"Come up with a good picture and she might see the error of her ways. She's a nice person once you get to know her." He paused. "Well, I have to run. Take care, now," he said and made his way down the stairs.

Rebecca watched him go, heard the door close again, and turned to the window to peer out. The scene was just as she imagined it, so she took out the sketchbook and started to draw. Outside, in perfect daylight, there was the colorful harbor and the graveyard. The clock was drawn backward against its translucent face and she drew the works of the clock inside in its dusty, brown-and-white image, using colored pastels only for the harbor and sky outside the window.

The clock ticked loudly. When it was about to chime, it let out a soft click, which was good, thought Rebecca each time she heard it, for the chimes were loud enough to be heard almost to the far reaches of the island and it was good to have some warning. She almost thought she would have to leave, especially since the chimes lasted longer the later she stayed. It was late afternoon and she had to go to work soon.

As she sketched, the pendulum swung and she thought about it, trying to imagine it in mid-swing so she could draw it the perfect way: still, showing movement while standing stopped in the air, almost invisible motion lines. She stared at it swinging and for a moment it stopped. She was startled, though she did not know why for the clock continued as normal. Again she stared, watching the pendulum to find the point where it looked best. She felt the ticking and soon was not herself. Then the clock struck once and she realized she was late. The drawing would have to go unfinished as she hurried down the stairway and out the door into sunlight.

Chapter 7

A Walk Past Homes of History

Outside the Dog, the street was a courtyard for three large hotels, Victorian relics of an era where the island seemed to remain, and the wind howled a flurry of snowflakes through the railings of their empty porches. The oval-glass doorways were locked, the hotels closed for winter, and some windows were boarded up for protection against the storms sure to come. Walking past them in the ghost-gray perception made one believe all the stories of haunting, the bride who hung herself while still in her gown and who can still be seen when lightning flashes, that sort of thing, but none of them had to do with Dave's ghost story.

From the Dog, he walked through the cusp of evening back to the main road and crossed it, then started up the lane toward his house. What the old man said before about a killing, how there had been a killing here long ago, that was the only murder the island ever knew. There was the time when the immigrants fought the natives away from this island. That they called warfare, not murder, for the natives chose to fight back. When they knew that they were going to lose, they hurtled themselves from the tallest cliffs, choosing to take their own lives rather than leave this place known to them as Manissus, Island of the Little God.

And of course, with Wianno being a fishing harbor, there were plenty of untimely deaths through the years. But the only murder happened so long ago that Dave couldn't see any connection. He had read about it in the journals that were kept in the library—part of the research he undertook for a background history of his own work.

People came to the island, mostly in summer, for many reasons, but mostly because it was quiet; the winters were not nearly as attractive. It took a few hours to get there on a ferry, but when folks first started coming, it was a good day of sailing, for the rocky, narrow channels forced the sailing ships out to sea. Most people left by December, before ice filled the bays, but one year a group stayed for the winter. It was in 1837.

Before Christmas of that year, the harbor was blocked with ice thick enough to carry the weight of a man. Eventually, when the island got popular enough and technology permitted, the harbor was cleared a few times daily by an icebreaker so boats could get in and out, but not back then. Then it was solid till spring. Dave had heard that it was tough living on the island in winter, but that year must have been frozen hell.

Eleven people stayed through that winter—two women and nine men, each with their own reasons. Some wrote in letters and journals that it was for religious freedom. Regardless of that, there was nothing to do but survive once the cold had settled into the harbor and the piers were pulled from the tide so they wouldn't be crushed by the ice. The people would gather at what is now the Dog Tavern and sit around playing cards, reading and writing, telling stories, staying warm. Life was slow.

It's easy to tire of someone when you spend too much time together. It is not that you no longer like them, though in some cases that is true, but you need your own space and time. Even in the most populous places, one often comes across the same people too often. The idiosyncrasies of someone else are too much to handle when you must deal everyday with your own. So it was in this tiny place that winter.

One night, two of the men started fighting for reasons unclear at first. The answer was written in only one of the last entries of the diaries preserved in the library, all of which Dave had poured through in his studies of the island. The fight was brief, lasting only a short time until the other men broke it up and one of the two left. Eventually, they all left and went home to their houses, some of which Dave walked past every day, little things with no insulation, just boards thrown up as walls and a roof. Summer shacks. In these houses, the cold of winter, unbearable, sticky cold, could be escaped only by the side of a body closest to the fire or the body of another.

The next morning, they slowly appeared back at the main building for breakfast, all but the two men who'd been fighting. After a while, a pair of men went to look for the other two, assuming they were still angry with each other and wanted to save face for as long as possible. They got to the home of one man, but he was out, as was the fire. They could see smoke trickling from the chimney of the other man's shack, so they went there and knocked, but there was no answer.

They had no idea what to think, so they went back to the main building and didn't think about it at all. The day went on like the others, too cold to do anything but sit inside and keep the fire burning. It was around noon when Captain William Nickerson, the man on the island who was considered the leader, came to the main building. When he heard that neither of the two men had been seen yet, he decided he would have a look for himself after he ate.

There was no answer at the first house, so, with a feeling inside, he forced open the door and entered. From the looks of it, the man had packed up and gone, though there was nowhere to go. He went to the second house. Again, no answer and again he forced his way in.

Nothing seemed out of the ordinary at first, though the door was bolted from the inside. There was no reason to bolt the door unless you were afraid of something. He paced the house slowly. The rooms were small and cold and he felt the cool embers in the fireplace. An inner sense told him something was in the next room. He hesitated and moved forward. The second room was brighter as the sun shone through the window. It appeared that someone had left through it, for the window was closed askew. If they had left in the dark, it would be hard for them to notice that the window was not closed all the way and the breeze poured in, and outside something had been dragged through the snow.

He went to close the sash all the way, that seeming the neighborly thing to do, but when he lifted the window to reseat it properly, he noticed a lock of hair with skin still attached. He bent down to study it closer and found blood on the floor in the shade of the windowsill. He heard footsteps and backed toward the wall. The footsteps were hurried and walked through the house to the back room and then returned. A voice called from outside: "Will?"

Nickerson stepped from the wall. "In here," he said as he knelt by the blood. It was dry and there was more of it outside in the snow.

"Will," said Tom Murphy. "Will, it's Ronnie. They found Ronnie down by the dock. He's dead, Will. Murdered."

Murphy led the captain down to the dock, all the while talking of the horror. "His throat's been cut, Will."

"There wasn't enough blood at the house for that," Nickerson said, but when they got to the dock, blood was all he saw. Partially buried in snow was the body of Ronnie Wilckes, simply a fisherman who wanted to be away from society. His eyes were open and frozen. His jaw hung and the flesh of his neck flared out.

"I wouldn't of found him," claimed Ned Martin, "if it wasn't for the blood. He was buried good and deep, but the blood flowed out and rolled down the hill here."

"Looks like he's been hit pretty hard. Why would he drag him down here to finish him off, you suppose?"

"Probably wanted to make it look like an accident. Probably knocked him out at the house, carried him down here to drown him and he woke up, so he had to slit his throat."

Nickerson looked at him with suspicion. "How do ya figure that?" he asked.

"Just figurin'."

"Well, there's no sign of a struggle here," said Nickerson. "Too many footprints around now to determine much. We can speculate all day long and it ain't gonna change the situation. You boys haul him out and I'll help you dig a hole."

"How are we gonna bury him?" asked Turner, the breath of his words curling skyward. "The ground's frozen solid."

"We can't leave him there!"

"What are we gonna do, Will?" whined Murphy.

"Scout out a place to bury him, if you can. Don't get too far from here, though. We don't know where he is or what he intends to do next."

Nickerson went back to the main building where the rest were waiting. One of the women was crying as the other consoled her. Still the question: "What are we gonna do, Will?"

"I haven't thought about it enough," was all he could say.

"We should find him and hang him," said Fred Miller.

"He's got his guns," said Nickerson, and that was the last of the ideas about finding him. They were left in the cold and all they could do was talk. The subject came up again and again. Some would tell the others to stop and bring up another topic, but the conversation would always fall into a lull and then the two men would come up once more. Another supper, then bedtime, and then another day passed; breakfast, lunch, supper, bedtime.

That night, one of the men stayed up late in his house reading a book lent to him earlier in the day. He heard a noise and looked out the window to see the door to the storage shed was ajar and slapped in the breeze. He put on his coat, turned up his lantern, stepped into the cold wind and went to the flapping door. He was going to close it, but decided to look inside and he saw a man. The man hit him hard and, when he fell, the lantern fell, too, its fuel spilling out in a fiery puddle that streamed through the shed and caught onto the barn.

The man who got hit was pulled away from the building by his assailant, but he did not wake up in time to put out the fire. When he came around, the other men were desperately trying to extinguish the flames, but it was futile. Even the dogs cowered at the sounds of the animals in the barn as they charred. The flames consumed the barn and the shed and most of its contents: the food that they stored for winter.

Dave came to the end of the road and climbed past the tree to the porch, stepping carefully on the wood so as not to be noticed by anyone sleeping. The door creaked open and the dog barked once, but knew who Dave was and started groaning, fully enjoying the petting. Dave opened a cupboard, took out a glass and filled it with water from the sink. The well came alive as he walked to the window and stared out.

A nacre moon floated on a cloud, animating the sea crashing ashore in stretching moonbeams. The room was peaceful in the cool light. Dave found himself comfortable in the darkened solitude and stepped around the furniture to a wall where an aged chart hung. The island depicted as it was fifty years ago resembled it now only in form, for much had changed due to erosion. Even some of the names were different. Hearing the sea whispering again and watching the moon by the chart on the wall, Dave realized something that had been staring him in the face all along.

The island was shaped like the moon at half-mast, the sea whirling round it changing only the cast, the future. It bobbed in the tide a balloon shaded by sunrise and tethered to the mainland far up the prevailing southwesterly. Crumbling as it curved, the island would eventually be but a shoal, the rocks it held up part of the sea bed. The windward tip rose from the ocean in low bluffs that rounded taller and taller to the east, where cliffs held high a lighthouse seen for decades, then tapered north into a spit that wrapped around to protect the bays and harbor.

It was at the same time both big and small, though bigger in winter and smaller in summer. Two bays forced their way inside the island, one after the other, near the north of the western side. The first, named Tranquility, was much larger and washed into the second, Serenity. Neither was very deep, so the harbor had to be dredged often for the ships. Not the ferries or fishing boats, mind you, but the large cruisers and fish packers that fouled the harbor and sometimes brought life from afar in their ballast tanks.

The island Wianno was not like other islands near it, not cut from stone but dredged up from the bottom by a glacier that receded after the last ice age. As such, it was both young and destined to die so, for the currents carried bits away every hour, reshaped the spits each and every month, carried its sand back to the sea floor.

It took a few days to perambulate Wianno, maybe five if you were fast, a pastime attracting more and more as spring reached summer. From the ferry dock, some went left, some went right, and everyone converged on the town in the center eventually. As summer ended and autumn fell to winter, the population tapered and time stretched longer, trees losing leaves, nothing to do, the cold.

It did not matter if you were white or black on the island, everybody was hated unless you lived there year round, or maybe every summer of your life. This was a place whose inhabitants knew each other so well that they greeted one another not with "Hi, how are you," followed by "OK," they simply said "K." So people walked along the town or the beach and when they came across another islander, they both simply said "K" and the message was clear.

At first Dave thought they were merely laconic, for even though he was with Thomas, people talked in strange jargon. Dave believed they wanted him not to understand. He asked and Thomas told him he was crazy, and from his look Dave came to understand that the islanders had simply varied the English language to match their own needs. It seemed strange, but when the history of language is taken in perspective, the question is not why, but why not? Languages changed over history because people were isolated from other groups. When isolation is in a place of desolation, when everything said has been said before, thoughts collapse into phrases, phrases condense into words, words into glances; people talk with their eyes.

And so it must have been back then as the year changed to 1838 and those people huddled around the fire in fear. They shared the lycanthropic nightmare where one trusted man changed in the night and vanquished the life of another. Now they were all threatened. They were alone together with no law enforcement but themselves, a killer on the island and dwindling provisions.

Entries in the diaries indicated a strong belief held by most: that the one who did the killing, Jacob Leigh, had no desire to do any more harm. But one woman wrote, "A man pressed hard in winter, with no food or shelter, a man who would hang for his crime, has no use for those who would testify against him in a court of law, no care for any but himself. He might just as soon kill us all and dispose of us so that he may go free."

After the raid on the storage shed, Nickerson wrote, "I have failed twice now. I should have taken their fight more seriously and gotten into the middle of it right away. And afterward, care should have been taken to secure the store house, perhaps even a sentry should have been placed. Now I fear that more shall die, if not from starvation, from actions taken in fear of what we must endure in the coming months, or even at the hands of this man whose plight could push him to more heinous acts of violence.

"I have ordered that the remaining food be taken from the store, inventoried and moved to the main building. Everyone is to move their things to the main building, also, including bedding. We shall stay together lest the mad man kill us all to save his own skin."

Hunting parties went out for game and fowl. No one was to hunt alone and no one was to look for Jacob Leigh. A dog was tied outside the door to keep watch in the night. The dog became the focal point. Even a whimper would raise bodies to elbows to listen from their bed. Often the question was asked, "Was that the dog… did the dog…the dog…?" And so the name endured.

Nickerson estimated from the stores recovered, less what was destroyed in the fire, that Leigh had taken about a week's worth of food, maybe two weeks if he went lean. If Leigh had good luck hunting, the rest might never see him again, but no birds were taken on many trips out and only twice did they hear the firing of a gun not their own. Furthermore, what was left of the food was barely enough to keep the remaining nine alive for the weeks it would take before a boat could get into the harbor.

The rations were minimal, but fear tore through their bodies more than famine. Prayers began to supersede the talk of what might happen, what to plan for, how to protect themselves. Soon they no longer needed to speak at all. They knew what everyone was thinking, for each had the same paternoster echoing through their mind.

Starvation left them without the energy to hunt, but they did and began to have some success, yet still their famine continued. Gathering wood required more effort because they had farther to go to collect it. They thought of tearing down buildings for wood, and they started with the home of Jacob Leigh and then the dead man's home, but no one wanted their place to go next.

The dogs knew it. They sensed it in their hungry guts and when they were called they came with slight hesitation. There was talk of eating the dogs, but they were needed for hunting, at least to keep watch at night, so they would go last. Hunger led to bitterness, then bickering and a fight, and from that they fell silent again, retrieving the same thoughts.

The winter dragged and they all began to believe that Leigh was dead. The cold was so much that one wrote, "too much cold for a man to survive in the wild." At that time the island was the wild, but it would not be the first time a man lived through a bad winter in the wild.

Out in the cold, Leigh must have been unnerved. Facing to be hanged by the neck until dead, he surely chose taking his chances on the euphoria of freezing. Alone, alone, alone, he passed beyond the pale. He was no less hungry than the rest and the hunger led him further astray. He went mad. They saw him one day, close up on a hill looking down at the village, laughing. He took a few shots and hit a window. The cold swam in as the women shrieked. Nickerson fired back and Leigh ran, howling like a jackal.

For the madman, it became a game to torment the rest. In the middle of the night, the dog would bark incessantly. They would find things left outside the building. He broke into the houses and left the contents strewn about the village. Then he began to burn the houses. He burned one to the ground and then another. The people inside realized it was time to fight, but he knew where they were and they had no clues as to where or how he survived.

Then one night they heard him shrieking and looked out the window to see him running toward the building with a flaming torch in his hand. He was laughing and running and he threw the bomb towards them, but it landed short and the container broke. The fluid inside spread flaring across the ground and he stood fiendishly behind it, laughing, then he disappeared. One man opened the door and tried to go outside, but a shotgun blast forced him back. Then another shot shattered a window. He reappeared behind the dying flames with a torch in each hand, giggling and talking to himself, finally yelling out, "You burned my house! Now, I'm gonna burn you!" and howling.

He reached back to throw one, watching it as he did, then a shot from Nickerson's rifle missed him, but hit the jar and it exploded, covering Leigh in flaming liquid. He screamed at first as he danced to a harrowing beat. It was one long, continuous scream, interrupted by only enough time for him to grab fiery air. They watched him as he turned and waved, sucking the flames into his chest as he breathed. Nickerson thought of shooting him, but he could only turn away. The women looked away, too, but the other men continued to stare as he fell to the ground and convulsed in the pool of flames.

In that instant, one half of their plight was relieved. With Jacob Leigh gone, they could concentrate on hunting and hunt the whole island without fear. The men went out alone to cover more area and each brought back game. They found Leigh's camp and the bones of his dog. One man shot a deer. They were saved.

Within weeks, the harbor broke free of ice and they prepared for the journey to the mainland. In those weeks one of the women began to reveal something as well. Clearly, despite her attempts to hide it, she was pregnant, having been raped by Jacob Leigh, her honor unsuccessfully defended. The image of him in her mind, as he lived and as he died, led her to drown the baby when it was born and she was committed to an asylum for the rest of her life. She had gone as mad as her assailant had there on the island.

Dave sat on the couch and stared out at the clouds, the moon hanging alone immortal, and wondered what it must be like to have been as alone as Jacob Leigh, living in semi-solitary confinement with the run of an island. He remembered a film about a man sailing solo around the globe. It seemed hard to imagine that as solitary confinement, but he ended up doing some pretty crazy things on that boat, as if solo circumnavigation wasn't enough craziness.

On the front page of yesterday's paper, there was a photo of a guy who believed in anarchy and had wanted to fight for it. Though he was dead, he was right in a way. What is a government for, anyhow? To keep mad guys away from society, of course. If you're left alone to play with the right things, you'll be fine. It's the guys who play with the wrong things that scare you, and some of them form governments, too, Thomas had said.

Thomas was famous on the island for a bumper sticker that he brought back from Germany. It was oval, like one of those European stickers that told from which country a car came, but it had only a question mark. He thought that, since his truck rarely left the island, the sticker would give the impression that either the car knew not from where it came or that the driver knew not where he was. The true meaning is clear: who cares from where a car comes?

Thomas traveled far and wide and had so many stories it was hard to believe they were true. His favorite places to go were in Europe, though winter took him south and to the Far East on several occasions. He had an envious life to some, for he made little money working, but was given an inheritance which he seemed to piss away.

His first trip took him to Holland, where he realized that the moon over Amsterdam was the same as it was over Boston, though the clouds were different over the landscape. He was impressed and kept going back, promising himself that someday he would live there. France and Germany were next, and he went so often that he began to make friends, and it became even cheaper for him to stay as he learned his way out of the hotels and into apartments and houses. Yet each summer he returned to paradise, back to Wianno, where all of his dreams began.

His roots were firm there and he was drawn back to his friends and the endless summer parties, the bonfires on the beach burning through sunrise. He met the woman he married on the beach at midnight. It seemed the perfect place to fall in love and he thought it was his destiny. The wedding took place on the beach and the band was his rock-and-roll friends from the island. However, the term "to wed" originally meant "to wager," and had life not turned him sideways, his wager might have paid. But it didn't, and he was left to his friends, some of whom by all rights would be considered odd.

Dave recalled going with Thomas to visit the island's only miner, perhaps one of the most unique excavators in the world, a man who left behind his tractor for a simple bucket. No shovel, just a bucket so he could take enough of the island as he needed each day. As if the beach wasn't disappearing to erosion fast enough, this man exported sand. He was an artist, though, so it was a little different.

He lived a few houses down the beach from Dave, and Thomas led Dave there with a promise that it would be enlightening. They walked along the reach of the waves until a spot where they climbed the steep dunes. When they came over the top, there was a little house asleep in a bowl before the dune rose again. Dave had already walked past that spot at least three times and never knew the place could possibly be there, atop a false summit, without having climbed up to see.

The house seemed shingled with lobster-trap buoys of all different colors that were found as flotsam washed ashore, so many buoys in fact that the layers of them made the house appear larger than it really was. As Thomas and Dave approached through the beach grass, they saw a man through a dark window who was working with flames. They got to the door and knocked. The man said, "Come in," but did not look up as they entered, the lights before him flickering when the door opened, the man entranced.

He sat in front of five candles, actually one candle with five wicks, and gazed at each flame in turn while he kept the men waiting among many large candles burning around them. He held in one hand a pair of fine scissors and when the time came he would cut off a wick and place it somewhere else. Where the flame was, he would sprinkle a bit of sand using half of a small hourglass and then dip the glass in a bucket for more sand as he cut another wick. He also used a small torch—an alcohol lamp with a wick and a pump that blew air through the side of the flame, bringing it to a fine point.

While the man worked, Dave inspected the intricate detail of the many candles burning around the room, fixing on one that was a small castle made out of wax and sand and tiny pebbles. As the flame wound down the wick, the castle would crumble into small piles of rubble, revealing the interior. When the wick was gone and the flame gone out, the castle would remain only as ruins.

They were all indeed works of art and Dave wondered why he would burn them. One was a spit of sand with a lighthouse on one end. The tower was built of stones, well to scale, and burned away first. There was another one just like it there, only lit much sooner. The tower was only rocks and half of the spit was gone. It was not really gone, but the wax had burned away and all that was left was the sand.

Eventually, the man finally said, "Ah, to hell with it," and blew out the flames in front of him, then tossed his tools to the table. He looked up. "Thomas," he said as he struggled to rise, six feet nine inches tall and a cast on his leg. The cast had a sticker that said, "Crashin' sucks."

"Hi, Dylan," Thomas returned, "this is my friend, Dave. He lives a few dunes down."

"How-ah-yah?" he said with that northeastern tone coming through the thick, long beard customary to many lobstermen. Dylan started to limp towards him, but Dave took two quick steps and shook his hand. Dave could not help but ask what he had done to his leg and he told the story of leaving a bar on his bike and crashing drunk on a tree. He had obviously hit his head hard for he not only talked too loud, but he seemed proud of wrapping his bike and his body around an elm.

It turned out that his ancestors made candles for as long as they had lived on the island. It was something to do in the winter. Dave asked why he was burning so many and he said he was trying to perfect them so that all that was left was sand when they were finished burning. These were tests.

He showed them around to many of the structures, some as beautiful as any man could make and selling for an unimaginable price. He told how he started a few years ago and sold a few at local crafts fairs. One man approached him and wanted to sell them on the mainland. He started working on efficiency after filling the first orders, but he just got a large order, so he hired someone who was to start the next day. Dylan still wasn't sure how he could use an employee. Thomas said to can the whole idea because the sand was disappearing and the island couldn't stand any more. The sand was sacred to Thomas and Dylan agreed as he held up a seashell covered in wax with a castle on top.

Dave began to remember Thomas so clearly. He was an environmentalist, a local activist working behind the scenes, talking to people so they would see his point and vote accordingly. He tried to do everything he could to preserve the island's frail and failing ecosystem. He disliked anything unnatural. He was a hunter-gatherer, stalking the sea for fish, diving for lobster, scratching for shellfish, gathering berries, growing a garden in clay pots so the soil wouldn't be carried away with the sand.

Thomas had a bat cave and nesting for swallows. The swallows would dart about the house in the daytime far more graciously than the bats would at night. The bats never bothered you, though, but the birds would sometimes disappear behind the house and then fly right at you to keep you away from their nests. The theory was that the swallows would eat bugs all day and the bats would eat through the night. Whether it worked or not was left to speculation, but at least the method seemed to promote a living food chain rather than the zapping destruction rendered by those ultraviolet lamp devices charged with generated electricity, whose effectiveness leaves you to the same speculation. Most noteworthy was the contrast to popular fear: the bats left you alone, but the birds would sometimes scare the bejesus from your body.

As a friend of Thomas, Dave was taken on a fishing experience that few of his guests would get in a charter since the risk became greater. As much as he enjoyed fishing, Thomas liked to take people to special places and would gladly put the boat wherever he wanted it. He had a fondness for a treacherous spot right near the north point of the island. He would come in from the deep ocean side to the east and creep in between two bars formed by the ripping tide. Generally, the waves came from the east and when the tide flowed from the west, the seas kicked up high. So he would back his boat into the trough of two standing waves, facing out to the open water for a quick escape, and then Dave would cast up toward the beach with live bait. The bait—a herring or an eel— would sink to the bottom and bounce along with the current, out toward deep water where the lunker fish lurked.

Even if they caught nothing, the feeling became a craving as the boat lay in the trough and standing waves changed to incoming breakers that flashed white water just feet from the boat. Then the water became deep once more and Dave watched the backs of waves breaking on the other side of the boat, the crests stretching to the beach, bleaching the shore with sheets of foam. The sibilance of the ocean breathing was heard above the idling diesel.

Thomas impressed Dave's boys so with his use of the gaff, that long hook used to bring big fish aboard. He took Dave and the boys out and they caught a big bass, so big that the line would have snapped if they had just hauled the fish out of the water by it. So Thomas took out the gaff and with one swing and a pull, the fish was in the boat flopping all bloody on the deck. The boys loved it. There's something about a gaff that really excites boys.

"That was so cool!" Peter howled, and Sam agreed.

When they got back to the house, Peter went into the basement and took out the gaff that was stored beside the staircase. The two boys marched around with it, faked at pulling the big one aboard, nearly gaffed the dog and each other before Dave had to yell to get them to put it away. When he went to inspect it, it was hanging with grass on it, the tip slightly bent and dulled. All he could think was, *Silly boys*, the same thing his father thought when he first played with a gaff, and Dave told them the same thing he was told:

"It brings you bad luck if you play too much with the gaff. And you don't talk about it too much, either. You just put it in the boat and don't touch it until you need it." Then he added his own twist. "What it does to a fish is karmically uncool," he said, which led to a long discussion of karma peppered with questions and side discussions.

"Some people believe in Heaven and Hell, and the Golden Rule —do unto others as you would have them do unto you," he told them. "Others believe in karma—that all of the things that you do, good and bad, add up and determine your fate when you die. It's basically the same thing," he went on as he worked on a bicycle, unaware that he was beginning to lose their attention.

He told Thomas the story the next time he saw him and Thomas laughed at the first part, but fell sullen as the yarn progressed to the discussion of karma. When asked what was wrong, Thomas muttered that he wished he could take back what he had said to his uncle at the beginning of the summer. Back then, Dave went with Thomas to meet his uncle at the ferry and they headed to the Dog right away. After a few stiff drinks, his uncle began to get loud after two gay men walked in and stood next to them at the bar. Gay people were far from unusual on this unusual island, but they were where his uncle lived.

"Before 1959," he practically shouted, "there were no gay men."

"That's right, Uncle Walt," Thomas followed, soberly hushed. "They were just fairly friendly."

"You're right!" he bellowed back, and then even more loudly, "When I think of two guys in bed, it just makes me sick."

"Uncle Walt," Thomas jeered, "why are you even thinkin' about it?"

Walt was taken aback. "I always wondered about you, Thomas," he said and shut up, knowing he was too drunk to compete with a sober man who didn't really care of someone's persuasion. He'd tell strangers, gay or straight, to "get a room" if they were making out in public. He just didn't want it in his face.

"Come to think of it, Uncle Walt," Thomas continued, "when I think of you and Aunt Rose in bed, why it makes me kinda sick, too." The guys gathered round started to guffaw.

"Don't speak of her again," came Walt's response, and he gulped his drink and walked off to the men's room.

Walt was Thomas' last living relative and he didn't live much longer past the time Dave met him. He died in his early sixties of a sudden heart attack. He felt sick, so Thomas heard, and tried to drive himself to the hospital, but he pulled over and died behind the wheel after bringing his car to a stop. It was sad because it was so sudden and it left Thomas completely alone. From that time on, it seemed that Thomas' mood had changed forever.

Dave knew about some of Thomas' past, how he had lost his daughter and then his wife, but he picked himself up a few years after that and started a respectable business building small wooden boats. He took the skills of his original trade, building houses, and applied it almost immediately to his true love of the sea.

When the building boom ended on the island, for there was little space left, Thomas had no idea what to do with himself. He had a child and a wife and no source of income spare what was left of his inheritance. Now all his money had to go to his family rather than the life of travel to which he was accustomed. Then, just as he thought he had it all figured out, Elizabeth tragically died and he started to drink. Then his wife left. But it takes a lot to drown a waterman's sorrows, and he soon realized that booze was more of his problem than anything else.

He gave up drinking and reassessed his situation. He still had some money left from his father, but his father always told him never to spend the principal. It was all right to spend the dividend income if he needed it, "but never, ever, dip into your capital." He had already spent much of the principal, but he needed money if he was going to fulfill his new dream of building boats. He needed a shop and new tools. And he needed materials. Add to that he still had to pay taxes and buy himself food. He needed advice.

He went to a man on the mainland who had worked with his father, told him what he wanted to do, and the man arranged a small loan, one that could easily be paid off by the interest generated by his inheritance. He told Thomas that he'd have to start small, that boatyards failed far more than they succeeded, but if he worked hard and put all his love in it, his had as good a shot as any business. He advised him to find a mechanic who could work part time and seek out people who wanted their boats taken care of professionally. Thomas must know plenty of people who needed their boats winterized and he could make money by taking his tools around to their homes. It would keep his overhead down and they could haul their own boats. The last thing he told Thomas was that his father would be proud.

So Thomas went back to the island with some money and ordered a few of the tools he thought he'd need: a table saw, a band saw and numerous hand tools specific to boat building. He also needed clamps, clamps and more clamps. He set up a steamer for bending wood and took a few weeks to make forms and jigs. Then he practiced for a month—he called it practice anyway—before setting in on his first boat.

He went to the library and took out every book he could find on boats and boat building, even getting some on loan from city libraries on the mainland. One of the things his early education taught him was how to learn about things through books and how to find the right books. He also sought the advice of older men, men whose lives were nearly over and all they wanted to do was help someone learn a craft from an era gone by, and there were many.

There were so many, in fact, that he had to thin out the crowd. He chose to confide mostly in the oldest, those not only with experience, but with passion, and those he could tolerate being around all day long. Soon fate drifted back in his favor. One old man lent his garage and Thomas set up shop. Together, they built Thomas' first boat, a twelve foot dory, the one he used for years, Lil' Bethy. There were some small errors and Thomas would gladly point them out if you wanted, but she floated true and was easy to maneuver.

Word spread almost instantly around the island that Thomas Soverge had put his hand to building boats and soon people were asking about it. Everyone knew he had mastered carpentry and was eager to see what he could do. The old man who helped him stayed out of his way for the most part, popping in every now and then to lend a hand or an opinion.

By the time summer rolled around, he had built three sailboats, with lines sweet enough to bring a gleam to the eyes of any true sailor, and the first few sold quickly. In addition to that, people with wooden boats who wanted them tended by a master hired him to launch and haul their boats, which gave him not only a source of income but a much more valuable lesson in boat building: seeing the way others had done it. He earned enough money that summer to pay off most of his loan and secure another.

He rented a shop, but was reluctant to leave the old man who helped him. The man assured him that he'd be by every day, and further boosted Thomas by telling him it was time to take on an apprentice, and he nominated his grandson. In less than a year, through books and through passion, Thomas had become almost a master and he chose boat designs that were proven in time to need little improvement.

The following winter he built six more boats, three of them ordered by customers. The going was slow at first. His new apprentice, just out of high school, was willing to learn and work hard, but he still made errors, some of them costly. The boy told his grandfather that things were not so well and the elder showed up the next day dressed in overalls and carrying his box of tools. Thomas wanted to pay him, but he refused, saying that all he wanted to see was his grandson learn a trade, even if it was a dying art.

"I want him to at least know what quality feels like," the old man said.

Of course, how could one be an environmentalist and destroy trees as well? Building wooden boats requires a lot of wood, so Thomas, holding fast to his environmentalism, sought out lumber from specific mills. He went to visit them and made sure that they used only younger trees that were specially farmed. He carried it to a point where some might question the quality of his boats because of the resins needed, but he eventually engineered his way around problems.

He worked tirelessly, sometimes being found asleep in the morning on a pile of sawdust. He claimed he got enough sleep, but people worried because he often carried dark circles under his eyes. It was hard for Dave to imagine sleeping just four hours a day, but now he was in the same situation.

Despite his attempts to fall asleep on the couch, Dave was still awake. Morning swept over the horizon and into the house, showing each piece of furniture in increasing detail as the room gathered light. It was not like the other day, all fiery and brilliant. It started the same, darkness to gray, but might stay gray all day, the island covered in cloud. Dave tossed the paper aside and walked out to the dune in what was left of the sunrise. From the cliffs, he felt half-seas-over with never a drop in the house. Perhaps the punishment of age is that you don't sleep as much, he thought.

Back in the house, the radio came back to life at six in the morning, the DJ happier than he need be. The weather was supposed to remain uneventful. Maybe that's why she didn't come, there isn't a storm, he thought. It figures she would come only when the weather was bad, but maybe it is because everyone is asleep upstairs.

The fire had gone dead. Dave took the first pages of the paper and made an attempt to revive it, but there was no more wood near the stove and he didn't want to bother anyway. He had spent the entire night waiting to find an answer, had not slept at all and had made himself worse by trying to remember an incident and thinking only of his friend. He still had no answers.

She, of all creation, was all he wanted to see, yet visions, as the word may lead one to believe, have little to do with eyesight. Though images may be used to describe or relate a concept, some concepts become clear yet can never be described. True thought requires no eyesight; it occurs with eyes open or closed. Open eyes tend to distract from the discourse of thought.

Her voice seemed a love song and viewing her led him to see more. In her clothing there were stories of mankind: wars, battles, ballet. Like a dream where you kept going but never got there, in each place she was different and she changed so frequently that soon the compass of his mind spun out of control.

She was a diaphanous daydream, a place in the brain where the mind wants to stay, an addiction. The morphine of his mind, her words nibbled at his ears yet cudgeled his heart, for she was not real in the sense that she could be touched, cradled in his arms or brought back awake with a kiss. She was iridescent, visible like sunlight falling through the window of a smoke-filled room; seen only when there is something to be seen against, even if it is just the lashes of eyes half-shut. As the rising sun slowly filled the house, Dave grappled with the notion that he would never see her again.

Chapter 8

A New Life

Rebecca walked through time, or so it seemed, for the road that she traveled turned from pavement to cobblestones and then to just dirt. Ahead at the corner, where the street lamp lit a dull circle below it, the cobblestones ended, as did the lights, and the road disappeared into night as two rows of fine stones separated by a grassy mound. Tree branches arched over the road forming a black tunnel. She hesitated when her feet first scraped the stones near two pillars marking the start of the passageway.

Even during the day this road was dark, but under a new moon nothing was seen and she would probably walk straight off the road and into the bog, she thought. Her eyes grew accustomed to the night, though, and she continued slowly with the sound of stones underfoot as her guide. The crunch was softened by pine needles as she found herself wandering from one side of the road to the other, holding her hand in front of her face should a low branch block the way.

As the road bent toward the bog, spring peepers grew louder into voices that filled her head from all sides. They were never seen, the little frogs, but their calls melded together in a deafening, multi-dimensional sound of twittering cheeps coming from the right and left, far away or just a few feet in any direction. And when they became loudest, at the point where they nearly made her shudder, the gravestones at Cobb Hill appeared through the trees and caused her to stop.

Staring at the gravestones silhouetted by a street lamp and then closing her eyes, the sound of the frogs bubbled through her with the pulse of thawing springtime. The cries surrounded her, repeating from places never predicted, yet sounding always the same. In their words, a voice was heard.

She opened her eyes and stepped along the road, those voices calling yet fading like the horn of a train, and soon all she heard was the rumbling sea as the road again became paved, but behind her something followed.

There were footsteps coming toward her, shuffling through the stones of the path she just crossed, getting closer. They were fast. She saw nothing. She should have ridden her bike, she thought, but it was too late. Something was behind her now, chasing. It came fast. Some kind of animal she couldn't outrun. She wanted to scream, to fray it away with some ghastly squall, yet as in a dream she couldn't raise her voice. It slid through the darkness hidden, slowing as it approached so as not to run right by, then wiggling in delight.

"Abbey!" cried Rebecca. "Hello, Abbey," she said, petting the dog who leaned against her, groaning a happy greeting. "You scared me to death, Abbey, sweetie. You are so cute. How could you scare me like that, though? Huh? Come on! Let's go!"

Then she had a friend to walk her home, even though the dog ran ahead, and she shook off the silly fear she let capture her. The way became slow again as the hill steepened, but the end was in sight. Abbey looked back at Rebecca, then kept on up the path. When she got to the stairs, she saw Ursa was awake and pouring milk in a glass. Trying not to frighten her, Rebecca made a gentle noise as she opened the kitchen door, but Abbey pushed her nose through the door and rushed in. Ursa turned.

"Hi, Ursa. I hope I didn't scare you."

"Oh, no. I'm just getting some milk. How was work?"

"It was fine. But the walk home, that was spooky. I took the short cut through the dirt road. Those peepers are really scary."

"I know. Isn't it, though? It's like voices calling from the graveyard. It's really eerie this time of year."

"Yeah, but then I was walking along and heard something following me. I couldn't imagine what it was, but it turned out to be Abbey. She ran up to me and I couldn't see her because she's black. Scared me to death!"

"That must have. But you'll get used to the place. There aren't any big, bad monsters here. Abbey kind of comes and goes. In the morning, she makes rounds of the neighborhood, stopping in to say hello to all the people around here. They all expect her and sometimes call if she doesn't show up to see if she is OK."

"That's so cute. She is such a friendly thing."

Abbey laid down on the floor with a grunt and a few slaps of the tail. Whack, whack, whack.

Rebecca blew into her hands to warm them. "I'm beginning to wonder if it will ever get warm here," she said.

"Don't worry, it will. Well, I'm off to bed. Good night, Rebecca."

"Good night, Ursa. See you tomorrow."

Ursa turned to the stairs and limped up to her bedroom, her steps slow and methodical on the wooden stairway. Rebecca sat down at the table and opened the sketchbook she carried with her at all times. Just a few pages had been used, but she studied them with curiosity, as she had all day long. Then she set to working, her pencil flowing until she looked to the clock. It was three in the morning.

She laid her head on the cool table, waking to find the sun up and Ursa softly padding from the stove to the sink with the kettle in her hand and Abbey following with her tail whipping.

"Good morning, Ursa." She yawned.

"Oh, good morning, Rebecca. I'm sorry to wake you, but that can't be a very comfortable place to sleep anyway."

"No, it isn't," she said as she stretched her neck and looked at the clock. "Wow, it's seven thirty. I've been sleeping here since three. I better go to bed for a while. I have to work tonight. I hate being a waitress."

"You're not a waitress, Rebecca. You are an artist. That drawing you have there is really beautiful. So many people equate what they do for money with what they are. Don't you make that mistake."

"OK. But I hate waiting tables."

"Have you ever sold any of your drawings?"

"No."

"Have you ever tried? Someone would buy the ones I've seen of yours. Maybe you could try to sell some at one of the fairs."

"Maybe. I don't think I have enough, though."

"I have a friend who displays at every fair. Maybe she could show some of your work, too. I'll ask her if you want."

"Sure. Why not? I could use some extra money. I could help at the fair, if she needs it."

"I think she might. I'll ask her today. In fact, why don't you come to meeting this morning? You can meet her yourself."

In Rebecca's mind echoed the words, "meeting? church?" Then aloud she said: "I don't know, Ursa. I'm not very religious."

"Well, I don't want to force you. It's a beautiful place this time of year and we're not really affiliated with any one religion."

"Really?"

"Yes. We try to keep an open mind these days."

She heard in her mind, *Your mother would want you to go.* And she asked, "What time does it start?"

"Eleven."

"OK. I need to get some sleep, though. Good night, Ursa."

"Good morning, Rebecca. I'll wake you up around ten-thirty?"

"Only if I'm not up by ten."

"OK, I should be back by then. Sleep well."

Rebecca left the room and Ursa placed the kettle on the stove, then went to the table, helping herself to Rebecca's sketchbook, even though she knew that she shouldn't. The drawings were striking, but mostly black and white and concentrating on the graveyard. She sighed and stood, walking to the sink to wait for the kettle with her hand on her cheek. Then she smiled and the kettle began to whistle. Ursa grabbed it, burned her hand slightly and dropped the kettle on a cold burner with a mild curse.

On a breeze above the path, tufts of candy-cotton blossoms flew from the arms of a wilting cherry and drifted on a pool of sand. The tree, half full, stood aside and the path rolled through a field of fallen petals dropped by the score of twisted trees lining either side. At the end breathed a simple house with doors swung open, revealing from a distance one large room, with people spilling onto the porch and stairway. The flowers floated all around, everywhere.

"It seems a shame to walk on them," said Rebecca, her eyes drawn down to avoid the gaze of strangers as she and Ursa neared them.

"Yes, but the feeling is grand," answered Ursa, inhaling deeply through her nose, her head held high as they walked their bicycles through a tunnel of pink flowers. "Don't be afraid, Rebecca. Everyone here is quite friendly. Especially on a day like today."

"I'm not. I just feel a little awkward."

"Well, don't. And look up. I want you to paint this and get away from that silly graveyard. Look at the colors. It's magnificent."

"Maybe I should go get my paints right now," she joked and the two laughed as they laid their bikes down on the fresh sprung lawn by the last tree.

"Ah, laughter, and never a better day for it," called a man as he walked from the porch with a cane.

"Mister Phillips, how are you? I haven't seen you since yesterday!"

"No, but it's a big island. So big that I've never met you, miss," he said, extending his hand to Rebecca.

"Hi. I'm Rebecca."

"Rebecca's my new tenant," said Ursa.

"Well, welcome to the island, Rebecca, and to our church." And with this introduction she met a man whose every word was a sermon, though he had yet to speak of religion. He wore no robes, but an understanding and enjoyment of life radiated from him as he moved from group to group, person to person. Rebecca had never before met someone so unassuming.

"He's the Reverend?" she asked in disbelief. "He's not wearing a robe or whatever it is that they wear."

"No," said Ursa, hinting with her hand that they should go inside. "He trained originally to be a minister, but he has studied all religions and claims he doesn't want a label. He's really a fascinating man."

People on the stairs began to move indoors and settle into the rows of oak benches. The Reverend began with tidbits of news, an announcement of a birth and Rebecca listened, though a noise from outside drew her attention. She stared through the window high above the pews that revealed from her seat only sky and gulls circling around in a commotion. After many minutes, she leaned toward Ursa to point out the birds, but her ears were caught by the words:

"I saw something the other day and thought, 'Perhaps, God is an artist' and with that came the words I have today. As any true artist, God sought self-expression in His work. There are many stories of Creation and many of them have a similar vein. If we look to the Bible, in Genesis we read that God created darkness and light, Heaven and Earth, the flowers and the animals. Upon creating mankind in His image, in that moment of self-expression He flowed into his creation and the universe was complete. His work was complete and He rested.

"An artist. What is an artist? Someone who creates something, no matter what, can be called an artist if their heart is poured into it. There is an incredible story about Johan Sebastian Bach. Even if the story is an exaggeration, it's worth sharing, for Bach was truly an incredible man and he was very strong in his belief.

"No doubt, Bach was an artist—a master. Bach was known as the master of the fugue. A fugue most often refers to a piece of music where one voice starts out and is joined by other voices. The same voice repeats itself over and over, and is enhanced by still other voices. A simple example is the song 'Row, Row, Row Your Boat' when sung by three voices that are staggered in time. A complex fugue builds and builds to a crescendo and then tapers. It could go on forever, I suppose, but the musicians would get bored or tired and simply stop playing, so the composer tries to end it in the best way.

"Life can be compared to fugues in many ways. For example, one person tells a joke to another. Then that person goes and tells the joke to some other people while the original teller tells others. Soon the joke is being told by a lot of people—with some variation —the voices repeating the same words like a fugue. Everyone shares in the humor such that it builds in a way. Eventually, the joke reaches a point of popularity—its crescendo, if you will—and then fades away when it becomes an 'oldie'." The congregation chuckled.

"Well, that is a funny example, depending on the joke. Let's look at another: the spring peepers. They are tree frogs. Has anybody here ever seen one? I haven't, but that doesn't matter. We know they are there. This time of year, around the equinox of spring, we hear them starting around dusk. First one starts, then another and another and it builds until the sound is almost deafening. The noises are almost identical and some build on others. Eventually, as the night wears on, the peeping fades again. If you have ever stood near a bog at dusk, you can hear this natural fugue.

"When humans appeared on Earth, by God's creation or by evolution, whichever your preference, there were only a few of us. As we began to speak, we would say things over and over through time. The things you say to your children, your parents said them to you. How many times have you said something to a child and then realized your parents told you the same thing?

"So it goes on and on. Since man first appeared, he has said things and they get repeated. The voices are different. The languages are different, too, but what people say is often very similar. You can get by in many countries by speaking only a limited amount of the local language: 'hi', 'how are you', 'I am fine', 'thank you', that sort of thing. So people walk around saying the same thing. And as more of us appear on the face of the planet, it is a fugue. Perhaps somewhere out in space, the whole thing sounds just like the peepers.

"When it comes to knowledge, things are repeated as well: 'Let's go over the ABCs', 'let's talk about the Civil War', etc. Knowledge progresses at a very slow pace, really. Only centuries ago, some people doubted there could be another world across the sea, yet then there was the New World. But we teach our children not only so they know what we know, but to push them into discovering things that we do not know. So, like a fugue, voices repeat each other and build on each other, pushing higher and higher into a crescendo. Just wonder what will happen when everything to be known is known by all. Omnipotence? Omnipresence? God? Will the universe then collapse and start over? Perhaps some civilizations have almost achieved that knowledge, only to reach their crescendo and fall or be conquered and that knowledge wiped out, lost forever.

"So, please go ahead and figure out what a black hole is, but don't forget to go help your neighbor." More chuckles. He paused, cleared his throat and turned a page.

"Bach was the master of the fugue. Throughout his life he worked on a collection of fugues known as 'The Art of the Fugue.' He was in a musical society that required its members to submit a new composition annually until they reached age sixty-five. For his last submission, Bach chose his 'Art of the Fugue,' which he had worked on for nearly his entire life. He had to complete it, though, and the story of its completion goes something like this:

"Bach, the master of the fugue, had lost his sight during surgery, and with the help of his son, worked to get the final compositions completed. In one of the last fugues, Bach decided to spell his name, as it were, in the music—to musically state himself at the height of a fugue. The story goes that when he reached the point in the music where he wrote the notes that said 'Bach', his eyesight was restored and he wrote no more. He died some days later. Perhaps he had reached full understanding and needed to go no further.

"God is an artist. As any true artist, God sought self-expression in His work. I'm not sure if His work is complete, yet, but that is one belief. The point is that you have only one life and you must pour yourself into it. We all do something, whether we paint grand masterpieces or fix cars or mow lawns. We all have talents.

"Everything we do must reflect the truth of ourselves. Do nothing poorly. Try your hardest, for inside you, in a place that only you know, only you can find, there is a gem in raw form. To some people this comes naturally, others have to work hard to find it. Meditation is how some people search themselves. Others commune with nature. Many people go round and round looking for answers and never find them. The answers live inside you.

"There is at least one more thing to say about fugues. The voices can build on or detract from one another. You can bring down your neighbor, if you want, by gossip and negative talk, but it is better if you both try to bring each other up. There's no need for lies or hypocrisy. Though, without making things up or glossing things over, we can talk of the positive, encourage each other. Help your neighbor and your neighbor helps you. We sing louder in groups.

"The Pope said that his strongest tool is silent prayer. Silent prayer. Meditation. There is clearly some sort of energy inside of us, an energy that must be fed. If we radiate some form of energy and if we concentrate or focus this energy in meditation or prayer, it would make sense that prayers can build on each other and raise themselves higher, just like a fugue. So, please, let us bow our heads in silent prayer and on this glorious day, reach up to the sky with grand thoughts and great wishes for our neighbors and our world."

And the congregation bowed its collective head for a moment, and then a while, and soon the leader called them back: "Thank you, friends, for coming. Why don't we meet down by the run for today." With that, the hum of agreement and small talk began to fill the room again, women offering to help with the food brought by many and men carrying tables and chairs outdoors. Young boys helped the old folks down the steps and everyone smiled.

"What is the run?" Rebecca asked Ursa.

"It's what all those birds that distracted you are fussing over. It's really quite a sight. Come, let's go see," she answered and said no more, taking Rebecca's arm and leading her out the door.

Ursa greeted each person she knew, which was probably all of them, Rebecca thought, and was shy.

The run was a place where fresh water flowed down from a pond through a series of sluices, some past a waterwheel, but most through channels of rock that simply directed it to small pools. In the pools swam thousands of small fish, herring, in from the sea to spawn. The fish lolled about the shallow stream in such a mass that one swoop of a net through the flowing water would surely catch fifty of the silvery alewife. It was an easy feast for the gulls that flocked there.

Rebecca came back after the meeting to paint this scene, the waterwheel and shed surrounded by drooping lilacs and swirling water, the meeting house high on the lawn with the cherry tree path, the surrounding forest. As these thousands of fish just idled through the day, she noticed that one of the fish was on its side, staring at her. Then it seemed that they were all on their sides, staring. Then they were normal again, with just the one fish staring, staring, staring.

God surely is an artist, she thought, recalling the sermon from earlier and wondering how she could express herself in her work.

She could not possibly detail all of these fish—as if matching the pink blossoms and almost metallic trunks and branches of the cherry trees didn't take long enough—but the painting needed something to stand out, so she decided to draw one of the fish in excruciating detail. The fish must match perfectly what it symbolized to her, one individual lost in a crowd, with an eye drawn so well that it follows you around the room.

As she went to the stream and got down on her knees for a closer look at the fish, she remembered a drawing by Escher, a self portrait with him holding a small, reflecting globe. The picture describes everything the reflecting globe sees, including the artist and everything in the room, drawn in an unusual, curving perspective, just as a fish eye might see it.

She reached in the pool and tried to scoop up a fish, but it wasn't as easy as she thought it might be since these fish were only resting before shooting themselves up the rapids to get to their spawning grounds. They could dart away quickly and the water she pushed with her hands only helped them escape. She finally got one, though, by forcing it into shallower water and throwing it up on the bank. She grabbed it quickly before a gull swooped in, and she felt bad because the fish was all sandy, so she gently dipped it back in the pool to rinse it off.

As it flopped and puffed its gills, Rebecca cupped the fish in her hands and studied its silvery side and dark bluish-green back. Its body was flat and compressed, its belly slightly saw-toothed and its eyelids were puffy and fat. Then, as she noticed how easily the scales fell off and shimmered on her palms, a voice called out her name and she turned to see the chief of police coming toward her.

"Hi," she said and put the fish back in the water.

"How are you today?" he asked.

"Great. Astounded by all of these fish! It's amazing."

"I see you're doing another picture."

"Yeah, I love the colors here and I was studying the fish to try and get them just right."

"I figured you weren't taking them for bait."

"Bait?"

"Yep. They're great bait. Unfortunately, you're not supposed to touch them."

"No?" she said, shocked at the thought that she might get a ticket.

"Don't worry. I can see you're not poaching, but the fishery is closed. People took too many and now they're protected for a while until the stock replenishes. Bet you didn't know that." She shook her head.

"Well, since you seem interested in them, I can tell you that the herring is an ancient fish, primitive. They've been coming here to spawn for as long as the island's been here. The natives relied on them heavily for food. So did the settlers. You can eat them fresh, smoked, salted, canned as sardines—and they are particularly good bait. They became an industry of their own, used for fish oil, fish meal and fertilizer. The scales are even used to make pearl essence."

"Hmmm," she said with mild interest.

"My father used to bring me up here and we'd take them by the bushel. Unfortunately, they were so in demand that everybody over-fished them and now we have to conserve. That's why I'm here: We send someone up here to make sure no one takes them."

"I let it go."

"Don't worry; you'd need to be up here with a bucket and a net to get in trouble. So, do you like the island?"

"It's beautiful. So many things to draw. And I'm meeting some nice people. Once it gets warm, I'm really going to enjoy it."

"Great. Well, good to see you again. I'll let you get back to your work. Have fun!" he said and walked back up the hill.

But Rebecca had to hurry again. She had to finish what she could of the painting and get to the art show as she told Mrs. Walker earlier. She was not sure if she wanted to go, for Mrs. Walker was a woman whose accent changed to British the moment her art began to sell. Her deep-blue blood was so cold you could practically hear the ice cracking when she moved, and now she held her head as though her moment of greatness had arrived. But in finding faults with everyone, Rebecca found in herself what she didn't want to be. Plus, she said she would go and wouldn't want to do something to embarrass Ursa, so she finished what she could and carefully packed the wet canvas in a case so it could travel. Then she loaded up her bike, rigged with whatever she could design to make her life easier as a bicycling artist. The heavy bike went downhill easily, but she found herself nearly out of breath as she approached the yard where the art sale was.

Frames were everywhere. Hanging on snow fences winding through an open yard, a thousand frames held pictures seen by one eye and expressed on canvas for others to interpret with their own. Even realism will miss some detail or add others, the artist's own opinion. Guided by the heart and teachings both chosen and forced upon it, the soul has a collection of knowledge from which to draw conclusions.

Frames of reference. Two people from opposite ends of the earth meet and speak the same language. They have a common frame of reference: the words of the language that they speak. They have both seen a globe and roughly know the location of the major cities close to each other's home. "I live fifty miles east of Paris" or "thirty miles south of Chicago". Using that frame of reference, they can describe their homes in more detail and the other will understand to some degree.

Frames are everywhere and the closer you are to someone, the more time you spend with them, the more frames of reference there are between you. You can predict their actions. You know what they are thinking and finish their words. Frames are everywhere.

On the snow fences, there were many frames with different pictures painted by different artists. There were many good ones. Mrs. Walker's were fine, but they didn't express any passion. They were just pictures, she thought. Still, they were better than what Rebecca had done to date (so she believed and would surely be told so by Mrs. Walker). With that thought, Rebecca resigned herself as an artist just as Mrs. Walker came to say hello in that phony British accent.

"Hi, Rebecca," she called like saying toodle-loo.

"Hi, Mrs. Walker."

"What do you think of our show?"

"It's great. Are these all local artists?"

"Well, local and not-so-local. Is that something you brought for me to see?" she asked, pointing to Rebecca's case.

"No, not really. I didn't think I was supposed to bring anything. This is something I was working on today."

"May I see it?"

"It's not finished," said Rebecca shyly.

"Well, you don't have to show it to me, but I would like to get a feel for your style."

Rebecca agreed to show it and slowly opened the case, carefully removing the painting. "It's still wet."

"My Lord, Rebecca. It's beautiful. How long have you been working on this?"

"Since about one o'clock."

"Since one o'clock? I meant how many days. Surely you didn't start this at one o'clock today?"

Rebecca shrugged, not believing the painting was that good, and a raindrop fell on the canvas.

"Oh, no, dear, put that away. I was afraid it would rain. Would you help us put away these works?" Mrs. Walker asked as she turned away. She fully expected the answer to be "yes," and

Rebecca did not want to say otherwise, so she placed her work in the shed and then helped move the others inside.

When she finished helping, Rebecca rode her bike in the rain back to Ursa's house and went to a shelf where there was a reflecting sphere—it was one of those things that you found in an old person's house. Ursa noticed Rebecca studying the globe and predicted her intention by simply saying "please," before being asked if she could borrow it. Rebecca smiled at having her mind read and took the globe to her room.

As she stared into it, she imagined what the fish would see, looking out from the brook. The warp of sunlight reflecting back from the surface would confuse the fish, surely, especially when someone was bending over to look closely. She tried to draw the perspective that Escher drew, but without herself in the picture.

She remembered the self-portraits she painted the winter before when the snows kept her alone in her room with nothing to do but paint or sleep when she wasn't working. Dodging the doorbell and unplugging the telephone, she began to wonder how many self-portraits she could paint without adding something original, and with all the sleeping she did she imagined a self-portrait of herself asleep. She put mirrors on either side of the bed so she could see what she looked like when she woke, and drew herself with lips pursed, curving down, a lock of hair across her face. She got to the point that when she woke, she'd keep her eyes closed and take note of the position of her body, her arms, the pressure of her eyelids. She opened her eyes slowly and studied herself in the mirror, painted herself almost on her back, arms crossed, facing up or face down hugging the pillow. She'd close one eye and scrutinize it in the mirror until she got the lines just right, and soon it would be time to sleep again.

Then she got an idea. She needed canvas and she had done about twenty self-portraits. If she white-washed over them, she could use them again. She could white-wash them and then paint scenes of nature as seen from the eyes of other animals. Perhaps the pentimento, the picture painted over, will show through and have some special meaning—herself in a picture of nature—some special meaning for her life.

Maybe, but what animals could she use? The fish was one. That was sure to be a weird one, for the fish had two eyes. She would have to draw two of these perspectives—two fish eye drawings side by side, one looking up and out of the stream and the other looking down at the bottom of the brook. What else?

She looked out the window and just outside was a black iron eagle atop the flagpole. It was an iron eagle, but the view it had looking down from the top of the island gave her the idea to do bird's-eye portraits. She thought of the osprey that she saw the day before flying over the harbor, and how it saw a fish from so high and swooped down on it. She wondered how that would have looked from the bird's eye. There was only one way to find out.

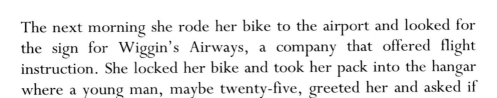

The next morning she rode her bike to the airport and looked for the sign for Wiggin's Airways, a company that offered flight instruction. She locked her bike and took her pack into the hangar where a young man, maybe twenty-five, greeted her and asked if he could help.

"I'd like to take a flying lesson," she said. The man told her that he was the instructor, gave her the price and asked when she wanted to go. "As soon as possible."

"We can go right now if you want. I don't have anyone scheduled until one." He led her to a plane and started going over the basics. "You have to start with an inspection of the aircraft," he said, and began to point at the engine. Rebecca didn't listen, opened the left side door and put her pack on the seat.

"Have you flown it today?" she asked as she took out her wallet.

"Yes."

"Then we can go. I've got a license." She unfolded a stiff, yellow paper and handed it to him. He studied it and gave it back.

"So, why do you want a lesson?"

"I don't really. I want someone who can legally fly in the right seat while I take some pictures."

"Why didn't you say that to begin with?"

Rebecca realized she had been brusque, but she knew he was going to ask her out, so she wanted to establish early on that she wasn't interested. She could tell by the way he had looked at her when she went into the hangar. *All guys are like that. All they want is sex and they are so nice, then they turn out to be jerks.* "Sorry," she said. "I'm in a hurry."

"Nobody's in a hurry on this island. What's the rush?" He thought to himself, What a bitch. Why are girls such bitches most of the time? Can't even be friendly. They just assume guys want sex and then they use it as a weapon. It's not worth it.

"I have to get some stuff done today," she said and climbed into the cockpit. "Let's go."

"How long have you been flying?"

"Since I was a kid," she said and the thought occurred to him that she still was a kid.

"This is a UNICOM airport. The station is set."

Rebecca started the plane, checked the oil pressure and the flight controls, and set the altimeter.

"You're not going to do a check list?" he asked.

"You've flown it today, I'll do the pre-takeoff. Why don't you handle the radio?"

"OK. Hey, what's your name?" he asked, even though he read it on her license. "Mine is Andrew."

She introduced herself and they shook hands, then Rebecca pushed the throttle in. The plane moved forward and she pushed her left foot to the floor to steer left down the taxiway. Andrew spoke into the microphone almost inaudibly because of the engine's low drone.

"It's a good day to fly," he said. "There aren't too many people up yet. Where are we going?"

"Just around the island. I want to see it from the air. Is an hour too long?"

"Take two if you want," he said.

"All right. Do you want to mark the Hobbes time?"

"I did," he said, embarrassed that he forgot to write down the numbers on the gauge that told how many hours the engine had run. He did write it down though, from the last time he was up. The engine had not been run since then, so the meter was the same. He told himself, You're being self-conscious.

The plane turned onto the runway after Andrew declared into the radio that they were taking off. Rebecca pushed the throttle all the way in and the engine screamed, the propeller sucking them down the tarmac. She pulled back on the yoke enough to lift the plane off the ground.

"Not so soon!" Andrew warned, but Rebecca leveled it off just a few feet in the air. They flew in what's known as the ground effect, a place just above the surface where the plane can fly at a lower speed because drag is reduced, the spiraling vortices from its wings broken up by the ground. If the pilot climbs out of the ground effect before the plane reaches a speed it can normally fly at, the wings will stall and the plane will come back to Earth hard. An experienced pilot would do this to reduce the strain on the landing gear, especially on a dirt airfield, but Rebecca did it to show off. In the ground effect, the plane accelerated faster and soon they climbed steeply.

"Sorry," he said, again embarrassed. "But you should tell people when you're going to do that."

The island disappeared in the distance behind them since the runway shot straight over the ocean. At one thousand feet, Rebecca leveled it off, throttled down and turned back toward the island.

"What's the plan, Rebecca?"

"I figure we'll do a couple fly-overs weaving back and forth and going about this far out into the water. That'll give us plenty of time to see other airplanes. If I see something I like, you take it and I'll shoot some photos."

"Anything in particular you're looking for?"

"The harbor, the house I'm staying in, the dunes. Some of the meeting house. There's a lot."

They flew over the island once and turned again. The engine sound changed as they turned back into the wind and the plane buffeted. The clouds were high and thin, though where the ocean met the sky there were none.

"I'm taking it down to six hundred feet," Rebecca said as she pushed the yoke forward and the engine tone again changed.

"We'll be better off flying the length of the island. There'll be fewer passes," he said, using 'we' as the pronoun because it gave his students the feeling that they were a team, with him as the commander of the aircraft.

Below was the budding island. They approached the tallest dune and the lighthouse and passed over, the plane buffeted more as they cleared the cliffs, the updraft lifted them and the ground fell away. Turning back steeply, the stall warning horn sounded and Rebecca pushed the yoke forward, but the horn did not stop.

"Better level off. You're too low to stall now," Andrew warned and began to wonder aloud. "When's the last time you flew?"

"A while ago. Maybe a year and a half," she said as the plane stabilized.

"You flew over a year ago. Huh, here I am thinking you fly everyday. Watch the cliffs. The wind shear can be extreme and I don't want to die today." He felt his ego filling back from the previous deflation. *Over a year ago! You gotta fly all the time to just take control. Man, I am an idiot! Watch this one carefully.*

"All right, you take it," Rebecca said. "Fly in as low over the harbor as you can."

"Do you want it wing low?"

"Sure, if you can."

"I can do anything." He smiled and she looked at him and smiled back, though she still thought he was just another pilot. They're all too cocky. He adjusted the plane so it flew itself.

Rebecca shot a few photos, but she soon realized that photography is an art in itself. In order to take good pictures, your efforts must be concentrated on all the aspects of camerawork. Photography is completely different than painting. In order to get ideas, she concluded, she must concentrate on observation and forget about taking pictures. She put the camera down.

"OK, Andrew. Fly me around the island. This is a sightseeing trip. Let me know if you need any help."

"Roger, Captain." He did not like her. She was unfriendly and too bossy, and she seemed prejudiced against him. That didn't matter to him, though. She's cute, he thought, but there will be plenty of those around the island in the weeks to come. No need to get hung up on this bitch. The nerve of her just showing her license and treating me like a shit. What a fool I am. She could have stalled back there and put us right into the cliff. Look at her now. Just another passenger. Shut up. Just take the money. This hourly thing is not worth it. I should be flying jets. Soon.

He was paying more attention to himself than to his flying. They were flying low and slow, one of the more dangerous things to do. When a plane is flying straight at another, the other one can appear about as big as a thumbnail held at arms length when it is just seconds away. Concentration on flying the machine is as important as watching the sky, especially in a UNICOM area that is not controlled by a tower.

"Here comes another plane," said Rebecca. "Better drop to the right."

"Where is it?"

"Just up to the left. See it now? He's climbing away."

"Yeah, I see him. It can get pretty full up here, especially around lunchtime. You ever eat at the restaurant at the airport?"

"No."

"You should check it out. It's got a great brunch. Lotta people come here just to eat. They say it's 'food worth flying for.' You could join me for lunch when we get back," he said with a smile and paused. "Why don't you fly more often?"

"It scares the shit out of me," she finally admitted to someone other than herself.

"Then lunch won't be so bad," he said and scanned the horizon.

Chapter 9

Going to School

The alarm clock paged at quarter to eight Friday morning. Dave threw a fist at the clock and sat up, still aching from the days before, exhausted from staying up until dawn, and he looked for his wife because she was rarely there when he woke these days. He heard her and the boys down in the kitchen. He couldn't sleep anymore even though he felt worn-out still. Downstairs, as the kids tried to help make their own lunches, Aimee was referee to the first event: a peanut butter fight. Dave climbed from the sheets and made his way down the hall and stairs as he wrapped a chilled robe about him. He felt that the boys knew there was more to the story as he felt the cold air from the kitchen tiles on the tops of his bare feet, yet they had nothing to say about it.

"Boys," he pleaded, separating them, "Do your mother and I fight with peanut butter?"

"Sometimes," said Sam.

"Yeah, I saw you spread peanut butter on her shoulder once."

"Yeah, then you licked it off. Ick!"

"Yeah."

"Well that wasn't at eight in the morning, and we weren't screaming at the top of our lungs," he said, animating the last bit. "Besides, we weren't fighting. Cut it out, all right?" He took the knife from Sam's hand and the jar from Peter's. "And good morning."

"Morning," they said together.

"Good morning, Love," he sighed to Aimee and reached for the coffee left in the pot, his eyes sinking deeper into the bags beneath them. "I'll take 'em and then go to the hardware store, OK?" She grabbed the sleeves of his robe and pulled herself close with a kiss to his neck.

"Shouldn't you get some rest, Dave?"

"I can't sleep."

"You still shouldn't be driving."

"Why not? I haven't forgotten how to drive. I'm not dizzy or anything." His insistent tone imported that she not argue and she didn't feel like arguing anyway. In her mind, she resigned that she'd drive and he'd come along for the ride, then they could talk. She looked at the bruise on his head.

"What do you need at the hardware store?"

"Just some things for the boat. No big deal."

"The boat? What do you need for the boat now?"

"Just a few things. Just something to do—to give me something to think about."

"OK, but be back soon. If you're feeling that good, I'll give you something to think about." She smiled, one eye slightly squinting with a hint of something else on her mind. "I need the car, though. I've got to go to the market. These guys are eating like horses and the garden is going thin. How about I drop you off and come back in half an hour?"

"How about I go to the store for you?"

She pensively considered the change in her plans and accepted it without really agreeing, but she knew she had only a few minutes to get the whole day moving.

"I'll jump through the shower and get dressed," he said and went back towards the stairs and up, slowing as he neared the top. He tossed the robe on the bed and went into the bathroom, turned on the water. He lifted a toothbrush from the counter and ran it under the sink, then looked at his naked body in the mirror. He saw a

130

different man. Lifting heavy traps, working on the boat, eating what he caught (though his wife and kids forced him to eat "normal" things now and then), he lost a lot of weight. His muscles were toned. The guy that he was back in the office, that guy was gone. He felt completely new.

After a few minutes under hot water, he quickly dried himself and pulled on some jeans. It was cool, but not cold enough for socks, so he didn't bother to look for them. A T-shirt under a long sleeved shirt, some deck shoes and he was ready, but then he stuffed two sweatshirts and a pair of socks into a daypack. He grabbed his wallet from the dresser and looked in the full-length mirror as he left the room, tucking in his shirttail. Combing his hair with his fingers as he tromped down the stairway, Aimee peered around with a mug full of fresh coffee.

"I don't know how you can look that good with such little effort."

"Well, maybe it's livin' in the country. You know, sleepin' late, no responsibilities, no worries... Sure beats the city." Their lips met and he hugged her neck. "Those guys ready?"

"They're out in the yard," she said as he walked toward the door. "Hey..." she called. Dave turned to see a look that asked, "Do you remember anything?" But all that crossed her lips were the words, "It does beat the city."

"I..." he said and forced another smile, pushed through the screen door and stepped down from the porch. The boys were chasing the dog and each other around the yard in a game of tag. A truck pulled into the driveway. It was Eddie Vanson. Dave walked slowly, a few steps towards the truck, then stopped, not knowing what to expect from Eddie, who had not only been in jail for a few years but also had won at least a hundred brawls. He was at one time Thomas' best friend and looked like he had been up all night with a bottle. Who knew what he was thinking?

"Morning, Eddie," Dave said to him solemnly as Eddie climbed down from the big pickup.

"Dave," he said, staring.

"Hi, Eddie," Aimee called from the porch. "Would you like some coffee?"

Eddie's face softened as he recognized her. "Hi, Aimee. No. No, thanks."

Aimee walked slowly down the porch stairs and over to Eddie. She hugged him and whispered how sorry she was about Thomas. In a circle, as the boys chased each other and the dog around them, they spoke of their dead friend. Dave had nothing to offer, nothing to say. He was fearful of Eddie, nervous, wondering why he would come so early to the house. He seemed to have had as much sleep as Dave. As they talked, Dave studied the clearing sky behind them, watching the clouds for wisps of the weather.

"What time is it?" he asked.

"That's right," said Aimee. "We have to get the boys to school. Eddie, what are you doing? Can you give the boys a ride and drop Dave in town?"

"I suppose I could," he said, and Dave was left wondering what had just happened to their plan.

"Great," she said. "I'll get a blanket so they can ride in the back." She ran to the house and Eddie moved his gear around in back of the pick-up to make space for the boys.

"What's that stuff?" Dave asked, just trying to keep the conversation from turning to where he knew it would go.

"I got some mason work. You know, that's what I do when it gets too cold to fish. Ain't much work around anymore, though. Mostly just repairs. No new construction. I'm the last mason who lives here on the island."

Aimee returned with a large blanket. Dave called for the boys to climb in the back and sit with their backs to the cab, then tossed the blanket over them. The dog watched for the opportunity to jump in the truck.

"No foolin' around back here, all right? I don't want you guys fallin' out and missin' school."

Eddie pulled himself into the driver's seat as Dave walked around to the other side and told the dog to get back, but it was useless. She wanted in the truck, so Aimee grabbed her and held her as she squirmed. The engine started and Dave opened the door and climbed in awkwardly with his pack. Eddie backed the truck out onto the road and drove down the hill rather fast. Dave wanted to tell him to slow down, but the kids were enjoying the ride and he didn't want to seem weak.

"So what the hell happened out there?" said Eddie over the hum of the tires as they picked up speed. "You don't still have amnesia, do you?"

He hesitated to answer. Pieces had come back, but he wasn't going to start telling Eddie. He will be the last person I tell anything to, he thought.

"Well, from the best I can recollect," Dave said, trying to delay his response long enough to make up a reasonable story as they went along. "I'm not sure, but we got on the rocks and waves started coming over the side. We tried to back off, but it was no use. The waves kept pushing us higher." He was lying. Lying always leads deeper.

"How'd you hit your head?"

"I can't say for sure, Eddie. That's what I can't remember, that and what came after. I just remember being stuck. You ever been up on the rocks in a good sea?" Dave said, trying to change the subject

"No, I haven't. Hope I never am."

Dave let it die at that, but Eddie kept going.

"What's it like?"

"It's pretty scary," Dave said, trying to dig more of the lie, unable to come up with words.

"I'd imagine so. But what happened? Come on, man, Thomas was one of my best friends forever! Tell me what happened."

Dave looked at him and shook his head. "I don't know yet. When a boat's in the waves like that," he said, remembering the time he slept in a large sailboat and woke up when a ferry came into the harbor at speed. The tide had gone down and left maybe a foot of water underneath the keel. When the wake went past, the waves lifted her up and then dropped down. The keel hit the bottom like thunder and they rolled from side to side to the point where water came into the cockpit.

"The keel hits the bottom and you roll way over," he said. "Then another wave comes and rolls you the other way. The boat nearly turned over. Things were flying off the shelves. Pots and pans, the charts, everything went everywhere. You know, when the keel hits the bottom, it shakes the whole boat, and when it can't go down any further, the boat rolls over on one side. I tell you, it woke me up. I was scared. I guess that's how I hit my head…slipped as she rolled and hit something."

He stopped the story. It couldn't go on or he would let something slip. Dave thought, he'll go straight to the police and they'll want to hear it and I am making the whole thing up. I cannot remember what happened and if I tell a story now, I will dig myself into trouble.

"So you got a concussion. How did Thomas end up dead?"

"I don't know, Eddie. I think we tried to get the raft over the side and maybe we fell in. I really just don't remember."

"Tom Berger says Thomas was shot. Shot in the head."

"That couldn't be true," Dave insisted. "Why would I shoot him? Be realistic, Eddie! Thomas and I were friends. Nobody got shot out there. It was dark. Thomas could have split his head open worse than me." Dave turned his head to highlight the bruise.

As they came to a stop sign, Eddie looked over at Dave, shifting his body so that he faced more toward him while keeping a foot on the brake pedal.

"What's this I hear about you talkin' to old man Hersey last night? Somethin' about a dead girl. Where'd you hear about something like that? Ain't nobody been killed here."

Dave saw something in the eyes of Eddie that he wanted no part of. The boys were looking through the back window, wondering why they had stopped. Eddie wanted an answer and he could be the one who... Dave slid open the back window.

"Boys," he said. "Climb out on this side of the truck."

"Why, Dad?"

"Just do it, all right?"

"It's OK, Dave," said Eddie. "I'll take you the rest of the way."

"It's no bother, Eddie. We'll be fine. I just don't want to talk about it anymore. I'm telling you things I'm not sure about and the police want to know what's going on just as much as you. This town's talking behind my back and I don't want stories flying around, especially to the police."

"Don't worry. I won't be goin' to the police. Can't trust them at all. They're the last ones I'd want to talk to."

"Just the same, I think we'll walk," he said and climbed out the door with his pack.

"Have it your way, Perfessor," said Eddie and he spun his tires in the gravel and flew down the road, Aimee's blanket still in the back. Dave turned to the boys and they looked up in bewilderment.

"Now what do we do?" asked Peter, the older boy.

"We miss school!" shrieked Sam.

"No. Now we learn how to hitchhike," Dave said.

"What's hitchhike?" queried Sam.

"It's when you stick out your thumb to beg for a ride," said Peter.

"It's not begging, and don't ever do it without me! And don't tell your mother. Come on, let's start walking. And another thing, hitching on this island is a lot different than hitching anywhere else. People here know one another and they'll stop for you. On the mainland, there are all kinds of weirdoes. Some who might hurt you. Do you understand?"

They nodded and then Peter asked, "Why did Eddie kick us out of the car?"

"I don't know," he said. He felt worse as the whole thing seemed to fall apart further and his confusion only led him to the side of the road. He began to walk and the boys followed. He could use this time to talk to them, he thought, but he hadn't the words to say. His head throbbed a few beats and he knew the boys wondered what they were doing, but didn't ask. Dave worried what might happen at school and almost had the words to say when a car came along slowly. Dave stuck out his thumb and the boys did the same as the driver pulled over immediately. Dave opened the passenger door and greeted a familiar face and her dog. "Hi, Mrs. Taylor, how are you this morning?"

"I'm fine, Doctor Wyman. Hitchhiking with your children?"

"Well, I knew it was you." He smiled. How could he not know it was her? "We had a little trouble with our ride. Could you do me a huge favor and drop them at school?"

"Oh, sure. I'm in no rush. I'd be glad to. I'm just going to the market."

"Thank you so much, ma'am. I'll put them in the back." He closed the door and turned to the boys. "OK, boys, Mrs. Taylor is going to take you to school. Be very nice to her, OK? And don't say anything about Eddie, all right? It's very important that you don't say anything. Do you understand?"

"Yes."

"Yes, but what's going on?" asked Sam, dragging the last word on and the question echoed in Dave's head. *What's going aahhhhhn?*

"I'll tell you later. Just don't say anything." He opened the back door and the boys climbed in. "Thanks, again, Mrs. Taylor. I owe you one."

"Oh, I don't mind, Professor, it's no trouble."

"You boys be good and remember to say thank you when you get out. Thanks again. Bye, boys." He closed the door and she drove off slowly. At least they'll be safe with her, he thought.

Dave started back toward the house, kicking a stone along the road for distraction, and recalled how he came to this place from the city. He was working as a biologist in Boston and maintained close connections with his university. Whenever he got sick of the day to day, nine to five office routine, he would return to school to take classes, do some research, or even teach. To him, school was therapeutic, but it drained his bank account. When the boys came along, he needed the higher wages that came with a real job and took one that started great, but soon his ideas turned into someone else's. He remembered walking to the train one day and it all came at once. Like every emotion rolled in a ball and thrown hard at his head, it hit him. He thought back to that day.

I awake and it is raining. The clock has yet to ring and already I am hurling curses at a boss whom everybody hates. The worst part is that the boss hates Mondays, too. Mondays, I curse them even in my dreams.

Monday is garbage day. On this day, no matter what time I leave the dingy-yellow house in this horrid suburb of Boston, there is always a dingy-yellow garbage truck and guys screaming "Hep!" at the door to greet me. To make it even finer, it starts raining harder as the door closes behind me.

Down the lane to the train I go, with this town's familiar rain glistening on the trash thrown about by those who like the place even less than I. I am late. As the most uncomely train station ever built looms closer and closer, swarms of people scrambling for their daily lives congeal onto platforms and await the departure of an iron serpent to take them to their loathsome hell. The boredom of another Monday starts the boredom of another week and threatens us with homelessness and ruin.

To think that mankind has evolved into this. If Darwin is right, then man emerged from the primordial soup and became so advanced that he dreads the start of every week. People crowd into vehicles and sit in traffic for months of their lives in order to please someone else, despite the fact that a thinking job can generally be done anywhere.

I stride under the bridge and the birds sitting above that led me to coin the term guanophobia—fear of being shit on. Some people think it's good luck to be shit on by a Toucan, but these skeavy pigeons whimpering above me know nothing but a wretched existence of which only they are unaware. They are free, free to go

138

anywhere, but where did they choose? A bridge by the side of the highway. In Boston. In winter. What fools.

I turn around. All this thought about the job has made me ill. By the time I get home, I will surely have thought of an excuse that no one will question. Today, my creativity shall be spent making up lies.

I go back under the bridge, taking careful steps around the mounds of dung; the law of averages, you know. Oddly enough, my stride has slowed to a saunter, despite the rain pouring down. I'm tempted to fold up my umbrella, but I'm no fool, I think.

The men don't notice me as they load up their truck with the things I threw out. The door seals behind me, muting the sounds from outside. Now I can think. No one can see me do whatever it is that I want to do. Whatever that is.

So, Dave was fed up with commuting to work for somebody else, but what else could he do? He felt helpless, gutless. He had some money saved and could live in the country for a year, if he wanted, but what would he do there?

The island seemed like the perfect place for an escape. All he needed was a little incentive, so he wrote a proposal and got a grant to do a study on the disappearing land. It started out fairly well; his oldest boy came home with a bouquet of flowers for his mom and it turned out that the flowers were on the federal endangered species list, but flourished in a spot nearby, barely noticed by anyone at all.

So he did his self-assigned job. He went around taking notes on everything, not just the biology of the island and sea, but everything down to the people and buildings. The den became a chart room with marine charts and geological charts and road maps from many different years stacked on the table, rolled up in a corner or taped to the wall. The locals started making fun of him because he was always with a notebook, squinting at things they took for granted. Not Thomas, though. He volunteered to be Dave's guide and took great pleasure in it, for he knew all that was right about the island and what was going wrong.

Nevertheless, Dave found himself studying the small details, just as he had in an office or laboratory for his entire career. He still wanted change, to study the macro part of life, something pressing. Then the conditions for lobster fishing changed, with a new phenomenon occurring with the food supply, water temps, etc., and he was already collecting data right smack in the middle of it, seeing first hand the boom and potential bust of the industry. His colleagues encouraged him and he started to get the real-world exposure he wanted. He spent more and more time on the water, going out in all kinds of weather, seeing the creatures that came up in the traps and the changes that tides and winds brought through the season. After some time, he realized that what drew fishermen to the sea time and again was the closeness of nature that didn't have to show itself for anything more than what it was.

When Dave got to the island, he began to grow into someone else, someone new. He remembered an old roommate from a time when there were five of them in a house at college. He was nineteen and in his second year of school. His friend was in charge of the house, given that responsibility by the woman who owned the place, and he gloated that the number of keys on his key ring was an indication of how responsible he was.

Now, Dave thought, I don't carry any keys. There's no crime here. The doors are locked only at night. The keys to the car are in the ignition. Where else would they be? People had been known to borrow someone else's car in an "emergency," which was generally a joke. It was a good way to keep people from driving drunk, too.

If someone's too drunk to drive, just take his car home without him. He could always get a ride. Everybody knew everyone else and hitchhiking was a standard way to get around and meet people in the summer.

Then he realized the opposite about keys, that the more keys you carry the less important you are. A janitor has a lot of keys. Those of importance need no keys. The President carries no keys. So he was happy to be keyless and all that he wanted was a beater truck that anyone could take and drive around the island.

And his mind raced: I came to this place to get away. I came here to write a book on marine biology, to try and do the world some good by describing the effects of industrialization vis-a-vis northeastern marine life. At least, that's what I told the people at school. What I really wanted was to take some time off and be with my kids as they grew up. And now here I am, September, with hardly a typewritten word and a suspect in a crime in a place without crime. I came here to try and live my life and find out something about life itself and I found out about this. Who the hell thought I would become involved in...?

The house was in view. Aimee was just getting in the car to leave and saw him climbing the hill.

"Dave, what happened! Where are the kids?"

"They're all right. Mrs. Taylor took them to school."

"Mrs. Taylor? What about Eddie?"

"What *about* Eddie?" he scoffed. "He came here with more questions than the police. My God, he wouldn't let up. With the police, you can just shut up, but that guy is really intimidating. I just had to get out, so we started walking and Mrs. Taylor came by. I hitched a ride with her. She took the boys to school and I walked home. I'm telling you, Aims, people are talking about this like I shot Thomas. Like I'm already guilty. Why would I do that?"

"Dave," she said, "it wasn't a fight over me, was it?"

"No. It was definitely not a fight over you. You see? That's just like the rest of them. Everyone's throwing out conjecture like it's a game of charades when it was just a boating accident. I'm torn, Aimee. I'm torn between trying to figure out what happened and why it happened. I think Eddie was involved in it."

"Involved in what?"

"I'm not one hundred percent sure, honey, at least not about what happened. But I am sure of one thing. This town is talking about it like nothing else is going on in the world. Rumors are flying. I talked with this old guy last night about nothing, about his model ships and legends of the island. Next thing you know, Eddie has it all confused and comes here this morning with it clear in his head that I killed Thomas. It's gossip ten times over. The lawyer told me not to say anything to anyone. Now I understand why. Freakin' Eddie. There's only one reason why he'd be so suspicious. They were up to something."

"Like what? Growing pot? That's not so important. Maybe he just wants to know what happened. We'd all like to know, wouldn't we?"

"Yeah," he said, touching his head. He took a breath. "Maybe you're right. I'm just really confused."

"So what do we do?"

"I want you to leave for the weekend, with the boys, please. I have to stay and try to figure this out, but I don't want the boys or you to have to deal with it. You don't know anything more than I do. I'll bet the boys get picked on today in school. Will you do that, please? Just go see your parents for a few days."

"And leave you here to do what?"

"Nothing. I just don't want you here and I can't leave the island without raising suspicion."

"What about your head? I can't just leave you here with a concussion."

"I'll be all right. The worst is over now. I just don't want the boys to see me like this. I just need to think."

"All right," she said reluctantly, "but it can't go on for more than a few days, Dave. Right?" her eyes asked before the words passed her lips. "If it goes on longer than that, I don't know, maybe we should move away from here, get them away from here. I feel it in them. I know they are…living through a major part of their lives, Dave? Dave? Are you listening to me?"

But he did not hear her for he was alone in his mind. "Come on," he said, putting his arm around her shoulder. "Take me to town. I just need some time to clear things up in my head. Come on, Barney," he called for the dog. "Let's go for a ride!" Dave took a bicycle from the porch and put it onto the back of the car, which always seemed to have had a bike rack on it since the day they bought it.

Chapter 10

A Walk Around

Morning broke with an overture of birdsong and a sky that could be no clearer, where stars flew low on the horizon and changed to seabirds as the light turned the nighttide. Rebecca woke knowing that she would spend her days off as many here do: walking the shores of the island. Despite the cacophony of reason and doubt calling her back to her room for one last forgotten thing, she took up her pack and turned her back on the room, the over-stuffed bag already too heavy to be carried for an entire day. She snatched her camera from the bureau as she left. She loped down the stairs with a rhythm of two beats and a pause and found Ursa, in her usual morning manner, lifting a kettle of boiling water for tea.

"You're up early," she said, then dropped the kettle back to the stove and put her burned finger to her lips. "I have got to get a new kettle!"

"Two days off. I'm going to walk on the beach the whole time."

"That's always fun."

"I'm going to paint mostly."

"What will you do about eating?"

"I'll just take this," she said, grabbing an apple from the fruit bowl without stopping on her way through the door. The last thing she wanted was questions about what to bring. The pack was already too heavy and she could always catch a ride into town and eat at the Dog. Ugh, the Dog. That's the last place she wanted to go. Maybe she should bring some food, and at that point Ursa called from the porch with a bag in one hand and the other gripping the rail as she hobbled down the stairs in a rush.

"Here, Rebecca," she said. "Some bread and some cheese and fruit. It might keep you for a few days the way you eat. I hope it doesn't spoil." And with that she handed over the bag and turned back to the house, knowing when not to speak further.

"Thanks," called Rebecca, wanting to say "thanks, Mom," in a joking way but stopped. "Thanks, Ursa."

"Someone has to look out for you crazy artists," she said as she climbed back up the stairs, her cane left in the house more often. "Have fun."

Rebecca passed the end of the beach grass, the cool blades still dripping with dew, and lunged down the dune, driving her bare feet into the steep sand, plunging down and down until the dune leveled off at the beach. Abbey followed down the dune part of the way, but turned back when Ursa called.

"Only one way to go," Rebecca decided and turned to the right, away from the near tip of the island. The morning was cool; the sun not yet high in the sky, but it would not be long until most of her clothes came off. Maybe she would take all of her clothes off and walk nude down the beach, she thought, cause scandal and outrage, but that had been done already and there was no sense in mimicking anyone. Something audacious was what she needed. Something to set her apart, be and define her. Something to attract attention through its own special grace.

The sun needed not to rise any higher, for the burden of the pack had already brought her to a sweat and she paused to take off her shirt, leaving on the black top of her suit and her shorts. Then she thought, Don't forget why you are here. She sat on the sand and squinted over the view, then closed her eyes and leaned back, her head in her hands.

"Oh, yes!" she called aloud, "this is why I came here." The sun idled higher and warmed her skin so it glistened with sweat. She opened her eyes and squinted even harder as she took out black glasses from her pack. Again, she ogled the view with a smile, but nothing was there to be drawn, so she closed the pack and stood, swatting the sand from her bare thighs.

As she toddled down the beach and the dunes grew taller, she forced herself to look at them for what they really were—piles of sand. They were just piles of sand, a few hundred feet tall, capped by dune grass and held up by reddish clay that streaked down the coarse sand to meet the fine sand of the beach. Swept up by the wind, they were the mountains of the island, looming high but made of tiny grains that tumbled slowly back down themselves. Larger rocks and stones eventually came loose from above and rolled to the bottom, leaving behind a trail on the dune that the wind covered back up in a day. In the places where the tide rose past the beach and ate away the dune, steep cliffs formed like desert canyons and the sand from above flowed down like waterfalls in hundreds of places. They never stopped, just flowed and flowed, the island a fluid formed by wind and water, rain and tide.

To see the dunes this way was easy, but to draw them was a task where one's mind must separate from the fingers holding a brush. She chose a place where the dunes were highest and the lighthouse could be seen, but the visitor center was blocked from view. Few people had come yet and she wanted to draw this before others arrived.

As Rebecca sketched this scene, she felt the waves slipping back to the sea in whispers, boiling in the stones and shells deposited at the ocean's edge. She turned her head to one side as if she'd heard a voice and turned to see who it was, but there was no one. She heard the voice again. It sounded like a cry and she stood and walked to the water, slowly, then quicker, and she peered around, holding a hand above her eyes like a visor, but she saw no one. A Laughing Gull laughed.

She was sure she'd heard it, though. It was so clear and plain that she refused to go back to her picture without searching the horizon for a minute or so, and as she walked back to her work she turned around to look again. Still, there was no one.

She returned to her sketch, almost ready for paint, and she noticed two fishermen walking down the beach, stopping at different places to cast in the surf. She continued, but kept watching the men as they got closer. She tried to put them in the picture. One man was ahead of the other, who seemed to be less fervent about the fishing. The leader cast and slowly reeled in not more than twice in a given spot before he started walking again, the eel used for bait slowly curling on the hook hanging from the tip of the fishing rod. As he got closer, Rebecca noticed that he was a boy, maybe sixteen. She laughed at herself because she thought the perspective was fooling her, but then the boy got a fish on the line.

The rod bent toward the waves and from a distance Rebecca heard the reel winding, line screaming out to the sea. The kid pointed the rod toward the fish and the screaming soon stopped. Out in the water, deep down by the bottom where the boy let his bait swim, the fish had hit the eel from the side and taken it a distance. Confident now that he had the eel, the fish stopped and adjusted it for the swallow. Once the eel was completely in his mouth, the fish ran again.

Back on the shore, the kid waited for a moment, anticipating the second run, then lifted the rod sharply when the run started, setting the hook deep. He reeled and snapped the rod upward two more times. Then he was into the fight. The rod came alive, bending in half and shaking. It was a big fish and Rebecca shared the excitement as the boy fought it, line screaming, then stopping and the boy pulled up and reeled in as he let the rod down.

As the boy fought the fish, a wave broke hard and pulled him down. Rebecca ran to help him. The other fisherman ran, too, and he set his rod down on his gear so the sand stayed out of the reel. The boy got back to his feet on his own and the fight continued, the pole still bent in half and pulling him to the water. The other fisherman held the boy by the hips and the waves sloshed around them. The fish broke the surface slowly, like a whale rising for air, its head, its back and then its tail thrashing the surface and driving it back toward the bottom.

"It's huge," someone shouted. A small crowd had gathered and more people were coming down the beach.

"It's a shark!"

"Sam, get out of the water," said the man holding the boy. They were both boys, actually. Most likely brothers, Rebecca thought. The fish kept pulling and the boys fought it and they fought the tow of the waves to leave the water. The fish broke the surface again as the boys made it to the edge of the water's reach.

"It's not a shark, but it's big," said another. The fish ran again, streaming line from the reel. Then the line went limp.

"I lost him," said the boy.

"Reel it in, Sam! He might have doubled back." That is what happened. The fish had stopped or turned around, and was fighting again.

"Keep him away from the rocks," one shouted. The line angled to the left, toward two craggy boulders that breached the backs of waves and were swallowed up with the next. The fish sought the shelter of the rocks and the line would surely break if it touched them. The boy pulled the rod to the right, trying to coax the fish back, and he did. The fish stopped and Sam raised the rod again and reeled fast on the down stroke.

The fish ran again and again, breaking the surface, but not jumping. Its head thrashed at the surface trying to shake the hook, but the hook was sunk deep near the swallowed eel that still curled in his gullet. Sam reeled the fish towards shore, seeing him in a wave that rose to a breaker.

"You got to time it right, Sam. When a wave is coming in, start reeling like hell!" But the boy did better than that. When a wave crested to break and the fish was in it, Sam turned around with the pole on his shoulder and marched up the beach, pulling the fish into a foot of water that disappeared as the wave fell back. The fish flopped a few times, but its weight out of water was great and it quickly tired. Another wave came and washed the fish farther up the beach and dragged it back some, but the older boy ran to it and struggled to get it away from the waves.

"That's gotta be a record," someone in the crowd said as the boys congratulated each other.

"I don't know how we're gonna get it home. We'll need a pick-up truck!"

"I have a station wagon," said Rebecca, and the boys looked up at her, but she did not see them. All she saw were his eyes and they stared at each other for a moment, then he stood.

"Hi," was all he needed to say. She smiled.

"It's not here, but I can call and have someone drive it here."

"Really," he said. "That would be great. There's a phone at the visitor center."

"I'll go call. Do you have any coins?"

"Just dial the last four digits of the number. It's free."

"You mean I've been here a few weeks and never knew that?" she said. "Watch my stuff for me, would you?"

She tried to run up the path that was cut at an angle across the dune, but toward the top she had to slow down and she reached the pay phone completely out of breath. She paused for a while, then went to the phone and dialed four digits.

"Hi, Ursa, it's me."

"Hi, dear."

"Can you do me a favor? It's not really for me, it's for some guys I met."

"I suppose. As long as it doesn't involve fish."

"It does."

"How many?"

"Just one. It's huge. You must see it."

"I've seen plenty of fish. Is he cute?"

"Well, yeah..."

"All right. It was just a lucky guess anyway. Where are you?"

"At the lighthouse."

"OK I'll see you in about twenty minutes."

"Thanks, Ursa," Rebecca said and hung up, laughing out loud. *A lucky guess.* That woman must be a clairvoyant.

Rebecca went back to the crest of the dune and watched the boys wrestle the fish toward the top. It was as good a show as them catching it, two boys fighting a fish up the dune, the fish flopping now and again, falling to the sand and rolling back down the hill. She stayed there until they got all the way up with the fish covered in sand.

"The car will be here in a little while."

"Thanks. Thanks a lot."

"I have to go back down and get my stuff."

"I'll go with you," said the one. "My name is Peter," he said, reaching out his hand, then wiping a slimy hand on his shorts. "Maybe we should save the handshake for later." He smiled. "This is my brother, Sam."

Peter and Rebecca walked down to the beach and retrieved her pack and drawings. Peter went to his gear, then to the edge of the water to rinse his hands and she followed him.

"I don't feel like running up the dune right away. Do you?" he asked.

"Not really."

"Do you want to go for a swim?"

"Not with fish like that in the water."

"Aw, come on. They don't have any teeth and they're really shy."

"It is pretty hot," she said and put her bag out of reach of the stretching sea.

He pulled off his shirt and ran into the breakers, diving into the face of a crest. He let out a whoop and shook the cold water from his face, but he swam a bit and dove under another wave. He surfaced, gazing at the dunes in the background of her smile. Then he swam back and climbed from the surf to collect his gear.

"How about that handshake now that my hands are clean?" he asked with a smile, his hand outstretched. "Nice to meet you, Rebecca."

"Nice to meet you, too," she said and he met her tidal-pool eyes. They touched. Her hand was warm and his cold from the swim.

"Sorry for the cold hands," he said.

"That's OK. I'm usually the one with cold hands."

"Do you need help with your stuff?"

"No, I can get it."

"Wow! You did that picture? How did you get those little rivers of sand so right? I thought nobody else ever even noticed that."

"Really?" she said with her hand covering a humble smile. "I didn't expect it to come out so fast."

"Are you sure we're not taking you away from your painting? We could find a ride from…"

"No, no," she insisted. "I offered."

"Well, I owe you one," he said "Tell you what. You carry the picture and I'll get your pack."

"It's really heavy," she said as he lifted the pack effortlessly and turned toward the dune.

151

"I appreciate your doing this for us."

"Not a problem. I can get this picture home and start another."

They walked side by side, then he let her go up the trail first. When they returned to the top of the dune, a small crowd had gathered by the fish and a young man was talking to Sam.

"Hey, Peter," screamed Sam. "This guy is having a party and wants us to bring the fish."

"What?" Peter asked.

"Hi. I'm Mike. You can come with or without the fish," he said with a smile and handed Peter an invitation. "It's an island tradition to have a party when you catch a big fish. Unless you want to mount it."

"I'd never mount a fish," said Peter as he read the invitation.

"Neither would I," Mike laughed. "Anyway, I'm throwing the bash of the summer tomorrow night. The band is incredible. I saw them at the Nail and they blew the place away."

"Let me see that," Rebecca said to Peter.

"Here, have one," said Mike and he handed her an invitation that said "Full Moon Bash."

"I saw these guys, too. They are great."

"Do you want to go?" asked Peter.

She looked at him and answered with her eyes, then said, "Sure."

"Great," Mike said as he started down the dune. "Bring the fish if you want, that's a lot of food. Definitely take it to the bait shop and get it weighed. It looks like it might be a record."

Ursa's car came into the parking lot and she knew exactly where to go because there was a crowd standing around a fish.

"Hi, Ursa," said Rebecca. "This is Peter and Sam."

"Hi, boys. Good to see you again," Ursa said as the boys nodded to her with huge smiles.

"Sam caught the fish."

"*You* did?" she questioned since the fish seemed larger than the boy. "Well, you're the envy of the island! I'll bet you get your picture in the paper with that fish."

Ursa felt like a grandmother with kids visiting for the summer. She brought plenty of newspaper to line the back of her car and she drove them to the bait shop where the fish was weighed. She knew the store owner and asked him to come outside and help with the fish.

The store owner (Bruce was his name, just one more name of the many Rebecca felt she had to remember because he was such a great guy) came out and gasped at the fish. "We'll have to rinse him off," he said. "He's pretty sandy. You didn't stuff sand down his throat, did ya, son?" he asked Peter.

"No, sir, why?"

"Just kiddin', but some folks'll put sand in a fish to make him weigh more. Didn't think you'd do that, but I figured I'd ask anyway. Let's get him around back to the scale." Sam grabbed the fish by the tail and pulled him out of the back of the wagon. The fish fell to the ground.

"Whoa," Bruce said. "Be more respectin' of that fish."

"Sorry," Sam said shyly.

"'S'all right, my boy. Let me get him," Bruce said as he slipped his fingers behind the fish's gill and lifted it up with both hands. "Wow," he said. "This is some fish. We'll have to get a picture of this one."

Bruce carried the fish to the back of the store and laid it down on the ground to hose off the sand. Then he picked it back up and hung it from the scale. It was a few pounds shy of the record, but it was nearly as tall as Sam. Bruce asked if they wanted to mount it.

"It's your fish," Peter said to Sam.

"I'd never mount a fish," Sam said, repeating his older brother's words from before.

"Wait a minute, now," Bruce said. "You caught that fish?"

"Yes, sir," Sam said.

"Well, I'll be damned. That fish is almost bigger than you are. Let me get the camera. We'll get your photo in the mainland papers. And stop calling me 'sir'! My name is Bruce. Don't wear it out."

He brought out a camera and took a picture of Sam standing next to the fish. Sam held the rod that he used to catch it. Then Bruce told the rest of them to get in the picture.

"Not me," Ursa said. "I had nothing to do with that fish."

"Come on, Rebecca," Peter said. "Let's get our picture in the paper!"

"I…" she said.

"Come on. Don't be shy. You look great."

"OK, but you stand next to the fish. I don't want to touch it."

They crowded by the fish, Sam with the rod on one side and Peter on the other side with Rebecca next to him, making sure she didn't bump into it. Bruce took a few pictures to make sure he got a good one. Then he insisted on writing down their names correctly for the newspaper.

"I'll call some of my friends at the paper and see that this gets published. It'll definitely get in the local paper. Now, what are you gonna do with this if you're not gonna stuff it?"

Sam said, "Some guy invited us to his party tomorrow and said we could bring the fish and feed a lot of people. Some kind of island tradition, he said. No sense wastin' it."

"That's awfully generous of you, Sam. And since I'm going to that party, maybe I'll help you clean the fish. You know how to clean a fish?"

"Well, sort of. I mean, I can filet a fish, but I've never done one that big."

"With a fish this size," Bruce said, "you're better off steakin' it."

"What's that mean?" Sam asked.

"It means cutting it into steaks, cross-wise. Let's take it over to that table and I'll show you."

"What should we do with the fish until tomorrow?" Peter asked.

"You can keep it in the fridge here. I've got some space and it'll keep well. Just come by tomorrow before seven with a cooler and some ice."

"Tell you what," Ursa said. "I have to go. Does anyone need a ride?"

"We're OK," Peter said, "but thank you, Mrs. Taylor. I hope your car doesn't smell like fish."

"No problem, Peter. Nice to see you boys again. Congratulations, Sam."

"Thank you, ma'am."

Peter turned to Rebecca and asked, "How should we meet tomorrow?"

"I can give you my phone number."

"OK"

"Do you have a piece of paper?"

"I can remember it. It's only four numbers."

"5928."

"All right. What's a good time to call you?

"Around six."

"Wait, now that's a lot of numbers." He smiled, placing his hands to his head. "5928 at six. I think I've got it. Talk to you then."

Walking to the car, Rebecca asked, "Do you know those boys, Ursa?"

"I've been acquainted with them for years. They've been coming here off and on since they were little. Nice boys. They've grown so much," she said as they got in the car. "That was some fish!"

"What?"

"The fish. It was big."

"Oh, yeah. Huge."

"My, Rebecca, are we head over heels?"

"No. He seems like a nice guy."

"Well, he seemed a bit distracted, too."

Rebecca turned and Peter looked up at her. Their eyes met and they smiled again.

Chapter 11

Back to the Stage

Dave's shoes slid down the asphalt shingles used for traction on the steep gangway leading to the floating dock. One sneaker squeaked when it hit the level surface and small stones, broken away from the shingles, followed him in a slow avalanche. The floats creaked as he tromped past the large boats down to the shallow water where the smaller boats berth.

His boat was a Cape Codder, or a Caper, a great sea boat wrapped up in only nineteen feet. Some of the local fishermen would go out in groups of these boats called the "Mosquito Fleet" because of the buzzing sound they made as they flew from the harbor in swarms. Locals took those boats more than fifty miles out in the ocean to fish the rich banks, knowing they could outrun most of the big storms and that there was safety in numbers. Dave's fearful respect of the fog kept his boat around Wianno, but this day was a different matter. This day, she would go to Stage Island.

She was powered by an outboard that popped to life after wheezing for three turns of the key. It stuttered and spit until warm. Her light gray hull pushed easily from the dock and the motor ground into gear with a chunk, gliding them into the harbor. Once past the moorings, she planed quickly and bounced through the small waves and channel. Around the sea wall, the waves building larger, the water was smooth and the sky a deep blue. The compass swung to the northeast and Dave settled in for a long ride with the helm held as straight as she would as he focused his mind on the past.

Dave's past didn't return to his mind as if he awoke in the morning. He had been awake for hours. So his whole life did not flow back from dreamland in one swipe at a shrieking clock. It returned in blobs, images.

And Dave thought, when you stop moving, you're dead, or on your way there. That was how Thomas looked when Dave came around and found him lying in the encroaching tide, dressed as a corpse, hands frozen to claws half clenched. Dave pulled him by his jacket, away from the rising waves and Thomas was limp. Dave thought he was still breathing.

Through the end of twilight, Dave saw the Elizabeth as she yawed like a log between rocks. The dingy on shore, flowing off and back with the sea, he went there to the edge of the island and hauled the little boat higher, stopping a while to rest and rid his head of the throbbing. When Dave returned, he knew Thomas was dead.

Dave awoke with his face flush to a stone and a wave rushing over him, yet he could not remember why, how, did they get on Stage Island?

His thoughts burbled again and brought back a memory from last spring, a memory of climbing onto the Elizabeth one morning and leaving the harbor. It was not a perfect morning, rather cold and foggy, but Thomas had no fear taking Elizabeth to sea in anything shy of a gale. He wasn't a fool, but fog rarely scared him.

That day, when the Elizabeth cleared the breakwater, there was nothing left to do, so Dave watched the radar for signs of Stage Island. The island was the only thing out in that part of the world except for a few buoys and it showed up strong because of the reflecting tower on it. Too many boats had perished there, so the

Coast Guard kept it well marked, but the electronics couldn't see it yet, far over the horizon.

"What's the story about this wreck you heard of?" Dave asked. "How big a ship is it?"

"Pretty big," Thomas said and adjusted the throttles to synchronize the engines. Dave was slightly annoyed, but he knew Thomas was deliberate in his response.

"Pretty big, huh?" Dave said. "Sounds enormous."

"I want to check the place out before we go for the wreck," Thomas said, repeating the words he said when he first told Dave of the ship a few nights before. "Let's just get there, look around. Dive for lobster."

"We agreed we'd do that, right?"

Thomas looked up from the controls and over at Dave with deliberation. "She was a four-masted schooner," he said. "That's pretty big. The story is that she came up from the mainland with a load of coal and supplies and wrecked. One of the interesting things to me was that the way those boats were built explains what happened.

"You see, those boats were popular back in the late eighteen hundreds because they could haul a big cargo, but they weren't as expensive to maintain as a square rigger. They had a simple rig that could be handled by a small crew. They had what was called a donkey engine on board, a single engine that could be used to raise the sails, haul the anchor, move cargo, even pump. The smaller crew meant they were more economical to run, but they had a few problems."

"Like what?" Dave asked, though Thomas was going to answer the question without being asked.

"Like they had a flat bottom that would pound in a seaway and the stress on the masts was so great that it caused 'em to hog, where they're lower in the bow and the stern than they are in the middle, shaped like a hog's back. That's not a good thing," he said with the knowing tone of a ship builder.

"To make it even worse, they had a tendency to hull twist when rolling in a heavy sea. Those boats had a life span of about fifteen years. A lot of 'em were lost in the eighteen-nineties, so many that it was hard to get insurance companies to underwrite 'em after a while. You get a big boat with a small crew and things start to happen, there's too many things for the crew to handle.

"This ship has a chilling story: She set out with a crew of ten and the captain's wife came along for the ride. Boats back then had to sail out to the east and then come back around the outside of the island, otherwise they'd have to tack through the rocks. You don't want to do that even today, let alone with a ship laden with coal. As it happens, the weather got worse out at sea and the waves grew heavy. The captain's log said that he heard a great crack and he ordered her to be held just off the wind while he went to inspect. The main beam had split when the ship twisted as she rolled, and the seams came apart.

"The captain's last entry was 'attempting repairs.' There's no sayin' how she ended up on the rocks, but she did. When they found her a few days later, her masts were the only things visible, stilled rigged with tattered sails and her bell ringing on its own as the waves rocked her. The captain's wife was found dead, lashed to the rigging above the waves. She froze there.

"Two days after that, the salvagers came out and hauled off the coal and they noticed that there had been a fire in the kitchen. When things start going bad, everything goes bad, I guess. They found a man with his throat cut." Thomas paused, almost dramatically. "It wasn't uncommon for a seaman in that situation to cut his own throat out of fear. But that woman, they said she was just as peaceful as could be."

They sat in the silence of the diesel hum and the island got closer and began to show on the long-distance range of the radar. Dave adjusted the screen to a shorter range and Thomas kept the boat aimed steadily toward the blip. Dave adjusted the radar again and again, but they saw only water until the radar indicated a half-mile and the mist yielded the black rocks. Thomas pulled back on the throttles to slow the boat down as they came to the buoy clanging slowly, the rocks just beyond it. He idled her in close as Dave went to the bow, unlashed the anchor and waited for his signal. The engines nearly silent to Dave on the bow, Thomas swung her into the wind and nodded for him to drop the anchor.

They got to the island around eleven o'clock, about forty-five minutes before the falling tide would slacken enough to let them dive. In the meantime, they made the last of the preparations quickly, checked the gear that they'd already checked. Thomas hoisted the dive flag and they sat on deck drinking herb tea, scanning out over the horizon and hearing waves cover the rocks and run back to the sea.

Soon enough, the current slowed and they could go over the side. They looked at each other for a moment, then Dave went in first. The water bit through the wetsuit for a few seconds, but was not as cold as expected, just a lot darker. He waited at the surface for Thomas, who splashed in and made sure again that everything worked. They gave each other the OK sign and let themselves sink beside the anchor rode to the bottom, holding their noses and blowing to equalize as the pressure gripped. Their regulators cast their breath in bubbles to the surface, which could no longer be seen after twenty feet. They fell slowly the rest of the way in cold blackness. At thirty feet, kelp slipped around them as they dropped until the rocks came into the lamplight and they leveled off on the bottom, at about fifty feet.

The kelp was thick and Dave paused for a moment to adjust his vest for neutral buoyancy, then he looked at his compass to head west, toward the island. He walked a step and a half then stretched out and swam along the bottom with a flashlight in one hand and a long, metal stick, hooked at the end, in the other. The rocks on the bottom were the gray in a black and white picture lit by the bulb at the end of his arm.

He slipped along the bottom, rising and falling with the rocks, until his first victim came into view: a two pound crustacean. The lobster retreated into a hole in the rock, but his mind was no match for a man. Lobsters swim quite fast, but only backwards, their strong tails pulling hard in reverse. In all other directions, they are slow and easily caught. Dave reached in the hole with the stick and tapped him on the back with the hooked end. The lobster, thinking there was something behind him, crept out of the hole and turned around to make his escape. With a pump of his tail, the lobster shot backwards, right into Dave's waiting hand. Too easy, he thought as he fumbled with the catch bag and a claw gripped his finger. Startled, he lost hold of his prey and it disappeared in the kelp.

"You loser!" Dave said into the mouthpiece. That was dinner for four somewhere. But Stage Island turned out to be an incredible place to find lobster. Despite the traps strewn a distance from the island, lobsters flocked in droves near the main cluster of rocks. Below the foaming surface, Dave spent the first half-hour dive collecting them like shells on the beach, only keeping the best. On schedule, they signaled each other to rise to the air, letting bubbles lead the way through the kelp and blackness. They stopped for a moment at fifteen feet and turned off their lights. The surface shined and shimmered like a mirror and they were suspended in the cold with nothing below them.

Dave broke the surface about six seconds before Thomas, who came up a few yards away and spit out his regulator to laugh.

"Holy shit, how many did you find down there?"

"I only kept six!"

"Ha, ha, I got seven, and they're huge!"

"We'll never eat all of these."

"I know. I don't know what we're gonna do for the rest of the time. We can't keep hauling these guys unless you've already made out a Christmas list!"

"Let's check out that wreck."

"Yeah. Good call comin' here. I'll never go anywhere else for lobster!"

The two converged on the boat, pulled off their fins and climbed onto the swim platform. They sat and let their legs dangle in clear black ink as a couple of seals scooted away from the rock island to dunk back to the sea. Smiling as they pulled the bags up for inspection, Thomas exaggerated the weight of his catch.

"Lookin' good there, Davy. How many did you get?," he asked, tossing his flippers, one after the other, over his shoulder and into the boat.

"Six."

"And how many got away?"

"Just one. The first one. You know, novice jitters."

"Yeah, right. I let a couple go myself. I must have had twenty in my hand, most of 'em keepers. I let a few out of the bag and kept only these guys. They're like two to three pounds, eh?"

"In your dreams, man," Dave said as he slipped out of his tank. Thomas was already out of his gear and climbed into the boat with both bags.

"Hey, don't get those bags confused. I want everyone to know who caught more," Dave called.

"Who kept more."

At the never-ending one-upmanship Dave laughed as Thomas dumped the lobsters into a holding box, then reached over the transom to hoist his tank onto the deck. Then he hefted Dave's. After the tanks were strapped in, Thomas took the long gaff from the rack on the gunwale and reached out into the water to hook plumes of kelp and pull them in to cover the lobsters.

"It seems a bit cooler up here," Dave said as he sat squinting over the horizon.

"Yeah, a little. Come look at this chart. That wreck is over here somewhere," Thomas said and ran his fingers in a small circle on the chart. They stared at the chart for a little while, Dave just looking and Thomas aligning his fingers to the chart and pouring over some notes that he got from a friend.

Though he had done most of the chart work back on shore, Thomas read over his notes as if stalling then returned his gaze to the chart. "The masts stuck out of the water for a few months, then another storm came and pulled her deeper. She must be pretty solid on that ledge, I bet. This guy says that there are three rocks in an 'L' shape and then two more side by side a little bit north. That must be these, right here. He says it went down here into about sixty feet of water. Can you handle it?"

"Are you talking?"

He aligned his fingers on the chart. "Check out how this lines up with the island and the two buoys," he said. "That means it's over there, just around the island." And with his other hand he waved a general circle to a spot only he saw for sure.

"Let's do it," Dave said and went to the bow. Thomas started one diesel and then the other. He pushed a throttle forward a little just to loosen up the anchor line. Dave took up the slack. The windlass pulled hard to free the anchor and hauled it to the deck. As soon as the chain raked over the bow, Thomas steered toward the spot he had chosen while Dave picked the anchor free of kelp.

"Don't get too close to the island."

"Yeah, I know, just keep a look out," he said through the windshield, which was hinged at the top and pushed out from the base.

They made a small arc keeping away from the island and rocks that came through the surface. Rounding from the lee of the island, the sea picked up and the hull showered a wave over Dave. He turned and ducked a bit, but the wave still coated him with wet salt. When he looked back up, there was something under the waves.

"Rock! Yo, a rock over here!" he shouted and pointed to starboard. Thomas put it in neutral and they passed a few feet from a submerged mass. "Go that way. We're gonna hit it!"

Thomas put full reverse throttle on the starboard engine for a second, knocking Dave off balance some, but keeping the boat off the rock. They slipped past it and then idled forward.

"That was close. Damn island is a death trap," Thomas grimaced and turned more away from the island.

"You sure you know what you're doing?" Dave asked, knowing full well that neither of them knew anything about the place. Without saying a word, their pride coaxed them on to a new world.

"Piece of cake," Thomas said. "Look at the fish finder."

Through the side window, Dave saw the screen of the depth meter and the outline of a sunken hull.

"She must have hit that rock you just missed."

"I just missed. Suddenly, it's me who's..."

"Yeah, yeah. Just turn her around."

Thomas spun the wheel clockwise and thrust the starboard engine in reverse, turning them around on the spot. They backtracked their wake and Dave dropped the anchor towards the wreck. The line slipped through his fingers as the anchor fell, then stopped.

"It only went down forty-five feet."

"Is it in the kelp?"

"No, I think it's on something."

"Good, it's probably right on the wreck," Thomas said and backed away from the anchor. More line slipped out before coming taught to the wraps on the windlass. When it held fast, Dave cleated the line and walked on all fours standing up, hand over hand on the handrail, around the wheelhouse to the stern. Thomas shut down the engines.

"Better mark that rock on the chart," he said.

"Good idea. Could you see the ship down there?"

"No, but it's pretty deep."

Again, they readied and checked the gear. They took the second tanks and fitted them to the buoyancy control vests, checked the regulators, did all the normal preparations. Then they sat and waited for a moment, making sure there was no good reason to stay out of the water. Thomas pulled his wetsuit on first. He took a thermos of hot water and poured it on the suit before he climbed into it. Dave did the same, but still his back curled as the cold rubber suit slipped around him.

"I don't know how long we should stay down," Dave said as Thomas held his tank and he slipped into the vest.

"Yeah, it's pretty cold and tide's gonna change soon. Let's just go take a look. Twenty minutes?"

"Fifteen."

"Twenty."

"All right, let's go then, but let's watch the tide. We'll cut it short if it starts running."

Thomas inflated his vest full and walked to the transom, opened the gate and stepped out onto the swim platform. Without another word, he heaved himself forward and kicked out his heels. He entered the water in good form, holding onto his mask and the quick-release of his weight belt should he need to ditch it if his vest failed to float him. Dave walked forward with a clumsy flop, flop of his fins, and jumped in after him. They met at the surface, their gear checked out fine, and they swam to the bow and grabbed hold of the anchor line. One last look at each other as the bow showered them in waves, and they deflated their vests and pulled themselves down the anchor rode, then swam alongside it.

As they got deeper, the water got black, though the white anchor line stood out the entire way down. Soon they saw nothing but the line and some of each other in their lamplight, then a little kelp, and then the gray hulk of a wreck.

The anchor hit fairly close and after they checked that it had set well, they swam to the ship, which sat deeper at the stern than the bow, a little on its side. As they approached, Dave recognized the shape of a sailing ship, though its masts had rotted to stumps and most of the hull was eaten away. Wrecks here looked a lot different to him than in warm waters. There were no real colors, just the dark mass as they swam towards it.

Thomas split off to the stern while Dave went forward and peered into the main hold near amidships. Below the deck was a black hole. There's no way I'm going in there, Dave thought, pulling himself around the square hole with his hands and carefully shining his light inside to see what might be there, ready to fly out at him. He panned the beam from right to left, then saw something flash. He moved the beam back to the right and it flashed again.

He floated for a moment with his light reflecting back at him and contemplated whether he could get up the courage to go in there. He reassured himself that there was nothing to fear and crawled in a little, just his head and the lamp. He thought, There's nothing in there, go deeper. But he lost what he saw. He took his eye off it and it refused to flash in the light. It was over here, he thought and searched, fully inside the ship's hold.

The hold only showed what his light hit, otherwise blackness. The light fought through a fog of thick flotsam, kicked up mostly by

Dave. He moved carefully, slowly searching for the thing that shined back. It's in here somewhere, he thought as the light hit some eyes by a pair of long tentacles.

A lobster! What the hell, just grab him, his greedy side called and he did, right by the tentacles. The lobster fought back, though, and clawed his small finger. Dave struggled to flick him off and pounced again as the lobster backed to the hull of the ship and crawled sideways. A waste of time it turned out to be since the lobster was shy of the legal length, and together they had kicked up so much silt that Dave feared it hard to find the way out, let alone what he came in to get.

Disoriented, he watched the bubbles float up through the turbid water and shined the light after them. Following them up to the top of the hold, he made his way back to the opening, at least where he thought it was, but couldn't find his way out. He got nervous; a few fathoms down and stuck in a hold. Think now, which way did you chase that fool lobster?

Then he saw it, the light shining back in his, and swam back down, kicking up more silt. The opening was clear and so was his prize, whatever it was. He stuck his face and lamp right up close and waved his hand to fan away the silt, but there was nothing. He dug deeper with his hand, yet still nothing. Then a round piece, like a coin, came out of the sand and then covered slightly again.

It was not a coin. It was a cross, a gold cross with a long chain that pulled endlessly from the sand. The chain was broken and slipped from the cross to bury again, but it was easily found. Dave put the cross into his dive bag, but the chain would fall through the netting, so he kept it in his hand. He dug for more, but there was nothing. Then he heard a tapping, metal, and floated up to the hatch and poked his head from the still water in the hold.

He knew at once that they were in trouble. With only his head outside the hold, he was pulled to the other side of the hatch by the current. Thomas tapped his tank with his light and Dave saw him.

They flashed lights at each other. Thomas moved toward Dave by clawing his way along the side of the ship, fighting the current that turned sooner and stronger than they had expected. They had to get to the anchor and follow the line to the boat, for they could not swim against the tide. Dave tried to climb through the hatchway, but the current grabbed his tank and turned him sideways, catching his wetsuit on the tattered edge of the deck. He had to retreat, to reorganize in the calm of the hold.

He needed to get rid of the chain in his hand, so he unzipped a few inches of his wetsuit and dropped the chain inside, then resealed his chest from the cold. He swam to the upstream side of the hatch, placed both hands on the edge and pulled himself clear and into the stream. The wood collapsed with a snap amplified by the water. He saw Thomas look back as he drifted up and away, but he turned and dove back down and caught the down-stream bulwark of the ship and dug his heels below the wall, leaning into the current.

Thomas shined his light at him and then at himself and gave the OK sign. Dave did the same and on opposite sides of the ship they worked their way forward, groping for hand holds. Dave made it a few more yards and shined his light to see what was ahead. The wood was rotten and split. The hull lay on rocks to starboard, but there was little to hold onto in that direction. Toward the middle of the ship, Dave saw a mast stump about ten feet away. I can make it, he thought. Swimming hard, pulling and kicking against the current, he fought to the mast and wrapped his arms around the stump, forcing himself around and to rest with his back against the mast. Sucking hard on the regulator, trying to catch his breath, his heart screamed its pulse through his ears.

One of us must get to the boat and he can rescue the other, Dave thought. He heard a clanging of metal, but couldn't tell where it came from. He couldn't assume that Thomas would make it to the anchor, and having his wind again, he swam toward the other side of the ship and along the outside of the hull. It was easier out there, though the current wanted to lift him over the top and carry him away.

He caught up to Thomas near the bow of the wreck and saw him clinging to a large boulder just ahead to port. The tide had overcome the wind on the surface and Elizabeth was facing the other way, the anchor line leading toward the island. Thomas turned and saw Dave's light and waved him to come ahead. Dave was breathing hard and sweating into the wetsuit. Three deep breaths and he dropped to the ground and clawed toward Thomas, grabbing rocks that at times broke away, leaving him to dig his hands and heels into the bottom for anything. The anchor slipped when the tide turned and threatened to tear free. Dave heard its metal clang, but it wedged in between rocks not far from where it first held and then they were at it, holding onto the line.

Glaring through his faceplate, Thomas gave the sign to stop. With his eyes and a motion of his hand he said, "Just relax. We're almost out of it." Hand over hand behind Thomas and their bubbles, Dave followed the line back toward the daylight silhouetting Elizabeth black on the shimmering surface. She was still afloat. She did not go on the rocks when the tide turned.

The line was both taught and loose at the same time, but the current was relentless, sucking a vacuum behind their tanks. The surface was just feet away and then they broke it, the waves opposing the current, moving slower, cresting. The regulator dropped from Dave's mouth and he gasped deep breaths of fresh air.

"Where the hell were you?" Thomas screamed as the bow lowered, slacking the rope that pulled tight again with the next wave.

"I went into the hold."

"You know not to do that. Didn't you hear me?"

He shook his head no. "I found a cross."

"That wouldn't do you any good if you were over there!" he shouted, pointing downstream past the island. "Come on. Drift to the stern. Don't miss the platform!" He let go of the rope and drifted along the waterline. Dave let go, too, and drifted down the other side, grabbing hold of the swim platform on the stern as Thomas climbed on and let out a sigh and a curse. "Shit! That could've been a bad scene, man."

Dave agreed and Thomas took his fins from him. Dave climbed the ladder, only to fail from exhaustion and fall back into the water. He held on there for another moment, then climbed out and sat and caught his breath.

The weather had changed some, slightly warmer, the fog had lifted a little and the wind had settled. The tide was rising and the water clearly flowed around the buoys and rocks. Much longer in the hold and I never would have noticed the tide, Dave thought. He might not have made it back to the boat. In those parts of the world, the current flowed so fast that you could only swim with it. Dave knew he screwed up. He should have signaled that he was going into the hold. Dangling from the platform, his leg caught the spit from the exhaust pipe as Thomas started the port engine.

"Get the anchor," he called. "I want to move before it pulls." Dave felt the chain slip in his wetsuit as he stood and carried his tank on board, then he dug deep in his suit for the chain and put it in the dive bag.

Dave hadn't had anyone angry with him for a while and he could feel it simmering within Thomas from a distance. He felt it even though anger had never before been expressed and neither knew how to act or how the other would. Dave had done something wrong, something very stupid, and they could have lost their lives together. Thomas had a right to be angry. Dave knew it and felt bad. It was their first dive together.

Probably our last, Dave thought. How could he trust me again?

Without a word, Dave followed his orders. Thomas drove the engines forward a bit when Dave reached the bow and pulled the slack rode, using the windlass to free the anchor from where it wedged. They were at cruising speed before he got the line and chain in the locker. Returning to the stern, he saw that his tank, left standing, had fallen and rolled to and fro with the boat. Quickly, he strapped it to the gunwale, knowing that Thomas had already seen it. Dave could tell it angered him further.

Still with guilt, Dave worked quickly to store his gear and clear the deck. When he found himself finished but not yet wanting to talk, he remembered the cross and took the dive bag to the bench seat behind the cabin and dug for it. Before he could study it, Thomas beckoned from the helm by slowing down one engine and speeding it up again. Dave looked toward him and Thomas waved for him to come forward, then adjusted the throttles to keep the engines synchronized.

"Take the helm," he said when Dave reached him, now with a way to break the ice.

"Look at this," he said, putting one hand on the wheel. "What's the heading?"

Thomas said nothing as he looked at the cross. He seemed as though he would say something, but he turned to go to the stern.

"Wait!" Dave said. "Let me get the chain" He left the helm. Thomas slowly put one hand on the wheel and drove without looking. Dave returned with the chain and Thomas stepped away from the wheel without a word. He walked away coldly uninterested. Dave took the helm and fought the wheel as he tried to study the cross and chain.

"What's the heading?" Dave yelled over the engines.

"Just go that way. You'll see the lighthouse soon."

"What's the heading? Thomas!" Dave yelled again as the boat caught a wave and lurched to one side nearly knocking them both down.

"Two-fifteen!" Thomas shouted as he began to wash off the deck and the lobsters with the salt-water hose. "Now pay attention to the boat!"

Dave took up the cross and paid half attention to steering through the calming sea. The cross was heavy enough to be gold and was about three inches long and proportionally wide. The chain was thick. It wasn't a normal cross, in the sense that most people think of crosses, but it had two transoms, or crossbars, the top one shorter than the lower and there was a slanting crosspiece below them. It had no markings, no stamp of purity. If it was real gold, it would have been made either long ago or in a place where such stampings were unknown. Dave felt some research coming and knew Thomas must be furious not to care about the cross.

He looked back at Thomas as he hosed the deck. Thomas had a love affair with as many boats as possible, but compared to Elizabeth they were all mistresses. When the day was over, he would leave the general cleanup to the others and then make sure the details were finished before taking the helm into harbor. He knew his boat through every inch, topsides and below, having stripped everything out and replaced or refinished it. Whenever a problem arose, as is often on boats, he was the one to fix her or watched carefully as the work was done. He never left the responsibility to someone else, never trusted anyone to fix his boat right, for a moment at sea can turn to disaster in an instant, like a snare on a rabbit's foot.

Dave kept looking back at Thomas as he played with the hose, washing the kelp and other debris from the deck. He glanced at the lobsters, packed in a box with wet seaweed. Then he watched forward through the clearing sky as the lighthouse came into view, guiding them back to their home. It reminded him of the cross he found shining back in his light, a quick flash as the beam swept past.

The sun began to set as they fell into the lee of the island and headed to harbor. The sea flattened and the boat picked up speed. Thomas returned to the helm for the last bit of the ride and Dave concentrated his focus on the cross, inspecting every scratch and nick and noticed his eye reflecting back in his glasses.

The Elizabeth moved through the small waves without bouncing, her forty feet and deep bronze keel making her near perfect for the seas around the island. She had two diesels instead of one big one, which gave her the reliability needed so far from the mainland. She could make it to any harbor in the area in rough seas if you wanted, easily.

She had everything a yachtsman could want and everything a fisherman needed. The helm had a spot that sat a foot higher, allowing the driver to stand with a longer view from a cupola on the main roof. Other than that, she was a classic lobsterman's boat, though she never hauled traps because of the damage they do to a boat. Her lines were that of a yacht, as was her polish, but her outfit never drew mocks from any fisherman considering the catch she brought back to harbor.

The pride shone in his eyes every time Thomas backed her into the slip using the throttles, then ran to tie her off single-handedly. He fussed with lines not more than once, the knot coming perfect each time, and he put her away as fast as he could. He spent so much time hosing her down, though, that people complained he was wasting water, got tired of waiting and told him they would be in the Dog.

Such was the case for Dave that day. He sat alone at the bar with his cross and sipped the remains of a beer, running the chain through his fingers, counting the links of gold. Thomas came in with a wave to the crowd and ordered a large glass of water, no ice, and slugged most of it down with three gulps.

"Man," he said, as he almost always did, "that makes me thirsty."

"Sorry I couldn't be of more help."

"Well, you know me."

"I think I'm starting to know you too well. I think you do that just so you don't have to buy the first round."

"That's it," he said, both of them knowing he would only drink one, if at all. But he ordered a beer and a shot of whiskey.

"What's up with the whiskey?" Dave asked.

"Just don't feel right. That's all."

"Look. I'm sorry. I screwed up—"

"You're damn right you screwed up! I was looking for you for five minutes. We could still be swimming right now. Or dead!"

"I know. I'm sorry."

"Don't be."

"What do you think I should do with this cross?"

"See that old guy there? His name's Ross. He's always in here and you can ask him about anything. He told me all the stories about that wreck."

"And to think I've been sitting here all alone."

"Well, you'll get to know people. He knows a lot about stuff like that."

"Yeah, but I don't know if we should tell anyone about the cross just yet. What are the laws about this sort of thing? Maybe the state can take it away. Maybe we should lay a claim. Maybe a claim has already been staked out."

"Any claim on that ship has already expired. I don't know. Maybe they don't expire. Just go show it to him and if anyone else asks, say you found it somewhere else. Besides, that wreck was picked clean a century ago."

"I don't know. Rumors spread fast. I could get taxed on it, or something."

"Or there could be twenty divers out there tomorrow, dying in the tide 'cause their buddy took off without—"

"Stop. I'm sorry. All right? That's it!"

"Yeah. That's it."

Reluctantly, wanting to say more about keeping it a secret in a place he doubted anything could be kept secret, Dave went over to a man sitting at a table with a few others, no one saying much. The man had a round head and round chest and belly piled like a snowman. His eyes and face shone red and his hair was cut short, the same length and gray color as his beard.

"Are you Ross?" Dave asked.

"Yep."

"Hi. I'm Dave Wyman. Thomas told me to come and talk to you about something."

"What's up?"

"Well," Dave said, again reluctant, but he continued. "I found something and Thomas thinks you might know about it."

"What is it?"

Dave motioned with his hand for Ross to come to another table and he slid his chair over.

"I found this cross," Dave said and placed the cross and chain on the table.

"Well, if you found it, you should take it over to the police station and turn it in—"

"No," Dave said, cutting him off. "I found it out there...in the ocean. Diving on that wreck you told Thomas about."

"You boys went to Stage Island?"

"Yeah. Dove for some lobsters and then on that wreck."

"And this came off the wreck?" he said, flipping the cross over in his hands as everyone does when they get their first look at a treasure.

"Yeah," Dave said. "Seen anything like it?"

"It's a cross. You know, a religious thing," he smiled.

Dave smiled. "But is it worth anything?"

"Oh, yeah. It's gold. I'll bet solid twenty-four karat. I'll give you ten bucks for it, right now." He grinned, deliberately giving away his deceit.

"Right. Why is everyone on this island always clowning around?"

"Yeah, it's worth something. It's worth whatever someone will pay for it. It's probably worth more than that to you," Ross said. "It's pretty unusual, though. Can't say I've seen anything like it around here. You might want to go to the library and see if they have a book on crosses. Maybe the encyclopedia or somethin'."

"I'm pretty good at going to the library," Dave said. "Now I've got something to do in there," he quipped, and thought to himself that's what he should have done in the first place.

Ross said, "Well, I'd be interested to know what you find out about it, but I wouldn't be rushing out to Stage Island to look for more. Place is pretty dangerous."

"Oh, well. I'm not destined to be a treasure diver anyway," Dave said and put the cross in his pocket. "Thanks. Nice meeting you."

"You, too, Dave."

Dave turned around and Thomas had gone.

That was in the spring, early in June, before Dave saw what he saw in a dream. Thomas and Dave had talked about going back out there, but never found the time. When Dave thought he heard Stage Island whispered, he knew he had to go back. He could have taken his boat, but he was more comfortable with Elizabeth. Thomas was reluctant, citing this reason or that.

"It's dangerous. The tide is too strong," was his best argument, but Dave finally convinced him to go for one more dive. He built up a story about grabbing as many lobsters as they could, hundreds if they were there, and coming back and throwing a party for everyone they knew. It would be an end-of-the-summer lobster feast. Thomas agreed that the idea had merit.

Then Dave pleaded, "I need to go out there and see the place. Just for a part of my work. We'll only dive if it's perfect and only at the wreck site. A quick one." The final straw that got Thomas to agree was when Dave said he was starting to cluck like a chicken and did a little dance with his hands tucked under his armpits.

He remembered the day they went back was as clear as could be. There would be no excuses, no reasons to turn back. Dave got to the docks a few minutes late and Thomas was ready. He dropped the mooring line and swung around to pick him up with a sweep past the pier. Thomas was a little ticked off because Dave was late and it was Dave's idea. In the last few years of his life, Thomas had gained a certain respect for the clock.

Now, as Dave's little boat sped toward Stage Island, he began to recall more of that day. The ride had brought on a headache, but he could see the island ahead. The sea was calm, the waves merely rolling, and he slowed down to figure the best way to get back on Stage Island.

Chapter 12

The Tantric

Some musicians say that heroin not only rids them of inhibitions, but increases a sensual awareness between them and the others in the band, and these guys were clearly on the same plane. They were led by an aged black man with the blues etched in his eyes and pulsing his ancient heart. Along a gold-capped tooth he slid a harmonica that breathed his music. His only drugs were booze, cigarettes and an occasional joint, but the others sniffed heroin to keep with him as he called the next song not by name but by saying to the drummer, "gimme something slow...no, a little slower... that's it," and puffed the mouth harp to start a rhythm and melody. The bass and guitar players smiled as they picked up the feeling and joined in with animated mastery, every note flowing from their bodies, through the instruments, and out of the stacks of speakers on either side of the stage. The drummer in a controlled spasm of fingers and limbs fought to restrain and released frustration with a cymbal out of nowhere or a cicada on the rim of the snare drum. But no one dancing under the stars noticed this performance for anything more than the control it had on their souls beneath the climbing moon. As they danced barefoot on the grass in shorts and short sleeves, you could feel the heat rising off of them.

Rebecca danced in her usual fashion, something slower and in time with the backbeat, and Peter danced as if someone were watching. Most of the dancers couldn't dance, but that's not what mattered. Scattered on the dune, the twisted trees looked like they were dancing, too.

The fish caught the day before was devoured; its head and tail stuck on the ends of a broomstick cut to the length of the original fish and suspended above a barbecue grill where a man in an apron kept food moving with fast hands. Some of the younger kids sneaked beer from the kegs and Sam bragged about the fish he caught.

"It's persistence," he said with the wisdom of a boy echoing the words of his father. "The more time you have a line in the water, the greater your chances of catching a fish."

The song ended and the band took a break. Rebecca fanned herself with one hand, sweat barely glistening on her tan skin, and the two walked to the side as the dancers splintered and picked up their clothes strewn in a semi-circle around them. The chill came quickly and they formed circles beside the two fires set away from either side of the stage area. Peter took her hand and walked to the fire where the guitar player stood alone with a beer.

"You guys are great," Peter started and followed with a quick complement, the type that anyone accepts without embarrassment or feeling annoyed. Then he led a question that would put any stranger at ease to feel welcome in paradise, which was where they were. They were atop a vertical cliff of sand and clay with the moon shining down on two fires overlooking the sea that had swallowed the sun hours ago, and all seen by this man with heroin in his nose and an exceptional ability to play guitar without a pick. His habit was unknown to the others around him and he smiled and stared at the flames as if the sunset never ended. The others might have admired him more if they knew he could be thrown in jail for the contents of his pockets, but the conversation continued without him, for without a guitar he wasn't there.

Rebecca and Peter joined the others in conversations bantered over the fire, stories told of stupid things done in years past. He touched her accidentally and she touched him back. Not moving away as though love at first sight could really exist, they went to hold hands at the same time and looked at each other with increasing frequency, their eyes meeting and not separating for moments and then not separating at all, even when they looked away to hear a story told by a guy named Demi, Demetre:

"A few years ago, I went to a party like this and got absolutely trashed. The next day, I woke up feeling like shit and went down to the beach with a joint and an air mattress, the biggest joint I think I ever rolled, and I smoked half of it and went out on the mattress just as stoned as I could be and closed my eyes. Suddenly, like out of nowhere, this ship's horn goes off, the loudest thing in the world when you're hung over, and I open my eyes and all I see is this huge bow, I mean, it's all I can see as I look up and the horn goes off again and I sit up and I'm out in the middle of nowhere. The island was way, way off. Almost invisible. I guess I fell asleep and the wind just pushed me away and I spent all day paddling back. If that ship hadn't come along, I would have been screwed. I went down to the beach at like ten in the morning and I was still way offshore when the sun went down, kind of a sunset like tonight, and I was practically naked and freezing my ass off and all I could see was the lighthouse and I paddled for it and finally got back to the beach on the north end of the island. I'm tellin' you, I was scared, man, cause of the current and out there it's like five hundred feet deep and the porpoises were jumpin' all around me and I had no idea what else was out there. I got back to the Dog just before midnight and I was just in my shorts and people were like, 'Where the hell have you been?' and when I told them the story, nobody believed me, except that my hair was wet and my shorts and then the girls started to hug me to keep me warm sayin', 'Oh, Demi, you poor thing,' and the guys bought me drinks and it started all over again. I lost the mattress and the lighter, but I still had the joint."

Throughout the story people laughed and some didn't believe it but went on to believe because others there did, and the guitar player sneaked away to join other members of the band in a back room of the house. The band leader came up as the story ended and said, "How y'all doin'?" Everybody greeted him like an old friend and he became the center of attention, telling stories that one would never expect and ending it off by saying, "How about I shut up and play some more music?"

He stood in the grass of the stage playing the mouth harp and the other men sauntered in behind him and again they were off in the rhythm and blues. Rebecca and Peter and everyone else stood around at first, then danced in place and soon everyone danced with each other, the whole crowd shaking the ground and the party went on and on, that old man never letting the band stop. Peter and Rebecca grew tired and went to the bar.

"I hear they brewed this beer themselves, just for the party," Peter said. "That's a lot of effort."

"It's a lot of party. Those guys are awesome. I think this is the best party I've ever been to."

"Yeah. Me too," said Peter, his eyes fixed in hers without trying.

"You want to go for a walk on the beach?" she asked and he agreed. They walked down a path through the bushes to a long, wooden stairway and took sixty stairs to the beach. The music followed like the smoke from the cedar fires. The sand was as cool as the night. She felt the breeze through her clothes as they dried on her body.

"It's cold," he said.

"Me too," Rebecca said with a slower voice and he stopped. Gently he reached his arm around her as she looked up and they clung to each other like the smoke to their clothes. Then squeezing some breath lightly from her, he brought his face down to hers and they joined lips. A soft kiss lasted for a moment, followed by a few moments more. He stopped and smiled and turned to walk on with his arm still around her, but she held him. He kissed her lightly on the neck and with a gentle pull on the side of his shirt she signaled for him to follow her down to the sand. The embrace grew tighter, the passion an artwork of slow kissing and sliding of hands. He felt her breasts against him and fumbled at her buttons. She sat up. Slowly, she slid her bra from under her shirt, exposing her breasts to him and the night, then settled back beside him on the sand.

"We can't make love," she said as she unbuttoned his shirt and pressed against him. He smelled the attar of clean sweat cooling off, everything soft and dark like putting your face to a white iris in the night.

"I don't love you, yet," he said. She felt his smile with her lips and her heart missed a beat. "So you couldn't call it that."

He rolled on his back and pulled her on top. She straddled his waist, her breasts hanging in fullness. He kissed them, sliding his tongue over her hard nipple.

"Are you cold?" he asked and pulled her chest to his, rubbing his cheek in the silk of her hair.

"No. But it would be nice to have a blanket." She turned her head to him and then kissed his neck, then a dozen more places on his face, quickly, and he laughed, then kissed her lips. "Uh oh," she said and started buttoning her shirt. "Here come some people."

The two stood up together, brushed the sand from each other and kissed again. A few more moments buttoning and they walked down the beach hand in hand, stumbling, bumping into each other and taking time to kiss and hold close.

"Where are we going?" Rebecca whispered with a laugh.

"On an adventure."

"An adventure, huh?"

"My house isn't too far," he said. "We can get a blanket and come back out to the beach. We can make a fire."

"Isn't that illegal?"

"Yeah, but I know the guy who patrols the beach at night. That's my place up there with the light on," he said.

"Is anybody home?"

"Shouldn't be. I live with my brother and he's probably still at the party."

His place was a shack that stood on stilts and the bay could wash under it. The stairs creaked as the two clambered up into the kitchen.

"Can I use your bathroom?" she asked

"Yeah. It's through there." He pointed with a glass in his hand. "Would you like some water?"

"Sure."

He poured water into the glass, drank some and filled the glass again. He took a bottle of wine from the refrigerator and uncorked it, twisted the cork from the screw and resealed the bottle. Then he took a few pages of newspaper and went to the porch. Looking around, he found a bucket and put the paper and some kindling sticks in it. He pulled a few logs from the woodpile and put them in a canvas boat bag, and then he felt he had all that they'd need. Matches. Don't forget matches. He went to the fireplace and shook a matchbox to make sure there were enough just as Rebecca came back to the room.

"What are you doing?" she asked.

"Come on. I've got it all under control," he said, and he took her hand and led her toward the door. "Wait. Gotta get a blanket."

"Are you sure you've got it all under control?" she teased.

"No problem," he said as he folded a blanket. "Now we're ready."

"Ready for what?"

"Look. You've trusted me this far. Trust me some more." He kissed her cheek and she followed him out the door. He picked up the bucket and spilled the kindling. "Hey, grab that bottle of wine on the table."

"Do you need some help?"

"No. I've got it."

Rebecca came back outside with the wine. He took the bottle and put it in the bucket, then gave her the blanket.

"This *is* an adventure," she said.

"You know it. Come on!" He nearly tripped down the stairs, but turned around to make sure that she didn't fall. Then he led her to the water's edge, put the bucket and the logs into a rowboat and dragged the boat to the water. "Here," he said as he kicked off his shoes. "Give me that and get in."

"Where are we going?"

"Over to the beach. It'll be easier with all this stuff just to row over there."

She climbed in and sat in the stern. When she was settled, he handed her the blanket and pushed the boat until it floated, feeling the mud in his toes. He picked up one foot and shook it clean in the water, then put it in the boat. He pushed off and rinsed the other foot clean as he clambered aboard. Rebecca let out a mild shriek.

"Don't tip us over!" she said.

"Don't worry," he said. "It's all under control."

He sat facing her and pulled on one oar to turn them. Soon, they were out in the masts of moored sailboats, some of their halyards clanking as they rowed past. The moon was almost overhead and the sound of the party carried over the water. Halfway to the beach on the other side of the narrow bay, he stopped rowing.

"Would you like some wine?" he asked as he picked up the bottle and uncorked it.

"No glasses?" she asked.

"Sorry. What was I thinking? Where is the romance?" he gasped and put his fist to his forehead.

She took the bottle and drank from it. "This is plenty of romance." She smiled.

"Too much?"

"Just perfect," she said and handed the bottle back to him. She stopped short and took his hand and kissed it and tried for a kiss on the lips, but the boat shook as she moved and she screeched and laughed. The moon glistened in their eyes and smiles, and he rowed again as the music from the party serenaded the bay.

They landed on the other side and the boat scraped onto the beach. Peter got out and pulled the boat further onto the sand so Rebecca could step onto dry land. He took her hand as she got out and the two kissed over the blanket she carried. Then he pulled the boat way up on the beach and took the bucket and logs.

"We just have to go over the dune," he said. "That way they can't see the fire too well."

"Who's they?"

"Anybody. The police, other people who might come out to join us."

"I thought you said you know the guy who patrols the beach."

"I do, but there's no reason to get anyone's attention, right? What if half the party tries to come out here? I'd rather be alone with you." He tried to kiss her again as they walked, but their bundles made it hard to do. "I guess I'll just have to wait," he said as they climbed over the dune and the ocean came clear into view. Breaking waves danced in the moonlight and swept over the sand.

Peter went a few steps toward the water, then dropped the logs and the bucket. "This should do just fine," he said. He took the wine out of the bucket and gave it to Rebecca. The bucket worked well as a shovel and he dug a small ditch, then assembled a fire, the newspaper first, the kindling stacked over that, the logs on top. A quick swipe on the box and a match flared and the fire began to flicker. He laid out the blanket as Rebecca watched, shivering.

"You're cold," he said.

"I'm always cold."

"Well, the fire should be going good pretty soon. We've got enough logs for a while. Come here," he said and sat on the blanket. "I'll keep you warm." She handed him the wine and sat next to him as he put an arm around her shoulder. She turned to him and they slowly fell in embrace to the ground. They held close and kissed, then put their heads side by side, his cheek much warmer than hers. She felt the radiance of the fire crackling behind her and the heat from his body warmed her quickly. Soon she turned and faced the fire as he rubbed her belly and breast and kissed her neck.

"You know, there is something we can do other than make love," he said

"Do you love me already?" She giggled, hoping to change the subject. *He couldn't possibly expect me to do that tonight?*

"No, but you have to like someone to do it right."

"Have I heard this before?"

"It's called the Tantric Kiss and it's hard to do without laughing. You see, we lie side by side and kiss. But first, you take a deep breath and I exhale. Then we kiss and I breathe your breath as you exhale, and we go back and forth like that for as long as we can. After about ten minutes, supposedly, our hearts will beat the same and our minds, well who knows. I've never done it, but it's some kind of ancient thing. A spiritual thing. I hear that after half an hour our spirits will meld together."

"Where did you come up with this?"

"Cosmo."

"No way," she said, elbowing him slightly and turning her head. "You don't read *Cosmo*."

"Well, no...not much. But my mom had a copy and I saw the article and read it. It was just the start of it, though. When I read that article, I sort of didn't believe it, so I went and read about it elsewhere. I've always had a feeling that I should study more than just what people tell me to, you know what I mean? You can't listen to just one person." He paused. "Do you ever do yoga?"

"No, not really. I wanted to sign up for a class...Tell me you don't do yoga" she said.

"Well, not a lot, but there are like...like rituals to achieve spiritual fulfillment. Yoga is part of it. This might seem weird because it goes into things that many people are afraid to talk about, but they're so ancient you can't just ignore it." He took a sip of wine and handed her the bottle. "Don't let me bore you."

"No, you're not," she said and took a sip also.

"The Tantric Kiss sounds great," he continued. "I don't know, though. I tried it a few years ago, but she couldn't stop laughing, so I never really brought it up again with anyone."

"Why me?"

"Why not? You draw so well, there's gotta be something deep inside of you. Besides, it's just kissing and this is a pretty good place to kiss, don't you think?"

"Yeah, I suppose there really isn't a much better place to kiss in the whole world," she said as she gazed over the fire and waves unrolled in the moonlight and stars. She turned to him. "And all we do is breathe opposite of each other?"

He nodded and hummed, "Hmmm, hm."

She reached up to kiss him and he stroked her hair. They hugged; he kissed her neck and softly tongued some of the fine grains of salt left over from sweat. Their lips met again, he breathed as she exhaled and without any signal they began to breathe as opposites. Awkward at first, they smiled and tried again and again as the waves sang and the fire crackled. Their lips parted just enough for them to catch up on breathing. A few moments later, their hearts beat the same and their minds filled with spirits and sparks from the fire set skyward to the stars.

Chapter 13

Back Again

Stage Island was so named because the sea swallowed it up, leaving only a small set of rocks; a platform with edges laced by black popweed and kelp. Some said the audience was the stones that stuck up around it at low tide, and many of those appeared only in the troughs of waves, but it was also a stage because its regular appearances drew the attention of people. Sometimes, they got too close in their boats and the other members of the audience grabbed them by the hull.

Arriving at the island, Dave nimbled his Caper between stones and slipped through kelp latched deep below to granite. The propeller fouled with weeds and the motor stalled, leaving him to drift in the still sound of waves slipping the last few yards to shore. He raced to tilt up the motor, dripping from the sea, and felt shells crumble as the hull slid onto the island of stone. He clambered ashore, though it was not really shore. With the anchor in one hand, he glanced around for a place in the rocks to wedge it. He stood quickly after securing the hook as best he could and fought the boat to keep it from beaching with the waves, then, turning around, he saw it all again clearly. Reliving even the pain, he knelt and sat on the never-dry algae, his temples pounding from the exertion of landing the boat.

The day returned to him and his image of Thomas was shattered. All he believed about him had once again changed; the image held in his mind was only a half-truth, the half that Thomas wanted his life to become after the tragedy. Dave remembered that now.

They got to the island just as the tide turned. It was already flowing, and the lecture Thomas gave on the ride out proved correct: Dave's being late precluded any chance of diving because of the current. They idled around the island thinking of what to do with the rest of their day, but Dave had not gone there to dive anyway.

"Let's go ashore," he said.

"What?" Thomas said. "Are you crazy?"

"Come on. We've got the raft. We'll just row over there and check it out. You've lived here all your life and I'll bet you never stood on that island."

Thomas was hesitant. So was Dave. It was crazy, but it had to be done, Dave thought. He just had to get on the island to see if there was anything, any clues or even a body, a skeleton, anything. They found a good spot to anchor Elizabeth, somewhere close and protected from the waves so the raft wouldn't swamp. Dave dropped the anchor over and watched the line until it stopped.

"How deep is it here?" he asked.

Thomas checked the gauge and said, "Thirty-six feet."

Dave questioned himself about the amount of line, threw out a few more yards and tied it to the cleat. Thomas joined him on the bow and Dave went to help him unlash the inflatable raft, but he already had it free and tossed it over the rail. It slapped on the water and bounced into the hull and Thomas walked the raft astern without ever looking at Dave, like he was not even there. He tied the painter to a side cleat and they prepared to go, deciding to row in rather than strap on the outboard because it would just clog with kelp.

"I want to get the camera," Thomas said and he disappeared below deck for a moment, leaving Dave to watch the sky and sea. He took longer than he should have, so Dave went to the companionway and was about to climb down when Thomas appeared.

"You all right?"

"Yeah, what's up?"

"Nothing. You took a long time."

"What's the hurry? The island's been there a long time."

They brought the raft close alongside and climbed in, Thomas first.

"You row," he said, shifting as Dave stepped aboard. The waves splashed as Dave pulled the boat into them, but the rowing became easier. The tide swept them toward the island and soon they stepped onto the Stage. The odor of decay was the first thing they spoke of.

"You'll get used to it," Thomas said of the smell.

"Yeah," Dave agreed as a wave crashed to the rocks on the other side and flew high. "Did I ever tell you the theory I heard about why we don't see visitors from other planets?"

"No," Thomas said, and Dave noticed a sense of uneasiness in his tone.

"I had this chemistry professor in college," Dave said while slipping around the tiny island. "We were going over the periodic chart. He pointed to the column with oxygen and said, 'When two atoms of hydrogen combine with one atom of any other element in this column, we get a compound that stinks to high-heaven.' His theory was that the similar compound formed by hydrogen and oxygen, that is to say water, stinks badly as well, and that we just got used to it. But extra-terrestrials can't stand the smell, so they don't stay very long."

"You believe in extra-terrestrials?"

"Sure, why not? To believe that man is the end-all of creation seems a little egotistical, don't you think?"

Dave anticipated a long, philosophical discussion, like the many they had in the past, perhaps one where he could talk to him about his experience, but Thomas came right out with it as Dave peered into a deep crack in the rocks.

"What are you looking for, Dave?"

"Rocks...I want to build a cairn," he said. "You know, a pile of rocks to mark that we were here. Doesn't look like there are any about."

"Surf carried all the rocks away, Dave. It wouldn't stand for long in the surf."

"I guess not."

"Then, why are you still looking?"

"I don't know, Tom." He hesitated. He had told no one his story and was afraid, but he kept looking around, slipping now and again on the slick weeds.

"What's going on, man? You're acting really weird."

"Am I? My life is weird, right now. Too weird to believe." Dave looked at Thomas and he was staring back. He was trembling just slightly.

"What are you looking for?"

"It has to do with the cross I found," Dave said, took a deep breath and sighed it out slowly. "I think it does, anyway. Just after I found that cross, I had a really strange experience. I mean really strange." He could not bring himself to say it.

"Tell me about it. Come on, you got this far."

"I saw a...well, I can't say that I actually saw it, but I communicated with some...with a woman, a girl. A dead girl."

"Come on," he scoffed.

"Don't laugh, Thomas. Please. I know it's impossible, but it happened. I'm having a tough time with it. I saw her and then I heard things, felt things. She said she was killed...I think she said she died on this island. It was hard to be sure. I don't think she spoke English."

Dave thought he stared at him in disbelief, but Thomas sank to the ground, sitting on the slimy rocks. "My God," he said slowly, with a look of fear. "Did she really come back?"

"You saw her?"

"She haunts my every dream." He began to weep. "When you found that cross..."

"Thomas, what happened?" He said nothing, sucked his cheeks between his teeth to fight back tears. They were together alone in their minds. Dave stood waiting for a response from him while he gazed into the temple of his hands. A wave slapped the rocks and showered them. "What did you do?" More silence hushed the sea. Another long moment passed.

"She was green," he said. "You know, seasick. When we pulled alongside and the green starboard light hit her face, I knew she was into it bad. I couldn't figure what she was doing there, but when I saw the others come onto the deck, it was clear that he lied to me."

Thomas went on to elaborate a story torn by grief and breakdowns, a story he seemed as reluctant to tell as Dave had been to tell his. Perhaps it was as much a lie as the truth, half hiding the real story, told by a man convinced of innocence through circumstance. It was not supposed to have happened, but it did and someone lost their life. There was guilt to be placed, responsibility to be taken, but no evidence to convict. Clearly from his distress, however, Thomas had taken the blame and suffered immeasurably, yet that did not absolve him.

"It was different than we planned. It was supposed to be a simple pick up. We did it before. All those trips I took to Europe. I met a lot of people. I can tell you, I guess. I guess it doesn't matter. I brought this gun," he said, taking from his pocket the pistol he kept on the boat below decks, "to kill you if you found the body. Huh, found the body. It's been years."

"Put that away, Thomas."

"Shut up, Dave! Just shut up!" He suddenly seemed to have an imbalance. Dave had never before seen his temper flare like that. "Don't worry. I'm not going to shoot you. There's no point in that. There's no evidence."

"Tell me what happened. Maybe there's a way out of it."

"No. There's no way out. All those nights I spent trying to find some way out of it. Nobody knew, but I can never forget. She was so young. She reminded me so much of my daughter. They would have been about the same age." He began to weep again. Dave stood fixed to the stones beneath him, not moving for fear of his life, not wanting to provoke his anger again. He wanted out. I did not ask for this, he thought. How could I possibly have known that the man I adopted as my best friend had murdered?

"It wasn't murder," Thomas said. "It was an accident. I didn't even know it happened until it was too late."

"Then you're innocent."

"No." He paused again. "No, I'm guilty. Guilty as charged. And I'm already serving a life sentence."

"What are you talking about? You're free."

"Free to suffer every night." He began to sob. "I can't explain. I could never explain it. All those nights I spent working, it wasn't to make the business work. I just couldn't sleep."

"Tell me what happened. Maybe I can help you."

After another long pause, he began, "We went out the day before. Took the boat up to the mainland north of here. You see, Dave, this island is like a shield, so to speak. I learned from a friend in the Coast Guard that the radar they use to monitor this area loses its signal around here, especially northeast of the island. Something about the location of the antennas on land and the markers out here causes a blind spot. Two boats coming in opposite directions can change course, meet in the middle and get back on course so that it looks on the radar screen like nothing had happened.

"I met some people in Europe. We became friends, just friends, you know. It didn't start out like business. I went over there and we met, got to talking about money. They said they had a connection. They needed a way to get things into the States. At first, I went along with it superficially, just talking. But they were serious. It sounded pretty easy. And it was pretty easy…and exciting. They had bearer bonds, a lot of them, from different countries. Paper. Just moving boxes of paper for a large fee. I told them about this island and the blind spot. It was perfect. It was so easy. I made a fortune, a fortune I couldn't spend. That's why my business does so well, Dave. It's a front.

"We went out as planned. Just like we had a dozen times before. We spent the night in a little harbor. It was a smooth night. We drank too much, smoked some weed. The next day was a fog. That's not a problem, the fog. It was good, actually. The weather called for rain. You know how it is around here. Damn weather can suck you up in a minute. I was a little nervous for some reason. Maybe I was just hung over, but something didn't feel right about that day. We had to do it, though. We had to go. If we didn't, people might go to jail. Or worse. We were in deeper than we knew. At least, deeper than I knew.

"We headed up the coast for a few hours, idled around the shore and then turned south when we heard the broadcast message. The goal was to meet the ship just out there," he said as he waved his

196

hand to point without looking. "We had it all set up, just like before."

He stared off for a while, then continued. "The seas were pretty big, which is unusual for a heavy fog. It means there was a storm somewhere kicking up the waves. The boat was running great, then one of the intakes clogged up and an engine overheated. We went along on one engine while I cleared it up, but we were already running a little behind because of the waves and the tide. Huh! Tides around here…"

It was obvious that Thomas did not want to tell the story he had never told. Dave just wanted to get him to say how she died, what happened to her just so he could know, but Thomas still had a gun dangling from his fingers and Dave didn't know what to do. He seemed distant, vacant, separated from himself, and for a moment, Dave separated from his body, too, and in his mind he saw the scene from afar: the two of them on the Stage with the Elizabeth out in the audience.

Thomas continued: "The fog was heavy. Between that and the night, it was impossible to see anything. When the time came close to ten o'clock, we had the ship on the radar. We were twenty minutes away. My nerves started flowing. It had to be done just right or the Guard would catch us. The whole thing should only take two or three minutes. There were never more than twenty or thirty boxes, but they had to be moved fast, and in those seas, I knew it would be tough.

"The lights of the ship were not in view until we got real close. I saw the name of the boat, the Brittle Star, as we came up on the stern. She was already into the wind and I pulled alongside. That's when I saw her. She looked like she had been sick for days. We tied up and the boxes were lowered, but then a ladder was dropped and people started coming down. Not a lot—five. The girl was with them. She came down third, after two men. I didn't know what was happening. I thought we were being boarded and I ran down for the gun. When I got back, Eddie was screaming, 'What the fuck are you doing?'

"I said to him, 'What's going on?'

"All he said was 'They're coming with us.'

"'What do you mean they're coming with us?'

"'Sorry, Tom,' he said. 'I would have told you, but then you never would have come. They're fleeing their country.'

"'What?'

"'You heard me. Refugees. Come on, move the boxes. We've got no time.'

"I knew," Thomas said to Dave, "I knew that he was right. There was no time to argue, let alone time to get them back up the ladder. They pulled the ladder up as the last boxes were lowered, then Eddie waved to some guy, a face I'd never seen, and yelled 'We're off,' as the lines fell to the deck.

"Eddie tended the lines and I went to the wheelhouse to back her away. A wave crashed over the stern and soaked everybody. I stopped when we were clear and went back to tell them to come inside. I felt like a host. I felt like a fucking host." He cried again, his sobbing drawing the story out longer than Dave wanted.

"As we wallowed there, not moving, just being tossed around by the sea, she got sick and went for the side. She had nothing in her stomach, but she still was retching over the side. Eddie came back and screamed at me. 'What the fuck are you doing, Thomas? We gotta go! We gotta make it out of the shadow on time or we're nailed! God damn it, Thomas! Don't fall apart on me! We can't get rid of them. Let's go!'

"He ran to the helm and put it in gear and we moved forward. The waves still controlled us for a while until the boat swung around on course. Then it smoothed out to some degree. I looked back. She was huddled in the corner, still dark green. We met eyes. She reminded me of Elizabeth. Would have been about the same age. She was holding a cross. It was around her neck, but she was holding it like she was making sure it was still there.

"Eddie screamed again. 'Take it,' he said. 'I'll get them to settle down.'

"I took the helm and looked over the instruments. We were out of the shadow and a little bit off course. I made an adjustment. I heard Eddie screaming at them, 'Sit down. Sit. Here, here.' I looked back again and he was gesticulating. I thought to myself, Great, they don't speak English.

"Eddie got them positioned, but the girl stayed where she was because she was still sick. Eddie switched on the flood lights for a moment to make sure the area was clear, that the boxes were all lined up right. I watched her face in the light. She was beautiful, even though she was truly green. I've never seen anyone so green. She looked like she was already dying. The others were three men and a woman. They were all dark, with dark, hopeless eyes sunk in their heads, life just sucked out of their faces. I knew they were hungry and tired.

"Eddie turned off all the lights and they disappeared. The only lights were the red lights in the wheelhouse. Eddie came inside, not saying a word. It was up to me to start and I started with rage. I was pissed. I said, 'What the fuck are you doing? Who are these people? What the fuck?'

"'They're illegal immigrants.'

"'From where?'

"'I don't know. I don't care.'

"'That's it? You don't know.'

"'I made a promise.'

"'You didn't tell me.'

"'You wouldn't have come.'

"'Damn you! This is a lot different. We can't just throw them overboard. How much could they possibly be worth?'

"'We're getting twenty-five hundred for each of them.'

"'Twenty-five hundred? Fuck, Eddie, we're making ten times that for the boxes. What the fuck is twenty-five hundred?'

"'The boxes aren't gonna be coming much longer. Times are changin'. We need another source of income.'"

"'What do you mean?'

"'You heard me. There might be another shipment, maybe two. Maybe none. After that, what are we gonna do?'

"'Don't we have enough?'

"'Enough for now. What's enough, anyway? Enough to retire? Not in this fuckin' world.'

"'I'm giving up, Eddie. I've had enough of this shit. What the fuck are we gonna do with them when we get to the island?'

"'We put them on a ferry and they're just like any other tourist.'

"'You've got it all figured out, huh? These people can't speak English, Eddie. How are they gonna deal, huh?'

"'That's figured out, too. Someone will meet them and take them on the ferry.'

"'You're a piece of work, Eddie. Oh, shit! Shit!'

"'What?'

"'There's a boat coming. Look at the radar.'

"'Let me see. Shit. It's a big return, too.'

"'It's coming right for us and fast.'

"'It's not that fast, Thomas.'

"'It's as fast as the damn Coast Guard, Eddie. I'm tossing the shit overboard.'

"'You can't. It's too deep here.'

"'I don't give a damn, Eddie. I'll take my chances with them, but with them and the boxes we're screwed. I'll tie on another hundred feet of line.'

"'Don't do it, Thomas,' he said, but I was already gone.

"The boxes were waterproof and each was tied with heavy cord wrapped around it like a net. We had a lobster buoy with a long line and I took the line and wove it through the cord and tied all the boxes on. Then I tied an anchor to the end, and if we needed to, we could throw the whole thing over the side and remember the location. The buoy had a timed release. People use them so the buoy will stay underwater for a day or two and you don't have to worry about boats running over your buoys and cuttin' the line, losing the traps. There's no pilfering, either. So we could throw the whole bundle over quickly and come back the next day. We would just open the door in the transom and toss the anchor out and all those boxes would slide right off the stern. We wouldn't even have to slow down. But we had these people. We couldn't even tell them what to do. There was no way to hide them. If we got boarded, we were going to jail. It would be the Feds.

"It was so stupid of Eddie to not tell me. We could have been prepared. I would have gone along with it. It was exciting. Really exciting. Just like when we were kids, growin' pot. It wasn't just the money. It was like being a spy, except no one really got hurt.

"When we were growin' together, Eddie and I would pass the crop to the mainland using lobster traps. We would wrap the crop in plastic and put it into the bottom of the bait buckets and then load the fish heads and other lobster bait on top of it. Not even a dog could smell it. Then we'd take it out to sea and we'd check the traps like normal, except we'd get to a spot and load a trawl of traps with the pot and tie on a different buoy, one owned by a guy on the mainland. We planned with the guy to fish the same area so our traps were close together. We used his buoy so that if anybody happened to see him, he was picking up his traps.

"The only hitch we ever had was one time when the harbormaster came by and saw me with someone else's lobster buoy. He wanted to know why I had it and I told him I got it caught in my prop and had to haul the trap or else lose it. I said I had a good idea as to who owned it and if he could confirm the colors I'd give it back.

"Otherwise, the system worked great. So well that we did it a few times with the boxes just to be safe. We'd chuck 'em off and then go straight into the harbor and have a beer next to the dock, right by the Coast Guard. We'd call to the guys when they came out and they'd come over and talk with us. Sure enough, we'd go back the next day at the right time, and once got there just in time to see the buoy pop out of the water. We hauled the boxes out and they were dry in minutes. When we got back to the dock, we were just another lobster boat unloading. Nobody'd suspect that there was a million dollars down below.

"I went back to tie the boxes and for a moment I met that girl's eyes. I saw in them, I don't know what, maybe it was a gleam of hope, an exhausted gleam of hope. I could see she was tired and sick, but she was almost home. When I tied all the boxes to the buoy and anchor, I went forward again to see if the other boat had turned away.

"'That's a few million dollars, man,' Eddie said. 'Don't be stupid. Just wait a little longer.'

"'I'm not going to jail. I'm not…I can't.'

"'Just wait a second, man. Just make sure it's the Feds before you do anything. We'll have plenty of time in this fog.'

"We watched for a while as the boat got closer. It was four or five miles away. We were going slower because of the fog, but the other boat was steaming. We discussed making a course change to see if they were going to follow us, but that would be too obvious.

There was only one place we could be going. I wanted to stop, to do something just to see if it was a patrol boat. Eddie convinced me that the boat wasn't going very fast, not like a cutter would if it were in pursuit, so we carried on. He was always so much cooler than me.

"I asked, 'What are we gonna do with them if it's the Coast Guard?' and Eddie just looked at me.

"We closed on the other boat at a ninety degree angle and after a little longer, I decided to slow down just a bit. I figured we had to do something; we were only a mile or so from contact. We were only slowed for a few seconds when the other boat changed course. It had to be a patrol boat. I guess I freaked out.

"'I'm gonna toss 'em over. We can mark the location and come back and dive.'

"'Thomas, man, he just made his way point. They just reached the buoy."

"'You're gonna take that chance? Fuck it. Remember the location. I'm gonna ditch them.' I went toward the door and Eddie grabbed my arm. You know how strong he is. He grabbed my arm and wheeled me around. I hit the throttles and the boat sped forward.

"'Stop it, Thomas,' he yelled. His voice told his anger. 'It's not a patrol boat, goddamn it. It's not! If it was it would have been all over by now.'

"I tried to fight back, but he had me pinned. I thought he would hit me, but one of the immigrants came in and grabbed his arm. That's not a good thing to do to Eddie when he's pissed. The man was saying something, speaking frantically. I thought he was trying to break up the fight, but Eddie smashed him backhanded across the mouth and knocked him down.

"The others came running in and Eddie picked up the gun and fired over their heads. It was like in slow motion. When he picked up the gun, it was one quick motion, but it seemed slowed down. Every detail was so clear. We had these people on board. We didn't know who they were. We couldn't understand them. For all we knew right then and there, these people could be trying to hijack us. Eddie took my gun, the gun I brought up, and wheeled around so fast and pointed it at them. Then he squeezed off a shot. I saw his finger moving so slowly. Despite how quickly he did it, I saw that finger move so slowly. He missed them deliberately. Shot over their heads. They shut up, all right. They shut up and cowered and Eddie started screaming 'Get out! Get the fuck out!' and he waved the gun over their heads. They backed out. A gun translates into any language, I guess. You just motion with it and people do what it says.

"They were saying something and one of the women helped the man Eddie knocked down, but Eddie was screaming. 'Get down! Down!' he screamed, waving his gun and pointing it at them. They still tried to say something, but Eddie wouldn't let them.

"I slowed the boat down while Eddie locked the door. I looked at the radar and sure enough the boat had passed.

"'I told you,' Eddie said. 'They would have had us a long time ago. No way we could outrun a Coast Guard boat.'

"I laughed and so did he. 'I'm always right in those situations,' he said, and he was. I'm not a good criminal. I guess I don't have the guts. We both laughed again and I turned around. The others were all on their knees, praying. That's when I noticed she was gone. She had fallen over when I hit the throttles."

A moment passed after the end of the story, and again Dave and Thomas were alone on the island.

"Did you go back?" Dave asked.

"No."

"Oh, Thomas!" he cried. "How could you not have gone back?"

"It was Eddie. I wanted to go back. I pleaded, but he wouldn't let me. At that point, I had no idea where to start, and in that cold water at night, she couldn't have lived for more than fifteen or twenty minutes."

"That's no excuse, man. You are guilty."

"Thanks. Like I need you to tell me that," he said as he slowly rose to his feet.

"So now what do we do?"

"Don't worry, Dave. I'm not going to kill you. There's no sense in that; you didn't do anything and I'm no killer. Huh, no cold-blooded killer, anyhow."

"Let's go back, then, Thomas. There's got to be some way to clear it up. I won't tell anyone. Maybe, if we talk about it, maybe there's some way we can—I don't know—fix it or make good on it. There has to be a way." All Dave wanted was out of it.

"There's no way, Dave, to make good on it. I don't know what to do. So many times I've thought of just taking myself out. I've got no reason to live and no right for it, either."

"Killing yourself can't be the answer, Thomas."

"I can't think of anything else. I can't sleep. I gave up drinking. Maybe I should start that again and drink myself to death. I'm too much of a coward to just pull the trigger."

Dave thought quickly. "When Gandhi was fasting once, a man, a Hindu, came to him and told how he had killed a young Muslim boy and did not know what to do. Gandhi told him to find a fatherless Muslim boy and raise him as a Muslim...There has to be a way, Tom. You've got a lot going for you. It was an accident. You can atone."

"No," he said. "It's no use. She's haunting me. I try to sleep, but her face just keeps me lying awake."

With that thought, Thomas put the gun to his head and stared straight at Dave, who was sure he'd do it. The look on his face became lifeless.

"Don't, Thomas."

"Don't watch, Dave. It's probably not too much fun to watch."

From beside them, a groaning scrape caused them both to turn. The rising tide had lifted Elizabeth and pulled her anchor from the bottom. She had drifted and lay on the rocks. Running across the slippery boulders, Dave lunged for Thomas and tried to force the gun from his hand. He just wanted to get the gun and throw it beneath the waves, but Thomas was stronger than him. He wrenched his arm from Dave's grip and with a backhand hit struck the metal across Dave's head. Dave fell to the rocks. The pain came after a few seconds, though he was groggy from the moment he was hit. When the pain came, all Dave could do was sleep.

He didn't remember how long he was out, maybe a minute, maybe ten. It could have been an hour, he still didn't know. When he came around, Thomas was lying in the water with waves washing over him. Dave thought he would drown. He saw the boat on the rocks as he ran to Thomas and pulled him from the water. The whole story had vanished from Dave's mind and he thought they had wrecked. He pulled him higher and went to get the raft, then stopped to rest. When he returned, he saw the gun and picked it up and threw it hard. Again, pain pulsed through his head and he sat down, lay down to rest.

Dave woke up and thought he saw him move, but his body was just settling closer to the stone. He became a monstrous affair, a gargoyle face, glacier blue beneath an ashen patina, a rictus to be reckoned with in the nightmares to come. His blood mottled hair rinsing in the waves, he scared him. Dave thought to let him go, to set him to sea in a proper sea burial, send him to a benthic grave, but he could not muster the strength even to think about it further.

Yet he could not stand to see him. His face, that face, he seemed in pain, as if something in his gut was torturing him even in death.

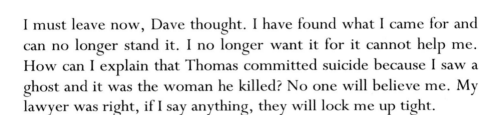

I must leave now, Dave thought. I have found what I came for and can no longer stand it. I no longer want it for it cannot help me. How can I explain that Thomas committed suicide because I saw a ghost and it was the woman he killed? No one will believe me. My lawyer was right, if I say anything, they will lock me up tight.

He got back into his Caper with the thought of escaping north or west, but there was just enough fuel to get back to the island. He plucked the weeds from the propeller and poled, then paddled, from the island, hoping it wouldn't rain or fog up or worse. Maybe if I perish at sea the whole thing will be left alone, he thought, but on the trip back he realized a ray of hope. If Thomas was guilty, then Eddie was guilty, too, and if she came back to get Thomas, then chances are good she would come back for Eddie. Perhaps he would see her again. *You are going crazy!*

He tore himself in half the whole ride back trying to assure himself he would see her, that he was not being used simply for revenge. She wouldn't do that to me. She is beyond that. Why would she come back, though? Why else would she come back? He wrestled with those questions as he wrestled the boat back to the dock and tied her off. Then reality set in as he walked off the dock and saw people. He assured himself it was just a coincidental dream; that the only ghost there was had haunted Thomas alone.

The first thing he did was head to a pay phone. It was only three in the afternoon, so his lawyer would be in his office even though it was Friday. His secretary answered the phone after three rings.

"Hi, this is Dave Wyman. Is he in?"

"No, I'm afraid he's at a conference, Mr. Wyman."

"When will he be back?"

"Late next week. Is there something I—"

"Next week! What am I supposed to do in the meantime?"

"Mr. Roth is covering for him, sir. I'm familiar with your case. Are you in trouble?"

"Yes, I'm in trouble."

"Are you at the police station?"

"No."

"Have you been arrested?"

"No."

"Then you're not in trouble."

"I need to talk to him. Can I call him at home? Has he left for the airport?"

"He left last night."

"Great. Just great. He didn't tell me he was going anywhere. If he calls, please ask him to call me."

"I will, sir. And if there is anything you need, please call back and I will make arrangements for Mr. Roth to counsel you."

And that was it. His trusted legal advisor had skipped town on a vaunt and he felt abandoned. So he could not tell anyone. He could tell this guy Roth his secrets, but he would have him committed before the day was out. It should make no difference, anyway, he thought. He did nothing.

So he rode his bike home, up the hill and to the house where he found Aimee and the children ready to leave.

"We waited as long as we could before the next ferry," she said.

"I'm glad," he answered back. She looked at him, still asking with her eyes, and he smiled and nodded yes.

"It's OK," he said. "I remember everything."

She couldn't wait to hear the story, but Dave hesitated in telling her.

"Boys, go play for a while. Your mother and I have to talk for a minute."

The boys went outside and, though Dave was still hesitant, he told her how Thomas died. "He shot himself, Aimee."

"What? Why?"

"Because I found out something I shouldn't have. He killed someone."

"How did you find out about it?"

"Do you remember at the beginning of the summer, you left with the boys for the day and when you came back I was in the chair and you came in and wondered if I was all right?"

"Yes. I suppose..." she said with a questioning look.

"Well, I wasn't all right. I told you about a dream I had. It wasn't *just* a dream... This," he said and went to the mantle where the cross was and picked it up, "this might have been hers. It freaked Thomas out. Now I know why he never wanted to talk about it. I found it out at Stage Island where she died."

"Dave, you're not all right. You're talking crazy."

"I know I am, Aimee, but you're the only one I can talk to. The blasted lawyer has gone out of town. I went back to Stage Island today and it all came back to me. We went out there to go diving again and the tide was wrong. It was running too hard. So we went ashore and I was acting weird and Thomas asked me what was going on and I told him. That's when he... he told me the story. It was him and Eddie. They were running illegal immigrants and one of them fell overboard. The woman who fell overboard and died, she had a cross. After Thomas told me the story, he tried to kill himself and I tried to stop him. That's how I got hit. I know it sounds crazy, but it's the truth."

"You have to call the police."

"No. I have to wait for the lawyer to get back or for something else to happen."

"Something else? Like what? Are you going to wait for Eddie to come around again?"

"He won't do anything. There's no evidence. I'm the one in trouble. He'll just sit tight and wait it out."

"Then why did he come by this morning?"

Dave had no answer.

She continued, "Dave, this is no time to fool around. I'm scared. What if Eddie gets drunk and does something stupid?"

"He won't. If he's into smuggling aliens, then he's not the boss and the boss won't do anything."

"Great. The boss. The mob. Just what we needed. I never thought Thomas would be into something like that."

"He wasn't. Eddie tricked him into it. Come on, I'll walk you to the car," he said and touched her shoulder. He pushed open the screen door for her and called out, "Come on, boys. We have to hurry if we're going to catch the ferry."

They walked holding hands and Dave assured her a million times over that there was nothing to worry about. He almost convinced himself, but she never believed it. She kissed his cheek and climbed in the car without another word. The car started and she turned it around, waving a quick goodbye. He heard the boys say, "Bye, Dad," their voices muffled through the closed windows. As they drove away, he saw his boys playing in the back seat and couldn't imagine them grown up, having kids of their own. Now he was alone again.

Chapter 14

Summer's End

To her, it was the last day of summer, although September had just begun and the final holiday weekend was still days away, but in a few hours he would leave. From what she remembered of the early spring she already felt she would be alone on the island. It'll be all right, she thought. If they were to be together they would be. She resigned herself to wait the final ticks of the clock with him even though he was late and she loathed the thought of the ferry horn when the boat pulled from the dock. She wondered if she should wait and watch it go or just kiss him goodbye at the gate and walk away.

"Enough of that," she sighed aloud and glanced about the porch of the Dog to see if anyone had heard her. No one had but various birds on the railing.

She took the last gulp of the beer on the table before her and wondered if she should have another or just wait, but the waitress came and asked and she said yes just to save time, chuckling at the thought that no one had checked her age all summer. When she came to the Dog and filled out the application she wrote that her age was twenty-one and after the manager served her a beer in front of everyone when she finished her first shift, they all simply assumed she was of age. She got into the other bars by going with some of the Dog staff through back doors and leaving through the front, stopping to talk and be friendly to all the doormen and soon the whole island was comfortable with her drinking. She rarely got drunk anyway and never out of control like many islanders.

Some people would get drunk and she would drive them home in their cars and then take the car to her home and leave it at the base of the dune. In the morning Ursa would say, "I see so-and-so had too much to drink last night." She remembered the one time she did come home drunk and Ursa told her to be careful, that not everyone on the island was as nice as she, and she could not believe it for everyone there seemed harmless, except for driving drunk. One of the hazards of the island that was often treated as a sport.

She remembered that night again for he had given her a ride home and wrestled her up the dune to the house and put her to bed. As he left he met Ursa in the kitchen as she went for a glass of milk and they sat there and talked for an hour. Later, Ursa said that he was such a nice boy and he was, but so much more. Anyone that Ursa likes, I like, she thought. She could not, would not, stop thinking about him and his smile and how perfect the summer was because of him. Or was it? Of course it was, she thought. He lifted her and she lifted him and they became invincible, able to withstand the island gossip, and she laughed aloud because soon it would be her birthday—if she could live through the next days. And when she told them all her true age they would laugh, too, for she had duped them. Yet still there was him and his leaving and the laughter seemed so far away now.

"Let me in on the joke," said the waitress, Melissa, as she set the beer down on the table. She had heard her laugh and Rebecca blushed softly as she reached in her pocket for money.

"I'll tell you soon enough," she said.

"Don't worry about it," said Melissa, indicating with her hand to keep the money. "This one's on me. But don't get drunk until he leaves. I'll get drunk with you later if you want."

"OK," she said, the quiver in her voice nearly noticeable. Melissa is a friend, she thought. She'll probably be the only friend I have when the summer is gone. She and Ursa.

Melissa was older and had slight jowls, yet her beauty still clung like a drying rose. Small folds of cellulite from years of partying and too much time working gathered beneath her breasts as she sat on her leg. She had washed ashore on the island years ago and found it better to stay than to pick up her old life again.

"First for love, second for money," she once said of her failed marriage. "Third for desperation," she joked and showed her equine smile, and they laughed together then, but now they said nothing and sat at the table alone with a yellow jacket becoming a bother.

"You hit them from the top," Melissa finally said as she whacked straight down on the insect, then crushed it under her shoe on the floor. "They can't sting you if you do it that way. I hate to kill things, but I won't share beer with anyone." They laughed and Melissa went inside to check on her customers.

Rebecca, alone again on the porch, took a sip of beer from the glass where the yellow jacket once landed. Don't think of it, she said in her mind. Just look at this scenery and feed the birds. She took up a crust of pizza that she saved for him even though he would probably want more and it was stale now anyway. She tossed a large crumb toward a sparrow on the railing nearby, hoping to coax the bird closer. When it landed by the crust, the bird looked so small and tried to swallow the whole thing twice and then shook it and shook it so hard that the crumb flew away from him and a gull swooped down where it landed.

"Too bad, but you might have choked on it," she said to the bird. "Then I'd feel even worse." She pulled a smaller piece from the crust and tossed it at the feet of the sparrow. The gull turned an envious eye as the sparrow moved closer for more.

And all she could recall was a summer of short rainfall and fair wind and days spent not working but sailing the bay and sometimes the sound and the ocean. They dragged their bodies behind the boat on a long line to cool off and landed on the beach in calm waves for lunch and wine. She remembered the talks and the time they left the boat on the beach while they made love in the dunes. He wanted to check the boat but she wouldn't let him go and the tide left it high and dry, impossible to move without help. They had to walk home and he wasn't angry for even a moment. Coming back the next day the boat was higher and drier and they needed the help of strangers to float her again.

Then they were off with the day and sailed the rest of the way around the island, once dropping the sails to make love on the bow while old men fished a mile away. They sailed nude, comfortable with each other, and coming suddenly upon the rip they had to sail past the point with shirts tossed on quickly when they felt a pair of binoculars watching from shore. They tacked between the markers and the house on the hill with that twisted tree alone in the yard, below them the rocks left from centuries past and the bottom rising to meet the centerboard.

Tacking, tacking, tacking, against the tide they worked to a sweat through the rapid waters at the narrows and finally past the point, came to a heading where the boat no longer needed to be steered, the play in the tiller not a fight anymore. God loved them, they smiled, for nothing else could bring them to such a place and such a point and they talked and wondered why people would fight and kill each other over something so small as a bottle of whiskey, as had happened days before on the mainland. It was because of their environment, they agreed. People learned from those around them and if all you know is hatred then all you have is hate and they looked at themselves and came silent before laughing as the sun burnt their skin dry and they in love fell downwind toward the moorings and beach. Why would you kill someone, they asked, when all you need is food in the belly, the friendship of strangers and the flesh of another at night and they came upon bad air, motionless air in the lee of the rotting marsh at low tide. Even paradise stinks now and then.

With him gone, she thought, she would be tacking through an eddy in her life where the wind went flat and the current carried her nowhere. All they did seemed a cartoon, a colorful promise that childhood had passed, and now they were ready for a shining

214

future, but the future had been set in the past and they knew it all along.

"I'll see you at Christmas," he told her, "or you can come visit me in Arizona." The University of Arizona, so far away. The other side of the continent. Two years of graduate school with lots of pretty girls all around him. Absence makes the heart go yonder.

For Rebecca, this had been the summer of her lifetime. For once she had done something that came only from her mind, a dream she dreamt and made into reality. The weather was nearly as perfect as anyone could want and she met a great guy who she fell in love with and who said he loved her, too. But still she was sad for he was leaving to a place so far away that even the phone bills would be too much to take.

Uncertainty had once again found a way into her morning and she found herself adrift on a sea of doubt. It was as when her friends all left before, bound for college or just somewhere else and not to be seen again, or maybe in a year, the next summer or Christmas, and it wasn't all that long ago that it happened. Those two years since graduation, the time just wasted. Why did she get a place there? She should have flown to the silent au vol in her heart. She should have done this so long ago, but she faltered. That was a bad time and just stop—don't think anymore, just stop thinking altogether. She fought back a tear as the past clouded her eyes. It's much better now. She forced herself to think of him again but her train of thought trailed away like a horn in the morning that wakes you and lulls you back to sleep. But today was just as bad and she knew she couldn't stay.

Absence makes the heart go wander, she thought to herself again as the sparrow hopped closer to the bread crumb in her fingers. Peter came around the corner of the deck of the Dog and stopped to watch her feed the bird, her arm outstretched and the side of her chin laid upon it. The bird took the crumb and flew, but she stayed there still. He felt as she did and softly walked up behind her and put his arms around her shoulders.

215

"Hi," he whispered, his soft breath blowing her hair.

"Hey, you're late," she said with an audible smile.

"I was hoping to miss the ferry."

"Me, too. I can't believe it's over."

"Are you dumping me?" he said and she shook her head with a sad smile as he sat next to her on the bench. "Don't say it's over."

"Seeing you will be the best Christmas present ever."

"You don't want to visit me out there?"

"Yeah. If I can afford it."

"You know, Rebecca, I've tried to hint at this without coming right out and saying it, but I really think you should go to school. I mean, you're a bright person. There's nothing wrong with school. In fact, there's everything right with it. If you stay here all winter and then another summer, then what? You made money working here this summer, but it will be slow in the winter. I don't want to try and make you do anything, but you might be wasting a valuable part of your life right now. Going to school now will change the way you think for the rest of your life. You should go. You're lucky. You can get your father to help pay for it."

"I don't want that. I don't want to be given everything."

"It's not giving you everything. Most people feel it's an obligation to send their kids to school. They feel that they owe it to them. One generation works hard so the next can learn more and then pass it on. I don't want to open the rift between you and your dad, except to say that you should get over it. He could die tomorrow and you'll have this unsettled business and then you're gonna feel worse about it. I've said enough. I'll listen to you if you want to talk about it, but I won't tell you what to do. I love you, Rebecca, and I just want you to be the best you possible."

Everything he thought of as he had walked there was gone. All the words and images he held he could not bring through his lips.

He knew so badly he was almost right, yet nothing he could do would bring a series of words to convince her to get off the island, not to succumb to the life of doing what she didn't really want to do. He knew what it was. She was insecure and felt like no opportunity existed that could make her happy, but opportunity awaits everyone who tries. Stay in one place for too long without changing, without learning something new, and no more opportunities come around. They don't all come to you.

They had met early in the summer, before it got warm at night, and right away they felt something for each other. Not love at first sight, though maybe, but he saw in her eyes a place he wanted to be. A distant place so close he could not look away. But he saw also someone who was afraid for some reason, afraid to assume that life wasn't a bad thing, afraid to believe that if life itself was possible, then anything else could not be so difficult. It only took drive and initiative, talent and luck. She had the talent, yet was afraid to believe it. Luck is what you make of it.

He thought of what she had done for him without even trying, without even knowing, but those words failed him, too. He was confused and frustrated because he wanted to be with her, but not only did he have obligations, he needed to change, to go somewhere different. He would be back, he knew, but now it was time to go.

He couldn't keep the physical attraction he had for her from clouding his thoughts. She wasn't the knockout bombshell men ogle in magazines, but she was luminous. Her body in the moonset, he'd never forget the first time they swam together at night after she got off work. Her skin so taught in the chilled northern water, and when they got out and lay on a blanket under the stars her breasts were still cool and shivery and formed into his chest as they warmed and relaxed. Their bodies together, drying in the breeze, the rise of her cheeks as she smiled and drifted to sleep, they often slept like that for hours and woke before dawn to go back to bed at his house. She smiled when she slept and woke with a liquid whisper, looking better than most people did when they left the house. They sipped each other for hours, ribbons of laughter breathing the wind.

Perhaps she knew to trust him from the first moment. Maybe there was some innate trust she saw in him. Soon she was sure he was there for her and he did things to make her happy. Simple things just to show he cared and appreciated the fact she was there. She wasn't a princess, expecting things to be handed to her from men who wanted her to be their queen. Perhaps that's what he saw in her eyes: Someone inside her who wanted just to be her, to be wanted just because of who she was. He gave her that without knowing at first and that's why he knew she was special, because she gave it back and each of them made things so much better for the other without asking.

When they went sailing the first time, he knew she had been before but she forgot it like she had blocked it out as a privilege meant not for her. She was actually good, though something kept her from pulling the knowledge from the back of her mind. It was easy, he told her, if you let your body become part of the boat, feeling the wind and the waves and the motion the boat made through the water, anticipating the gusts and lulls. You fly it like a bird flies its body, using more than just sight to know what to do. When the boat needed more than one to sail correctly, they worked together tightly as a team.

At first he drove, but she took the helm as her confidence grew and she lost the dogma of sailing classes she had taken as a child. She realized that the art of sailing was intuition and feel. They knew their weight distribution was important and she drove upwind so his weight could be near the mast. He'd lean out as the wind puffed up, flattening the boat before she'd have to adjust the helm. Then he'd drive downwind, sitting in the stern to keep the boat just right as the wind pulled them along.

They were fast together and he wanted to race, but she'd sleep in after a night at work rather than wake up early on the weekend to get out on the water, so he went with his brother. Then they'd come back and his brother would go fishing and he'd climb into bed all chilly at first and they'd lay there together with the wind in the screens. Then they'd fill a pack with blankets and food and go out on jaunts through the harbor, which was more fun than a race. Without the concentration required for racing, sailing with her was just a day together and the beauty of it all.

Then he remembered the first night they slept together. He placed a candle on the table and looked up to see her drop the shirt from her shoulders to the floor. For the moment that they gazed at each other, he saw her eyes and the look that wasn't a smile but simply the happiness in both of them. She was beautiful and he told her so.

She laughed and said, "So are you," and blew out the candle on her way under the blanket. "The moonlight is better, but I can't believe it's this cold," she said and sidled next to him, her shivers subsiding as she pulled close. The next morning they awoke with smiles and laughter, hugs and more kisses, wanting never to leave the bed they made together before breakfast. They did not make love, but were content in knowing they would and that it might be.

And it turned to love by midnight. Another fire in the dunes, words flowed from one another until there was nothing more to say and they'd lay by the fire with the same gleam of transcendence in their eyes.

But he had to go now. They walked quickly together and kissed goodbye over the gates as the ferry crew locked them.

"I'll call you when I get there!" he said and the horn blew and echoed off the dunes.

Chapter 15

Dog Stories

There were five dogs sitting outside the Dog, each in the back of a pickup and nervously eyeing the others, something more worthy on their minds yet too well trained to leave their posts and chase each other near the water's edge just a few yards away. They wouldn't step farther than the tailgate as Dave walked past, each dog's wagging tail and anxious eyes begging to be the first one petted, each face a visage of wonder as to why you would leave. Dave's little dog headed straight for the truck with the largest dog in it, a dog that seemed to be part wolf, and tried desperately to jump up there with him. The large dog stared down in wait of what would be just a tasty morsel, but the wolf wouldn't leave the truck without permission. The little dog wouldn't heel or follow, but couldn't get into the bed of the truck either, so he left them all together and went inside.

"I like to keep hard candy for the youngsters that come into my shop," said one of the old guys to the others who met there each morning. The group stopped talking and looked to see who had entered. After a pause, the oldest one said, "Good morning," and Dave wondered if he knew the story, if he was oblivious to the whole situation, or if he knew more than the rest put together.

"Good morning, gentlemen," Dave returned.

"Morning," muttered the rest of them.

Dave looked down at the paper stand and realized how early in the day it was. Yesterday's paper sat waiting to be taken away by the man from the first ferry who refreshed the rack every morning. Dave sat at the bar, away from the others who went on chattering, and ordered an egg on a bagel, toasted, to go, and a large coffee, which he sipped while he awaited the food like the wolf for his dog. Through the window he could see them, the wolf motionless, staring down at the bouncing, tireless terrier.

"That's some dog you got there," said the oldest man as he approached with a mug. "Mine would gobble him up easy, but yours would still go out fighting. Probably take off his tongue on the way down."

"Is that your wolf?"

"He's part wolf, ten percent, however they figure that out."

"He's beautiful, but I've never been sure whether I should pet him or not."

"Well, he's pretty friendly. Pretty smart, too. Good thing, otherwise it could get ugly out there. Mind if I sit?" he said and positioned his cup on the counter.

"No, please do," Dave said and made a feeble attempt to stand out of reverence, but the man put his hand on Dave's shoulder as he worked his way onto the next barstool.

"Don't bother to stand, thank you," the man said.

"Mine's part Jack Russell," Dave continued the conversation, "but who knows which part. The damn thing has a mind like a cat. Won't do anything I say."

"It's all in how you treat 'em," he said as he settled himself and abruptly changed the topic. "I hear that you had some trouble the other day."

"Yes, but I don't remember much about it."

"Really? It's rare that amnesia would last so long. I can't blame you for not sayin' much. Rumor has it that you killed a man."

Disconcerted by a stranger being so forthright, Dave sipped his coffee, hoping to appear as cool as possible, and turned slowly toward him. He saw eyes gleaming from a muscular face of soft skin chiseled from an island rock, swarthy, a wadmal sweater over work pants, rubber boots with the familiar smell. His dress indicated that he, too, was going out on the water. Still, the eyes asking...

"Rumor, huh?" Dave said. "Seem to be a lot of rumors in this place."

"Small towns talk, you know," the man said, his words vivifying the island, and the waitress came to pour him more coffee. He thanked her and gestured to the men talking at the other end of the bar. "Maybe there's just nothin' else to do." He admired the scent of his coffee before taking a sip.

"Thomas is dead, but I doubt I killed him," Dave affirmed. He kept his voice from traveling farther than a few feet. "The sea is a dangerous place."

The man's look of incredulity softened. "Well, nobody's innocent, but I don't think you're guilty of anything, either. I suspect that those boys were up to something."

"I'm sorry, but I didn't introduce myself. I'm Dave Wyman," he said and lifted his hand. The man smiled and reached out.

"Stuart Ashton," he said as they shook hands. "The place is so small, I just assumed everyone knows everybody else. They call me Stu."

"Pleased to meet you, Stu. What did you mean by those boys?" Dave asked.

"You know who I'm talkin' about," he said, dangling on the thought for too long.

"I'm afraid I'm not sure what anyone is talking about anymore."

"Thomas and Eddie."

Dave became more interested, though he tried not to appear so. He sat upright and turned to place both elbows on the bar. What does he know? he asked himself, but said nothing and scanned back into the man's eyes, waiting for him to continue.

"You knew about Thomas and Eddie, didn't ya?" he said.

"They were friends," Dave scoffed and looked forward. He put the cup before his face without drinking. "Life-long friends."

"They were more than just that. You knew they got into trouble together, right?"

"Back when they were kids."

"Well, all kids get into trouble when they're young, but Eddie went to jail. You knew that, right?"

Dave felt toyed with and wanted to say so, but he wouldn't risk seeming to know what happened, what only he truly knew at least. He slackened his face impassively and said, "He went to jail for growing pot."

"That's right. Damn good stuff, I must say. I hear they built bat houses and collected the guano for fertilizer. I guess you use the bat guano at a certain time of the year, when the plants are about to flower. Something about the balance of the fertilizer and it being organic. They perfected growing it. It's a simple science. You can't get too hooked on anything, though, and that's what got 'em into trouble."

He paused and reached for a paper napkin to blow his nose. "Excuse me," he said. "This time of year, something always gets my hay fever going." He tried to put order to his thoughts. He wanted to establish a framework, not wanting to say things too fast, repeat the unnecessary or play out more than Dave needed to know since neither could ever know all the details of two lives spent so close. He crumpled the napkin and tossed it to a wastebasket.

"You see," Stuart continued, "Thomas and Eddie grew up together. And they started smoking pot. Then they started growing it. I got no problem with someone growing a plant or two. What the hell, liquor's a lot worse, seems to me, with people crashing cars and ads trying to make you believe that pretty girls and booze come together. Course I never took too much of anything," he said and wrapped his fingers around the coffee mug.

"Those boys started growing a lot. Too much. They started making money and they were stupid about it. How can a kid around here make enough money to do what they were doing? They had hot cars, partying all the time, no jobs. They flaunted it. Smoking dope at the beach, by the lifeguard stand, in the parking lot, sometimes in front of parents with their little kids, and always with someone new. It was clear that something was goin' on.

"This is a little place where everyone knows everyone—and what they're doing. That's especially true when the summer is over and all the tourists leave. There's a lot less people around here and that's when the harvest begins, just like most of the crops in the world. Did you know that marijuana is one of the biggest cash crops in this country?" he asked almost rhetorically to give Dave time to catch all he was saying. He wanted to make sure that he wasn't just talking to the wind and turned toward him.

"They couldn't keep it a secret. Hell, they thought the place was theirs anyway. They knew it inside and out. Knew everyone, every little place. Some of the cops were still afraid of Eddie from high school, you know what I mean? And Prence, well he sort of felt sorry for Eddie and kinda looked the other way. But kids would come here in the summer and they'd be lookin' to get high and those boys loved to make friends, thought they were cool and that nothing would ever change.

"Who knows what exactly happened. Maybe someone got arrested on the mainland and talked or maybe someone just talked too much, but the state got wind of it. They sent some guy over here, some cop who wanted to be tough. The way the chief talks about that guy to this day. It's amazing how someone comes into the community and imposes himself. He just about took over the whole police force here, even if it is only a few men." Stuart motioned goodbye to a fellow who was leaving and turned back to Dave, leaning a little closer.

224

"Anyway, he came over here and just took over the whole show like it was the biggest thing happening in the world. Like it was gonna make him a star back on the mainland. Brought some men with him. I guess he'd been here before, doin' some kind of surveillance undercover. Asking around or listening in the bars. Somethin' like that.

"He didn't tell any of the local cops, let alone the chief. Before anyone knew it, he was here with three other troopers all dressed in black with radios and cameras. They staked out a few fields and caught Eddie and Thomas red-handed at the harvest."

"But Thomas never went to jail," Dave asserted.

"Yeah, that's the rub. You see, Thomas' father was a judge who helped the prosecutor with the election. When Thomas got arrested, his father was on his deathbed and the prosecutor wasn't gonna press charges out of respect for the man. Least not against Thomas. He stuck his neck out further than you could stretch it with a rope and he found some way for Thomas to get out of the charges. That cop from the mainland was furious. He wanted two convictions to add to his resume and he made a stink, had a quote in the paper. Someone cooled him down though, before it completely ruined his career. Can only imagine what he thinks about it still. Rich kid gets off on a technicality of arrest.

"Poor Eddie. With no connections and no money, he went to jail, of course. Damn shame, too. He blames Prence to this day, even after all the things the chief did for him as he was growin' up. Hell, I know he broke the law, but it was just grass and just his first time. The stash they said he had was a stretch beyond what anyone believed. They trumped up the seizure just to make a conviction stick. Then they threatened him with more jail time if he didn't snitch on his friends. Said he was part of some big conspiracy. The judge was the only one who believed it. Worst thing about it is that it made Eddie worse, not better. No sense puttin' a dope grower in with thieves or worse, especially if the police are gonna lie to do it." He let out a sigh.

225

"Eddie blamed Prence, at least he used to when it first happened, like all kids, you know, thinking nothing could ever be his own fault. Barely waves to him when they pass on the road even nowadays and that took forever. Truth is, neither of them knew it was happening until it was too late. State cops show up, what are the locals gonna do? Call Eddie and tell him?

"Prence blamed it on that cop from the mainland, Kipridge was his name. Those two have had it with each other for years because of this. Prence made a stink that they should have let the locals know what was going on. Not only because of jurisdiction, but he could have stopped it before they came and made a big thing out of nothing, took it to court, wasted money. Prence claims that Kipridge will never get past sergeant because of the way he handled himself. Huh!" he said and jostled himself on the chair, his coffee wafting before him.

"Big thing out of nothin'. Maybe it was big to someone. You know they use helicopters and planes to search for the stuff now. Imagine the cost of that for a few plants? Hell, there's hardly anyplace left to grow something without it being seen, 'cept maybe the old Krupsky farm…"

"Why are you telling me this?" Dave asked, cutting him short, probably too short he thought after he said it.

"Well, I figure you're in trouble and should know…"

"What if it was only a boating accident?"

Stuart's face went plain and he pondered the question with a slight glance upward, then he smiled slightly and lowered his eyes to meet Dave's. Shook his head. "I don't know. Just a hunch," he said and he pushed his way to his feet using Dave's shoulder with the same force as when he sat, and then patted it a few times. "Just a hunch."

"Well, I hope everyone will come to see that it wasn't anything more than a tragic accident."

226

"I'm sure they will, Professor," he said as he steadied himself. "I'm sure they will. I'll see you around."

"Good morning," Dave said and watched him walk out the door. He moved pretty well for a guy his age and pointed and said something to Dave's little dog. The damned dog went where the finger aimed. The dog would never do that for Dave. The old man reached over the back of his truck and stroked the hair of his friend, who forgot about the terrier as soon as his master appeared. He pulled himself into the truck using the steering wheel and backed out of the lot. The dogs watched them drive off. Then the terrier started jumping again beside another truck with the next largest dog, who looked down and then over at the others in disbelief.

His order came and Dave paid a different waitress who appeared to be asleep on her feet. She fidgeted with his check, her soporific mind unable to press the right keys until the register burst into some type of alarm more than once. "Keep the change," he said and bid the others farewell and stepped into the gray sunshine, calling for a dog who wouldn't follow until Dave picked up the bucket he brought and it was clear they were going for bait.

The fetid decay behind the fish pier, where vats of innards were filled for the free taking of lobstermen, was familiar to most of the islanders, who had probably lobstered at least once in their life, and it was a favorite place of canines. The smell would mask any canine scent and give them a distinct advantage over their prey, which could be anything of inverse proportion to the size of a terrier. Not that a mouse wouldn't be taken for fun, but very few things presented a challenge if the mind was set right, or steadfastly wrong, whichever the case.

Dave offered a piece of his breakfast and tricked the dog onto a leash tied well away from the vats before he ladled chunks into small netted bait bags brought back from the last time he went out to his traps. Ten traps, ten bags in the bucket, fat rubber gloves to keep the odor from following him home to the wife...

He peered through the door and saw the men working in rubber overalls and fat rubber gloves and knew they took the smell with them over to the Dog after work, for they, like everyone on the island, were friends of Thomas, and Dave had met them there. It was Thomas who first brought Dave to the back of the fish pier. Not his father or grandfather or uncle or brother or mother or some other relative who showed him the ways of the island as had been done for generations. Thomas. They came here and filled up a few buckets and went in to say hello to the guys and Dave wouldn't have known them again except for the smell. The smell gave him the idea that diving for lobster had to be better than slopping traps full of bait, stinking the boat and the whole of their being.

"Can't sell 'em if you dive for 'em, though."

"Thought you weren't going to sell them."

"I'm not. Besides, how are we gonna know what's up with the fishery if we don't use traps?" Dave said, including Thomas in the 'we'.

One of the workers sprayed the floor with a hose, pushing chunks together to be placed in a vat, and saw Dave looking in. He nodded hello with a lift of his head, then his face dropped out of countenance. Some of the others noticed the motion and looked over, briefly wondered if Dave was going to come in, but another basket of fish came up from the docked boat and they went back to work. They tipped the basket onto a stainless steel chute guiding fish to a long cleaning table where others worked filet knives and turned out pieces of meat to be packed in ice and chunks for the vats, a separating link in the food chain. Some food moved up and the rest moved down as bait.

Dave picked up the dog and the bucket and carried them both until they were away from the fish pier, then unleashed the dog, who led down the dock and jumped in the boat and took a place in the bow. Dave untied from the dock and they drifted, the water a moat to make his dog think twice before chasing down the dock while he stowed the bait and tacitly prayed the engine would start right up again. Soon they were off in the Caper, out in the bay, moving through the cool daylight, drops splashing up and spattering his stained orange slicker as the waves built and the motor wah-uuuun-wah-uuuun-wah-uuuun-ed as the boat leapt.

The traps were spread across the bays to study each area. He had to traverse a fairly wide range to get to them, but only the middle of the coves was rough. He took the traps out there first, idling up to them, placing the engine in neutral as he swung the gaff hook to grab the buoy line, wrapped it over the pulley, hauled hand over hand until the trap thudded against the side of the hull. Then he heaved the trap over the gunwale and onto a shelf set up for cleaning and re-baiting.

They get heavier, he groaned, as the weeds grow on them through the season. He picked the traps clean as part of the experiment. The lobsters probably didn't care if the traps were clean, but he thought it best, sort of like a control group in the experiment. Keep all the traps as clean as the others so they remain similar enough that nothing could throw the research.

He put the various growth in plastic bags, noting which ones came from which areas, kept general notes on conditions, time, temperatures, water temperatures (a little thermometer on each trap), everything that would later go onto a chart, and somehow after a year he would make some sort of deduction. He noted the number of lobsters in the trap, if any, their length, if they carried eggs (notched the tails if they did so others would know it was an egger) and then gently dropped them back to the sea. He made sure it got around the docks that he threw them back so that other lobstermen wouldn't cut his lines. They hated competition, especially from someone who's only in it for fun. It was Thomas' idea to tell them, but Dave began wondering if he was catching the same ones over again so he began tagging them with tiny numbered pieces of plastic, making notes when he picked them up again and sometimes moving them deliberately to another area. The strategy evolved over the summer and his notes filled a variety of books.

At first he thought trapping lobsters would be fun until he realized you had to break your back all the time. Rain or shine, snow or whatever, even the mail wouldn't make it to the island sometimes. But you have to keep checking the traps or the captives will eat each other. It was a few days since he was out, but no carcasses among the leftover bait in the traps so far. He picked out the growth and tossed out the crabs and snails and whatever else was in there, spilled the remnants of the old bait into the trap and put the new bait bag inside as he closed the lid. Then he checked that the line and buoy were ready to go over without catching something, drove the boat back to the same location and hefted the trap back over the side, another backbreaking endeavor.

The dog was bored, but sometimes hunkered down low on all fours to keep balanced in the waves. Only a few more traps. Ten traps. "Thank God it's only ten traps," he told the dog as he pushed the fifth trap over. The work made his head pound and dizzy. He thought of the past few days awhirl and recalled a circular dream, walking along a circular wall that never ended. A stone wall. Round and round and never an end, never a corner, a ledge. The vertiginous dream, sinuous, vinous, climbing, stone by stone, reaching for light, branching, climbing, no place to hide.

Sentient with a start, out in the bay, alone with the waves plashing, the dog asleep, quiescence, shimmering sleep in the sunshine, cars moving on the island an anthill, golden refraction over the hills, a place blocked from sight. A field.

The old guy called me Professor!

You couldn't take the road to the old Krupsky farm without being seen for it passed many houses before entering the property, but you could take a small boat around to a salt pond that filled deep with high tide. Dave poled his boat into the runnel that sliced through a stony beach. Small waves washed to the pebbles with the sound of bagged marbles passed hand to hand slowly. The creek carved through a marsh but opened into the pond after twenty yards. Then he paddled the boat across it and into the tall weeds on the other side.

From there, Dave crept up a path that barely broke through the thicket and forest and led to a rolling field of tall, blond grass. The path disappeared and he cut through the field, once used for corn, occasionally stopped by a briar. He passed an old farm machine rusting to the earth, some forsaken hives, and then a few gravestones. A stone wall stood falling, marking the entrance to the farmyard, most of whose buildings had been swallowed back into their foundations. Besides the birch trees that took many years before, the only wood still standing was the silo, its shingles carved with time into shapely splinters and covered with an iridescent moss on one side. Beyond that, way back in a thicket, was the remainder of the house.

The owners had lived here for three generations before giving it away as a preserve. The first building was simple and small, just one room for shelter and cooking. As the farm came to life and tribulations subsided to chores, more buildings arose. The shed, the barn and then an addition to the house that was bigger, formed the shape of an "L", where more rooms were added. In there was the living space, the bedrooms, a room on the second floor for the children who kept the family moving forward through time. In the original structure remained the kitchen and below it, built of island stone with a wooden stair, the root cellar, built in a circle so spirits would have no place to hide.

The only vestige of the house was the circle of stones holding open a hole in the ground. The floor was littered with wood scraps and a few broken bottles, and one side of the wall was covered with ivy. Dave jumped into the hole, hitting the ground with the realization that he wasn't as young as he used to be. He straightened his aching knees and found himself in deeper than it seemed from the top, the stones now over his head.

A circular wall. No place to hide. A place blocked from sight.

He searched the floor of the hole for signs of unrest, kicking aside some of the scraps. There was a board, but it covered only the ground. No sign of disturbance. No place to hide. No way to get out. He studied the mason work. There was a reason for a root cellar to be round, he thought. No place to hide.

A noise came from above and Dave peered from the hole, pulling himself high enough so that his eyes cleared the stones. Two trees rubbed together in the wind with a sonorous groan. He dropped back in the hole and kicked the board again, only to notice a splatter of mortar.

He remembered the morning when Eddie came by so early, but looked like he had been working already, even though he hadn't worked in days. The tools in the back of his truck. "Ain't much work around, though." Eddie is a mason. "...the last mason livin' on the island." He could have reset some of the stones. No place to hide. A place blocked from sight. Behind the ivy.

Another sound from above and there was his dog, forgotten since the boat.

Chapter 16

Ghost on the Roof

Part of the world holds an ancient belief that existence is comprised of the living, the dead and the near dead. An animate creature is certainly alive when breathing. When a man lives, he interacts with others. He becomes their friend or enemy, no one of consequence or merely a passerby. Yet those he comes into contact with know him to some degree. They know what he looks like, how he acts, things that he's done. When he dies, those still alive remember him, can draw pictures of him, and tell stories of what he did and how he affected others. At that point he is near dead, not alive, but not forgotten. He lives on in the memory of others. When everyone who knew him has died, then the memory of him is gone and he is truly dead.

And to live on as such a ghost surely couldn't hurt if many people remember you and speak favorably of you through the ages. Those who do much for others carry on in the memory of civilizations and even the brave act of someone who saves another would not be forgotten for as long as the saved one tells the story. The unknowns, who die too young to have achieved anything, who die alone with no one to leave behind, might simply disappear despite the one person who prays for the souls of the lost. But to be caught...to wind up in someone's dream by accident...alone, pale as candle wax and moving like a time-lapse cinema with a different scene at each blink of the eye. Unable to empty the lungs of the air that tells their story or the story of a sapping tree, a bursting flower, a bird diving in flight or a wobbling duck in a bathtub of bay, it all comes so fast and then fades just as quickly—a strange dream, a vaporous, celestial dream, reality caught between living flesh and what we call expiration, cessation, decease.

Rebecca did not mind living as a ghost, having disappeared from life and choosing only to be seen by selected faces on Earth. She knew no one now but a few people from town and Ursa, who left her alone to her studies and whose music flowed from the piano and into her inspirations. It seemed that was all that they did lately: Rebecca sketching or painting and Ursa stroking, pounding, thrilling the keyboard. They stopped to rest, to take tea, to eat, and to talk. Sometimes they shopped together, though they often took turns once they agreed to keep a communal list.

When Rebecca first saw the note that brought her to Ursa's house, the note implied that she would need to take care of an older woman, and when she first saw Ursa hobbling along, recovering from a broken leg, she thought it would require some work. To the contrary, however, Ursa seemed to take more care of the both of them. That broken leg healed completely during the summer and Ursa seemed so alive now. Rebecca even said that Ursa's constant chores seemed effortless and made her feel lazy, but Ursa assured her that this was the easy part of her life, hardly a job like working at the Dog. Even more so, Ursa seemed to simply float along. Her piano playing had attracted people to come and hear her, and they had even convinced her to play at town hall. She often revealed her soul as she finessed pieces from the heart with her eyes closed. With all that had been done for her, Rebecca felt she owed Ursa something more than rent, so she took it upon herself to peek through the window at Ursa as she played the piano overlooking the sea. She sketched out the scene and kept a painting that she worked on at night and would soon have a portrait she referred to as "Mother Pianist."

No one knew that she painted over her self-portraits. At first she was too embarrassed because she didn't have the money for new canvas, but then she liked the concept more and more as she painted beautiful scenes over herself. Then with the portrait of Ursa, she chose one of her sleeping self-portraits so she hoped it would signify, at least to her, that of a young woman waking to a full life of artistry, for Ursa had almost magically brought back a talent that lay dormant for years.

Rebecca thought of how the place had changed. Early on it was stark dunes and budless, windswept trees with sprig branches. The porch was barren until they moved blotchy pots from the shed, filled them with dirt from the compost heap and placed them about the deck. Rebecca had offered to do most of the carrying, but Ursa chugged along, telling stories of how they used to can and jar things from the garden and how she found pots easier to maintain. Rebecca questioned if it was worth the effort—putting out the pots and taking them back in every year so they wouldn't freeze and break—but the change over the summer provided more than just flowers and herbs. She had so many still life paintings now, with the sea and dunes behind flower pots covered with moss and dripping thyme.

When they first transplanted seedlings from the cold frame, she wanted to label the pots, but Ursa told her not to worry. Then as everything came up looking the same, she was certain they should have marked them, but as the plants matured and turned into themselves, Ursa taught her how to recognize each of them and arrange the pots based on height. Ursa would see perennials emerge and address them as old friends. She had a morning ritual with a watering can in one hand and a cup of tea in the other. She'd gently sprinkle those that needed it and notice the growth of each plant. Then came early harvests, primping the plants for the most growth and simple foods turned into sumptuous meals. Each morning produced new flowers and the harvest was ample enough for them to give things away ("used to jar those," Ursa would say). She'd joke about herself being "land rich", because her property was worth so much, but where would she go if she sold it? She lived richly on such modest means that she sold flowers just for the fun of it, but those dollars went to the market for the things she didn't grow. A boy from nearby sometimes brought her fish that he caught to trade for his sister's piano lessons—a little deal she worked out with their mother, she told Rebecca later, because they couldn't afford to pay money.

All of these led to picture studies, too: "Lady with Watering Can and Tea", "Lady by the Stove", "Flowers for Market", "Piano Lesson" and "The Gift of Fish", which she had to embellish because the boy actually brought fillets wrapped in foil.

All over the island, the changing weeks brought new life. Once it was white, wild roses blooming in the treetops and another time it was honeysuckle swaying in the breeze like a fire hose let loose. Queen Anne's Lace stretched long in a snapdragon field of apple trees, scraggly and twisted, sprouting leaves and flowering, their fruit growing slowly and ripening to gold and red. The last time Rebecca saw that field, the trees were half full of bright apples and the other half dotted the grass in fragrant decay, the aroma overcoming that of the paints on her palette. Giant sunflowers hung over themselves now and she painted them with a goldfinch eating the seeds by dangling upside down.

She was finally at home on the island. The tourists, or tourons as known to the locals, had stopped coming in hordes and the ferry had changed schedules to two boats, so its horn only bubbled from the harbor a few times a day. Rebecca had shifted her job to part time, but she hated it still and avoided it as often as possible, telling herself that she took the money only for paint. The scenes that surrounded her made it easy to draw. Another sketchbook neared full and she again needed more canvas. She focused on the elusive, the reflections and shadows of reflections. Most importantly, however, was that as daylight passed at this time of year it turned to a gold that couldn't be matched yet with paint. The other day, Rebecca had to run for different colors and still missed it, but this time she was ready with all of them.

She sat on the roof sketching the scene with Foamy the cat twitching her tail by the chimney, waiting for the sun to reach the right place in the sky and cast its shadowy tincture on the house and dune across the street. From the left, the road wandered up from the town through a valley separating the dunes. Ursa's house sat on one dune and another house sat on the other, and the dunes kept rolling. Her eye, trained from the pictures of the clock tower and lighthouses, picked up the details of the rusted gate latch and the white-painted fence turned silver with age as she waited for the sun to reach the right spot in the sky. This day was different than the other day, more amber and red, and she dabbed paints on her palette as the light changed quickly. Just when she got the colors nearly right, Ursa called from the doorway.

"I'm up here, Ursa."

"Up *where?*" said Ursa as she stepped through the kitchen door and looked up. "What on *Earth* are you doing up there, Rebecca?"

"I'm trying to match that color," she said, trying not to look away from her work.

"How did you get up there?"

"I climbed up the corner post."

"Oh. Well be careful coming down. The phone's for you. Should I tell them to call back?"

"Who is it?"

"I don't know. I didn't ask, but it's a boy calling from someplace loud."

"Peter," she said softly. "I'll be right down, Ursa."

"All right, but don't fall."

Ursa didn't like him at all, the young man who came to visit Rebecca. She didn't trust him, nor did Abbey, which was a rarity. He seemed nice on the outside, but her feeling was that he was hiding from himself, wearing a demeanor just so people will believe him or accept him. He came to the house shyly and took Rebecca straight to her room. Why couldn't they go for a walk? she thought. He seemed angry. She placed the kettle on the stove and tried not to listen, but the voices from upstairs were fevered and pitched.

"You just packed up and left, Rebecca. Why didn't you tell me you were leaving, huh? I had to search all over town, all summer, and I never would have found you if it wasn't for some stupid picture of you with a fish! Huh, this year's record, or something like that. Is that your new boyfriend?"

"Tim, you know why I left. I don't want to be with you anymore."

"Why not? Just because we had a fight? Damn you, Rebecca. You only think of yourself!"

"Tim, we're only twenty. How are we supposed to know if we're right for each other...forever?"

"I love you."

"You think you do, but you're just addicted to me. It's no different than you are with any other woman."

His rage inflamed, he backhanded her across the face. She settled to the bed and began to weep as he stood with eyes of a thorn bush.

"Damn you, Rebecca. You think you're just some other woman to me? Just some other—"

"Tim, please go. Just go. Just leave. I don't want you! I don't want you around me. It's not right for me."

"Me, me, me. That's all you think about. What about *me?*"

"Tim, we were only together for a year. It's not like your life is over. There'll be another."

"Don't talk to me like I'm waiting for a bus, damn you. I'm not someone you can just throw out."

"I'm not throwing you out, Tim. You were the first. Do you think I can ever forget you?"

"Great. Where does that leave me? I give my heart to you and you just grow out of it."

"If you gave me your heart, I'd want to stay."

He became furious. "If I gave you my heart. What the hell do you think I gave you?" he yelled and hit her with a closed fist.

"Fuck you, Rebecca, fuck you. I'll show you my heart."

He reached back to throw his fist again, but he stopped as the door opened and the dog rushed in with her tail whipping. Ursa stepped in behind, looking through her glasses at an angle in disbelief.

"I think you should go now," she said, cocking her head as she read his mind. She said nothing as she watched him lower his hand.

"We were just—"

"I know what you were doing and you'll be leaving this house RIGHT NOW!"

He looked to Rebecca for her to ask him to stay, but she found the courage to be rid of him.

"Just go, Tim."

He lowered his shoulders and head and moved toward the door, followed by Ursa. They stepped down the stairs and toward the front door. Ursa couldn't pass up the opportunity to lecture the boy.

"Young man, you'll never win someone's heart by ruling their body with your hands. That's not love. It's stealing."

He threw open the screen door and trotted down the porch stairs. Ursa called to him, but he didn't look back. She said, "Every cop on the island has had dinner at this house. You come back here and I'll make sure they meet you." Ursa closed the door and locked it, turning to Rebecca, who stood on the first landing, tears dropping from her eyes.

"Come here, honey," Ursa begged. Rebecca dropped down each stair slowly until Ursa wrapped her arms around her. "My God, Rebecca. I didn't think he would hit you. Let me see your face. It's all right. No bruises. Don't cry." She pulled her close again. "Rebecca, no man is worth taking that from. Do you hear me? There are so many people in the world, and no one should ever hit you. Please, please, never see him again." Rebecca nodded on her shoulder and the kettle called from the kitchen. "Go on upstairs and wash your face. Then come down for some tea. OK?"

"OK, Ursa. Thanks."

"Don't thank me. I didn't shoot him."

Rebecca cracked a smile and ran up the stairs. Ursa walked quickly to the kitchen and pulled the kettle from the heat, slightly burning herself on the handle. She dropped the kettle on a cold burner and put the scalded finger to her mouth.

"That bastard," she said to herself as she noticed her finger trembling against her lip. "He'd better not come back here for his own sake."

A little time passed and Rebecca came to the kitchen and leaned in the doorway. Ursa looked up from chopping carrots and smiled. "You OK, honey? Do you need a hug?"

"No. Thanks, Ursa." Rebecca smiled, though her eyes couldn't hide the feelings.

"I'll pour you some tea. Have a seat. Do you want to go for a walk before dinner?"

"Maybe, but…I have a lot to tell you."

"You don't have to tell me anything. Certainly not now, if you don't want."

"I also have a favor to ask."

"Yes."

"Well, it's a lot to ask, maybe, but…"

"Go ahead, honey, the only dumb question is one that isn't asked," she said with a rising inflection that seemed to mock an elementary school teacher from the past.

"I was wondering. Do you think I could have my father visit for a few days? He could stay in the third bedroom."

"I think that would be fine. Why don't you call him now? Don't worry about the charges, just dial direct."

"OK. Thanks."

"It's all right, Rebecca." She continued chopping the vegetables as Rebecca walked from the doorway. "As long as he doesn't snore. Thin walls, you know."

Chuckles spilled from the hallway.

Chapter 17

Growing Confusion

Now on foot and awaiting the night to conceal him, Dave thought through a combination of events that brought him to a place he couldn't explain. Back when he was just a newcomer to the island and out for a walk in the sunrise by Krupsky's farm, he heard a rustle from the thicket. There was Eddie all by himself, startled from the bushes as if he'd been sleeping on someone's private property and awoke from a haze to slip off leaving only suspicion. He didn't respond and had almost hidden his face while walking away, as if anyone could ever forget his appearance.

A few days later, Thomas introduced them and Dave almost said something like, "Yes, I saw you that morning..." but stopped before a word eked out. Eddie had a silencing effect, an inimical glare that kept you from wanting to know him. And when they shook hands and he held on for just a moment too long, he made it seem like he never wanted to meet again, either.

When Eddie was out of earshot, Dave mentioned to Thomas that time in the forest and it was blamed on a bad hangover, and from the way Eddie drank it seemed perfectly feasible. But now, looking back, with everything of Thomas coming unwound, scattered truths washed up in congeries on the beach. Now it was Eddie who was more truthful without saying a word.

The night Dave met Thomas, he was just a guy who lived on the island, someone with similar interests and enough dissimilar interests to provoke conversations lasting way beyond closing time. Left in a corner, sober and feeling sublime, while the staff put chairs on tables and slugged beer and came up with recipes for booze shots and garrulously frittered away at one end of the bar, two worlds apart, two worlds melded together.

Once talk turned to why Dave came to the island, Thomas quickly offered to help, to show him around, set him up with some traps, give him a sense of where to put them. He knew the island so well, he said, that he'd save Dave a lot of time and would enjoy working on a project that might save the place he loved. He told Dave where the last unseen sights were hidden, took him there or pointed to places on maps. Only after a friendship had kindled did he find out his wife had known Thomas from so many years past. It was merely an odd coincidence that they each chuckled about together and alone.

He wondered how long it was until Thomas told Eddie that Dave had seen him that morning at Krupsky's.

And so Dave felt himself compelled down a path back to the root cellar, if only to find out what was there, but knowing he was getting himself deeper into something he needed no part of. He was suspect enough. If he produced evidence that linked him further, then he'd be accused and Eddie would walk away free. Why dig his own grave? Why bother to solve the problems of a place that had problems it didn't even know about? Why take the chance when he could sit somewhere warm with a fire and food and a wife and some children and a job and simply exist like everyone else?

Something drove him—curiosity, disbelief, want for a tatter of evidence to parry suspicion if Thomas came back to shore—and he formed a plan. He had to go to Krupsky's by water or he'd pass by too many houses. Someone might find his bike. And what if he had to carry something? The boat slip was far enough out on the dock that no one would notice, without specifically looking, that he had gone out. So he rode his bike down to the pier. To foment his secrecy, he brought his dog with him to stifle any complaints about the inevitable howling of the dog left alone. As he pedaled, the dog followed closely, not wanting to be outrun.

He left the bike just off the road, behind rocks at the far end of the dock, and walked away from town, over the dune toward the ocean beach where no one would be at this time of day, this time of year. He left a small bag of tools and warm clothes there, too, safe from theft. No one would take them. Nobody's here. He'd take a long walk where no one would see him and come back after dark, an hour or so, pick up the bag. He could consider the plan closely alone.

When he got back, he'd make sure that no one was looking, wade quickly out to the shallow end of the dock and roll onto it. The dog would swim out and he'd grab the scruff of the neck. They could make it to the boat without anyone noticing, but he'd have to make sure the docks were empty. Otherwise, he'd simply go out to the dock like he was just going fishing. But that wouldn't happen. He'd silently paddle from the docks and the lamps that illumed only so far, start the motor and idle away without lights, increasing his speed only so much so the sound wouldn't carry and catch the attention of anyone nearby. Once in the bay, he'd navigate by the lighthouse and make his way past buoys that were ingrained in his mind. Even with the cloud-covered moonlight, there'd be nothing to worry about except in close to the shore over by Krupsky's. The small flashlight he brought would be fine. He'd not hit the rocks.

Once he got close enough to shore, he'd anchor the boat and wade the rest of the way. His pants would already be wet and he couldn't risk grounding the boat on an outgoing tide. No one would see it there. He'd make his way to the path with the dog on a leash or carried through the thickets. He should have sent the dog off with the rest of the family, but along with getting out of the pit again, he'd simply have to manage.

Meanwhile, as Dave speculated about mortar and chisels and which rock to take out and which to put back and what might actually be found, Barney, his terrier, bounded down the beach unconcerned of all but what might be hidden in clumps of weeds. Barney, by the full name of Barnacle, was a small dog, whose dark head, white body and gray tail lent the name. Those terrier jaws could latch onto anything and hold fast, the feathery tail ever waving, giving the look of an adnate barnacle fixed to a pier with its fanning cirri collecting food.

Of course, Barney was a girl. Dave's kids came up with the name and asked if he knew the difference between a girl barnacle and a boy barnacle and he told them that they are both— hermaphrodites. That confused them a little, so he sidestepped the rest of the questions and they were content in having a dog named Barnacle. They called her Barney because a two-syllable name was easier for getting a dog's attention, but she'd rarely take a command without the offer of food.

"No wonder she's confused," the kids would say. "She doesn't know if she's a boy or a girl."

Dave watched her now and despite her insolence, he knew her speed and spirit never ceased to amaze and amuse. Other dogs wouldn't bother to chase a ball if Barney was there to outrun them. She treed a bear once simply by barking in circles around it. Another time, she clamped onto the tail of a horse that spun and bucked and spun and spun and finally kicked the dog off and she sat up, panting with what had to be a smile as the whole group of people laughed. All the commands in the barnyard couldn't keep her from trying to grab on for another ride, but the horse kicked again and she learned her lesson.

Small dogs like Barney have a short life expectancy because they get into situations they should never survive. That's Barney, always picking fights with dogs four or five times her size. As cute as she was, she was still a killer, part of her lineage bred to kill rats, and you could never be sure if she would attack just for the fun of it.

She had a knack for digging at doors until they somehow opened and she'd slip out, showing up with a howl to be let back in some hours later. The household worried she'd be hit by a car or lost in the snow. A few weeks after one sojourn she became thick, a mongrel portent of calamity. She had five pups and they found homes for only three of the odd, unknown little breed. Soon, the neighbors joined forces against them since someone would inevitably leave a door open enough so the dogs could scratch their way out. They'd escape and kill whatever they could. The police were summoned, lawsuits threatened, angry words shouted about the dogs' disposition for cats.

The pedantic biologist, Dave studied them as they developed, but his dismay grew with the pups as they became a pack. The dogs packed with speed, outrunning a quarry until it became winded, then turning as a group, outnumbering, bewildering, succumb. Barking, a common goal and some wave of teamwork, they knew which way to turn at the right time and catch the break of an opponent or prey. They'd take on anything, that pack of three, once stretching out a German Shepherd, who ran away the living fright of death after the dogs were kicked from him. That's when they got rid of the other two pups and kept Barney, but he always recalled their packing instinct when something caught Barney's eye.

Her youth still showed as she tried to climb a rampart dune, jumping with all her might to hurdle the vertical wall only to spring up straight, see over the top and fall to roll down the dune to the beach. Undaunted, the task forgotten, she took off like the birds she chased, stopping shoulder high in a wave of foam. She looked back at Dave and shot off out of sight as the sea pulled away.

Dave came upon a pram turned over, to keep the rain outside it, and heard from within a scratching sound and he knew the Barnacle was in there chasing something, digging for it, outside. He couldn't help but entice the dog, so he prowled up to the boat and scratched back, causing her to stop, listen (Dave could see her cocked head in his mind) and then she dug even harder. When he called her, she knew she'd been deceived and crawled under the transom on her side through mealy sand mud. She'll have to be hosed off before she goes in the house, Dave thought. Perhaps a little carpet freshener, too, he joked in his mind.

She ran farther down the gravelly shore and disappeared behind an outcrop of rocks. Dave wanted to take a path into the dunes, his solicitous plan calling for night to fall just as they arrived back at the docks. He called for her, but she wouldn't come. He walked to the pile, calling the dog, but she still disobeyed, so he climbed up and over the rocks to find the sight, a sight that could never be lost, of Barnacle nosing around the remains of Thomas Soverge, his body days dead.

Dave was so lost in thought he hadn't noticed the birds circling in song. As he went to fetch the dog, he saw her ears fall back, her ginger step toward the corpse and snuffle, couldn't hear the soft whimper of recognition. Her countenance bewailed lament as she trudged to Dave, glanced back at Thomas, the birds keening from a pitying sky.

Dave kneeled down to stroke her and they gazed back toward the turgid body pushing and pulling the shore. He rose to leave when he noticed the crabs. Thomas had crabs crawling on him. He was helpless, nothing he could do. Dave lifted the dog and walked around the rocks, through the stones and toward the path, praying all the while that the soon falling night would hide the body and give him one more day.

Was the tide still rising, pushing Thomas up farther, or falling to leave him to dry?

The stones made balancing a task, though the dog was calm and tried to lap his face, knocking the baseball cap from Dave's head. He held her in one arm and caught the cap before it fell. When he took his hand from the brim, a crab fell into view and onto the rocks with a clack, just feet from him, dropped from above by a gull that hoped to eat it by cracking it on the stones. The bird couldn't be seen for the brim of the hat and Dave looked up to watch the steep landing near the crab.

The crab didn't break, though, and crept at an angle toward a puddle, claws in the air. The bird hopped toward the crab, now half-underwater and disappearing under the sand, but the gull stuck his head below the surface and took hold of a spiny leg. The points of the other legs poked at the bird as he winged to the air, straight up on a breeze, then dropped the crab smack on a stone.

From the puddles, Dave knew the tide was going out. The body was still there. What was left of his eyes stared at him from the arched-necked head of Thomas wound in seaweed.

He turned and walked up the path, but a boy and a little girl came toward him. My God, his mind muttered. I can't let them see that, please, please. They walked past him.

"Hey, mister," called the girl.

"Yes?" he said, already turned round to watch where they went.

"Can I pet your dog?"

"Sure," he said. "But I don't want her to run off right now, so I have to kind of hold her."

"That's OK."

Dave dropped to a knee and placed Barney down and she tried to shake herself free. He watched intently to see if she was going to bolt, one hand on her shoulders. With her head straight, she turned her eyes up, shifting them side to side. The girl knelt down and lightly smoothed the small head with the tips of her fingers.

"What's his name?"

"Barney."

"He looks like a Barney," and with the mention of her name, Barney leapt up and licked the little, paper face. The girl screeched and giggled as she wiped her cheek and pushed the dog away.

"You're all sandy, Barney!" she yelled and giggled again, happy to have made a friend, unaware that just behind the rocks a few yards away lay a sight that would change her forever.

"Come on, Lissa," called her brother. "Let's go."

Dave lifted Barney and watched as the brother and sister ambled down the beach. Slowly, he carried the dog to the path, hiding behind the dune as his eyes followed the children. His lips passed a soft prayer, "Please, don't go to the water. Please, God, please don't let them see that." He would stop them before they got there, he thought, but they shrank away to footprints around a flowing bend, unaware of the birds causing a commotion.

They were gone. He pondered as the darkling lowered around him. The birds calling. He could wait for the night to come, but in the morning the body would be found with an avulsion of its head and a lot of explaining left to be done. The tide could carry it all away. He remembered the tale of a despondent woman who left her clothes on the beach and swam out with the tide, her body carried away, never found. He could bury Thomas at sea like he wanted back on Stage Island. He could be rid of the evidence that left questions washing on the beach. Repulsion of a corpse, his friend, shied him from the beach as he thought the process through, another plan, a by-play to the original.

He infused himself with resolve, let the dog out of his arms and strode down the beach to the rocks. People surf naked in cold water, he could do this. He checked the beach in both directions as he approached the rocks where Thomas' body lay, shooed the birds with his presence and began to undress. He stripped to his underwear, laying his clothes high on the backs of the rocks where they'd stay dry, checked the beach again and stepped out of the rest of his clothes. There, naked, he took one more look at his friend, exhaled all lurking fear and stepped toward him. He grabbed an ankle, spongy clothes over pappy flesh, and tried to free him, his leg a mooring rode to the anchored body. He lifted the other ankle and leaned backward, strained naked toward the sea as a wave came and floated the body enough to be pulled deeper. Knee high in the water, the body afloat, Dave let go of one leg and faced the ocean, pulled hard and splashed. He kicked a rock and tripped, falling into the frigid grip of white water. Alongside the corpse, swimming with one hand, hardly noticeable from the shore, he bumped atop another rock and ducked under a wave. The body followed, pulling back toward the beach as the waves rode over, then he felt the tide pull sideways along the beach, then outward. A hundred yards from shore in no time, deep, he pushed the body with one hand and let go as though waving goodbye with short gasps as he forced his chest to breathe through the clamp of cold water. Away the body drifted as Dave swam backwards. The waves lifted and lowered and moved on. Thomas dipped and passed under a crest and didn't surface again.

The current pulled from the shore and Dave swam across it until the flow slacked and he could swim to the beach. He was far away from his clothes when he got to water shallow enough to stand. The waves left him naked and cold before covering again, knocking him sideways. He found the right depth and waded, but wading was tiresome and slow. Shivering, nose running, blowing water from his lips as he stood again, the waves flailed him like a shutter in the wind. He slogged from the waves, the undertow dragging him back. Stones and weeds washed over his feet. The night was almost down as he raced the rest of the way to the rocks where his clothes waited beneath the red-ribbon sky.

He wiped his shivering body with his undershirt and heaved his pants over each leg. He couldn't think of anything but the cold as he forced on his shirt, almost tearing it.

Barney was gone.

He glanced around the rocks, down the beach, through the darkness. He saw nothing but tracks in the sand. He could follow them, but the timing of the plan was slipping away. He called for her. Called again. She barked. Down the beach came a flashlight. He saw Barney with the two children. He looked at the water. No Thomas.

He walked toward the children, who came laughing, Barney running ahead. She came to Dave's feet with head bowed and tail wagging shyly. He told her what a good dog she was and she leaned into his petting hand.

The boy asked, "Did you go swimming, Mister?"

Dave feigned a smile and looked up at them. "Sure did."

"That's crazy," the boy said.

"Aren't there sharks out there?" asked the girl, her nose twisted as her cheeks rose up.

"If so, they're as cold as me," he answered. "Thanks for watching her. Come on, Barney!" He whistled the rising descant to lead the dog away, but lifted her and held her close to warm himself, leaving the two children perplexed with a flashlight and an unasked question about a dog named Barney, who was a her.

Through the dark street he walked himself warm again, the clothes not damp enough to stop him. He came to the turn before the harbor and stepped over the rail to where his bike lay, put down the dog, took up the bag. He couldn't get back in the water. He'd never get warm again if he waded out to the pier, so he chose to walk down to the gangway, spied it and strode fast with the bag over a shoulder. Barney charged ahead.

Silence suggested another time. Except for scattered lights, the town looked as though all humanity had left it forever behind, a whirlwind of dust from a dried river of rain. From the Dog glowed soundless warmth, shadowed heads in veiled windows, a glass of wine pressed to lips. The place looked as quiet as the day a lone boat slipped through the uncharted harbor. Dave came to the pier with its docks half full.

A truck drove down from the hill and Dave saw his overwrought plan coming undone. The truck, with lights atop, stopped in the harbormaster's parking spot. Chief Prence stepped out and shined a light on Dave.

"Wyman, is that you?"

"Yes, sir."

The chief came closer, his head bobbing but the light fixed in one spot from above his body. Dave froze with a hand raised to shield his eyes. "Someone called to complain about a man swimming naked. From the looks of it, that would be you."

"Kill the light, Chief."

"Was that *you* swimming naked over there?" the chief's voice raised. The light shined on.

"I wasn't naked. I had my boxers on."

"It's a bit odd to be swimming this time of year, isn't it?"

"For some, maybe."

"You look cold."

"I've got some more clothes with me," Dave said and flounced the pack gently enough so the tools wouldn't rattle. The light stayed on a moment longer, then clicked off. They both put down their hands.

"Are you OK?" the chief asked. "With all that's going on, you're swimming alone in the dark. Seems unlike—"

"My wife's taken the kids to her parents. I'm just tryin' to get myself together about this thing. You people are nuts, thinking I killed Thomas. Are you so bored that you have to make things up just to keep yourself going? Just to have something to do?"

"Now hold on, Wyman. No one has any answers here. Certainly not you and you were the only one there who's alive. Tell me what happened and we'll leave it at that."

"I'm not saying a word to you without a lawyer. You come over and swab my hands, stories floating around this place—"

"That wasn't my idea. The police on the mainland don't like to leave anything uncovered."

"Who led them to believe…Never mind. Like I said, I'll leave it to a lawyer. See you later."

Dave walked away.

"Where are you going?"

"My boat. I'm going out fishing."

"Hold it."

He walked back. "Chief, I've got about ten gallons of fuel. Where can I go? The mainland? I don't want to go back to the house. I slept or watched TV all day the other day. I just want to go out there and drop a line in the water and think. OK?"

"We're not going to have to rescue you again, are we?"

"I hope not. I'll swim home naked if I get in trouble. I promise."

"I don't know. You're gonna drive me batty with this thing."

The chief watched him walk away, mutely knowing how Dave felt. Once the cops from the mainland got involved, hell, no wonder he'd want a lawyer. This was probably just an accident, but the way people think, he's guilty of something. He has to be. Even if he didn't shoot Thomas, he's still responsible for screwing up somehow and causing Thomas' death. He's the "Professor" who came here to tell people what they've been doing all their lives. He doesn't know anything in the minds of those who work on the pier and boats. He gets in the way even though he tries to do his part and actually does know his way around boats. He just tries too hard to be accepted, but he's too smart to be so stupid.

The chief almost asked Dave if he could go with him. *Better not. Better get on home.* He watched Dave climb in the boat with the dog already placed at the bow, start the engine and sputter away, the lights on, the engine droning faster, yet growing silent as the distance gathered.

Chapter 18

Arrival

Every year when the season ends, fewer planes come to the airport and as the day grew older Rebecca was the only one there to notice the hum of an engine and squint up through the drizzle to see the landing light of an approaching plane. Through the slight rain and darkening sky, the light looked like a flame flickering in the wind as it closed in on the runway. The misty rain swirled in spirals behind the plane as it descended. She knew it was her father's plane and felt a tightness in her stomach.

In the cockpit, her father, Richard Foster, again pressed the push-to-talk button on the control yoke and spoke calmly into the microphone of his headset.

"Wianno UNICOM," he said and declared his plane on final approach. He reached for the flap controls and set them to full extension and settled back to feel the plane down to the runway. Another glance around showed no other aircraft approaching or on the runway. He checked his airspeed again and the runway came up fast. The wings gently stalled as he pulled back on the yoke and adjusted the rudder, and the main landing gear grabbed the runway paint. He pulled the throttle back and the engine idled as the plane rolled down the runway with the nose wheel high. It settled and he turned off the runway and made for Rebecca, who was waving him to a tie-down spot. He kicked the plane around, revved the engine up and then shut it down. Rebecca went to the plane as her father climbed from the cockpit.

"Hi, Dad," she said with a slight quiver. "Nice landing."

"Hi, Sweetheart. Nothing like the feel of a good landing!" he said jumping down from the wing. "I wish you'd get back into it."

"It scares the shit out of me," she said. *That should break the ice.*

"Nice talk," he said and chuckled. "Come here, give me a hug." He grabbed her and squeezed tight. He was a big man, but gentle; fifty-five years old and still jogging twenty miles a week. "So, this is home for the winter, huh? Looks cold even from the air. Do you think you can handle that?"

"I guess I'll find out," she said

"Come on, help me tie her down. Then I'll take you to dinner. I'm starved. Any good restaurants on this island?"

"The woman I'm staying with is cooking us dinner. She's really nice."

"But can she cook?" he asked with a smile.

"You're hopeless. Let me have one of those," she said and he handed her a short rope. Together they tied down the plane, and then he climbed back up on the wing and took a paper bag from the cockpit before locking the door. He jumped down again and pulled a leather bag from the cargo bay.

"Now what?" he asked.

"I have a car over there," she said and they started walking.

"Who's car?" he asked.

"It's Ursa's."

"Sounds like a good deal, place to stay, use of the car. How much is she charging you?"

"Not very much, Dad. We don't use the car that much, anyway. The island is so small, I just ride my bike most places. I have a candy bar if you want it."

"That'd be great. I'm starving. I forgot to get any food when I was in Jersey."

"Jersey, what were you doin' in Jersey?"

"Fuel. I was in such a hurry to get here. I forgot I'd get hungry. You didn't sound too good on the phone the other night. Are you OK?"

"Yeah, I'm better."

"Well, Rebecca, I don't want to meddle in your life, but I didn't like him anyway. Besides, you're young and there are a lot of guys out there."

"I know. I still love him, though," she said.

"Yeah, but did he love you? I mean, really love you? Or was he just proud to have a pretty girl on his arm?"

"Dad, I'm not pretty."

"Oh, bull!" he said as he opened the back door and put his bags on the seat. "Don't fool yourself. Your mother used to say that. 'I'm not beautiful,' she'd say, but every guy wanted her. It's a damn shame, what happened."

"Yeah, but what about you? Flyin' around like..."

"Eh, but if I die flying, then I died happy."

"You're nuts."

"No. It's just my third love, you know? You and your mother come first."

"All right, cut it out. Let's lighten up a little," she said and got in the car.

He opened the front door and looked back at his plane. He glanced around and took a deep breath through his nose as he closed his eyes. He could hear the sea. Rebecca started the car and he climbed into the passenger seat.

"So, tell me about this woman you're living with."

"She's great. You'll like her. She's constantly doing things — gardening, playing the piano, cooking. Her place is beautiful, overlooking the ocean," she said and started driving. There was a silence for a while as they came to the top of a hill and the ocean fell into view.

"This is a beautiful place," he said as he took it in.

"Yes, it's gorgeous. I'll take you around tomorrow. Sorry I have to work tonight."

"That's OK. I've brought a book to read." More silence continued as they drove into town. "I love these old hotels!"

"They're cool, huh? That's the place where I work," she said pointing.

"The Dog Tavern. How is it?"

"It's fun. It was fun, anyway. Kinda getting dead. Speaking of dogs, you'll love Abbey. She's a black lab and just the sweetest thing. She'll probably be waiting for us at the bottom of the hill."

And she was. As they came up the road, there was Abbey, sitting with her tail wagging, just like she was when Rebecca left. They got out of the car and the dog went to Richard first, then over to Rebecca and then up the hill, looking back to make sure they were following. Richard took the bags from the car and closed the door using his elbow.

"Lead the way," he said.

"Just follow Abbey," she said and they made their way to the path.

"This hill alone will keep you in shape," her father said as they reached the end and saw Ursa sitting on the porch. Richard placed down his bags.

"Hi, Ursa," Rebecca said as Ursa stood to greet them. "Ursa Taylor, this is my father, Richard Foster."

Ursa extended her hand and Richard took it in his right hand then clasped his left hand over hers as well. "Pleased to meet you, Mrs. Taylor. You have a beautiful house. Thank you so much for letting me visit."

"Oh, you're quite welcome. Your daughter and I seem to have become friends very quickly."

"Well, she's a kind soul."

"Dad, now please don't embarrass me."

"Sorry, Rebecca."

"Come in," Ursa said as she opened the door. "Let me show you to your room."

"Thanks," Richard said. They climbed the stairs to the second floor and Ursa led him to a bedroom.

"I hope this will do," Ursa said bashfully, mildly embarrassed because she felt that a man his size might need a larger bed.

"This is perfect, Mrs. Taylor," he said as he placed his bags on the floor and smiled at her. She smiled back, feeling the warm countenance behind Richard's eyes.

"Please, call me Ursa."

"Ursa. That's a pretty name. Short for Ursala?"

"Yes, that's right. They used to kid me and call me "Bear" as a child," she said. "Now, I've put out some towels for you. Just let me know if you need anything else."

"May I wash up before dinner? Something smells terrific."

"Certainly, the bathroom is just over there. I hope you like beef stew," she said as she moved to the stairway and looked back. "It should be ready soon."

"Thank you. I won't be long."

Ursa returned to the kitchen and Richard washed his hands and face and changed shirts. Rebecca sat on the porch reading a magazine until she heard her father softly step down the stairs, then she joined the other two in the kitchen.

"I brought you a gift, Ursa," Richard said, "and a bottle of wine. A lucky guess that I should bring red to go with the stew."

"Oh," said Ursa, "Thank you. That's very nice, but I'm afraid I'm not much of a drinker."

"Well, there's a big difference between drinking wine and getting drunk. Besides, my doctor says a glass or two of wine is good for you. Would you like some?"

Doctor? Rebecca thought to herself.

"Sure. I guess I will," Ursa said, scooping rice onto a plate. "I know you're hungry so I'll open your gift after dinner. How much stew would you like, Rebecca?"

"Oh, not too much. I'll get some glasses."

"Where might I find a corkscrew?" Richard asked.

"In that drawer there," Ursa said as she handed a plate to Richard. "Would you put this on the table, please?"

Richard took the plate from Ursa and set it on the table, then went to the drawer for a corkscrew.

"And you, Richard?"

"Oh, I wouldn't want to be rude, but I haven't eaten since breakfast."

"You can't be rude by eating what I cook. I'll give you some and feel free to have seconds. There's plenty."

Richard opened the bottle and noticed the herbs hanging by the window above the sink. Ursa and Rebecca sat at the table and Richard poured wine into the three glasses that Rebecca set out. He sat down and Ursa quickly led into grace.

"Lord," Ursa began, "we thank You for this food and the grace of Your company. Amen."

Then Rebecca and her father followed in unison, "Amen."

"I think I understand the secret to this terrific stew, Ursa."

"Oh?"

"It's hanging around the kitchen. Did you grow these herbs yourself?"

"Well, they grow themselves, but I've been growing vegetables and herbs for I don't know how long."

"It's wonderful," he said. "You'll have to give me the recipe. If you don't mind, that is."

"Certainly. There's not much to it, really. Do you cook?

"I used to just grill things, but as I'm slowing down at work, I'm taking time to enjoy things like that."

"What do you do for work?"

"I used to own a few businesses, but I've sold most of that off and now I help businesses get started. It keeps me thinking."

"How long will you be staying, Dad?" Rebecca asked, changing the subject.

"A couple of days, if I may," he said and looked at Ursa.

"Certainly. You are welcome for as long as you like."

"Thank you. I have an appointment next week; I can't be here past Thursday, weather permitting. And I'm not one to sit around doing nothing. I can swing a hammer if you need anything fixed. Don't be shy about it."

"I'll think if there is anything. Thank you."

As they finished eating, Rebecca told her father that she wanted to show him some of her pictures.

"I'll get the dishes," Ursa said. "You go on upstairs and show him."

"No, no, let us help."

"No, there's really nothing to it. Would you like some tea?"

"Well, then sit for a moment," Richard said and retrieved the gift from the counter. "Open this up," he said as he handed it to Ursa.

It was wrapped in paper that had been painted by hand.

"It's beautiful paper, Richard."

"It was done by one of the kids I met through a charity. He is very challenged, but he makes nice things."

Ursa unwrapped it as carefully as she could so as not to rip the paper. The box was big and from a store she had never heard of, a marine supply store. Her curiosity was genuinely piqued and she opened the box to reveal a new kettle.

"I asked Rebecca what you needed, and she said a kettle. It's a special one, though. When it whistles, it makes the sound of a bosun's whistle announcing that the captain is on board."

"My husband was a captain."

"Well, I hope that's a pleasant coincidence."

"It's wonderful. I've been meaning to get a new kettle and I'm glad I haven't. Thank you so much, Richard. It was very thoughtful of you. I'll use it right now. Now you two go on upstairs and I'll finish up here. Won't take but a moment."

Rebecca led her father upstairs to her room where some of her paintings were hidden behind a portfolio.

"You don't have to lie, Dad. I want your honest opinion."

"I won't lie, Rebecca, but I'm sure they're beautiful."

She pulled back the portfolio revealing the first of the carefully arranged paintings. She wanted so much for him to accept her. She wanted to put it all behind them, to start over. *We have to start over.* The first painting was of the church and cherry blossoms. *Please let him like it. I need for him to accept…*

"My God, Rebecca," Richard said as he knelt to get a closer look at the canvas resting on the floor. "You did this?"

"You like it?"

"Like it? I want it. You can't let this go. It must stay with *us!*"

"You're just saying that."

"No, really. Is this place here on the island?"

"Yes. I'm going to do another now that it's fall. The colors are so different now."

"I must see it. Then maybe come back and see it in the springtime. No wonder you like it here. Are there more?"

"Yeah," she said, and flipped the canvas forward to reveal the next painting, the best in her series of deliberate pentimenti. She thought she couldn't explain it, but he understood the style immediately and was genuinely pleased. She felt next to him again, like when she was a little girl playing in the yard and there were no expectations. He told her how proud he was and then how glad he was that she called.

"What's with the doctor?" she asked.

"You know I have to see a doctor regularly to fly," he said. "Don't worry. He's says I'm good."

Then, slowly, Rebecca told why she had called, what had happened, how it had happened before, and she broke down in his arms to cry. He wanted to cry, too, but he knew that's not what Rebecca needed. She needed him to be strong, strong and gentle, and he held her tightly until she stopped sobbing, saying, "It's all right, Rebecca." After a moment she stood straight and wiped the tears from her face.

"Forget about him, Rebecca," he said. "That's not the kind of man you need. He won't change, even if he promises. If you don't end it, you could be locked into a horrible lifetime, a lifetime wasted in fear."

"I feel sorry for him, though."

"Yes, but if you stay with him, you'll end up feeling sorry for both of you. I'm not going to lecture you. I've done enough of that. I've missed you so much. We've lost your mother. Let's not lose each other."

They hugged for a long while, until they both felt the sobbing subside.

"Rebecca," he said. "I think you should just get away from here. Just to see the world. Go somewhere warm."

"Dad, I've told you already. There's no way I'm going to Florida. It's—"

"You don't have to go to Florida to be warm," he laughed. "And I won't bring up school, but I want you to know that the insurance money from your mother's accident, well I've set it aside for you. I want you to have it. I don't need it. I'd give it all away if it'd bring her back. Please, take it. Think it through and put it to good use. Make something good come out of something so terrible."

She went to hug him so he wouldn't see her cry. "I'll think about it," she said. "But I better get ready for work."

As Rebecca walked to work and reflected on her father's words, the coins in her coat pocket jangled. She wanted to call Peter, but she would do it from the pay phone outside work. Abbey led the way, sometimes stopping to smell something, but always staying close. She turned onto the dirt road towards town. She wanted to walk, to give herself some time to think, but there was only a question and no answer: *What do I do?* Abbey looked back at her. Rebecca saw the light up ahead on the cobblestone road.

"Abbey," she said and bent down to pet the dog. "You've got to go home. Go on now!" She pointed and Abbey reluctantly turned around and walked off. Rebecca watched her go and then turned herself as a chill breeze blew. She saw the gravestones at Cobb Hill under the moon and walked on.

When she got to the pay phone, she put a few handfuls of coins on the shelf, picked up the phone and dialed. An automated voice told her how much to deposit and she dropped the coins down the slot, sometimes letting them fall to the ground and not bothering to pick them up. She just took another from the shelf, using two hands until the voice told her she had a credit toward overtime. The phone connected and rang and then a voice came on the line.

"Peter?" she said.

"Nope. Hang on a minute," the voice responded. She heard the man set down the phone and call for Peter. "Hey, Peter. Some chick's on the phone."

Some chick? she thought, and then she thought again. She had not considered that it might be over, that he was already with someone else. What if she was there right now? How would she know? He'll act weird, she told herself. She wanted to scream in the phone. *This is costing me coins, damn it! Pick up the phone.* And he did.

"Hello?"

"Peter?"

"Hey, Rebecca, I was just going to call you."

"Really?"

"Yeah. I was out hiking today and I saw some scenes that made me think of your painting. I wish you would come out here. Some of the things you could paint would keep you busy for years."

"Well, I might just come out. If you really want me to."

"I'd love it. I miss you, Rebecca. When can you come out?"

"I'm not sure. My dad is here visiting."

264

"Your dad? Wow! That's pretty big. How's it going?"

"Good. He flew himself here. He seems a bit different. I probably should have called him sooner." She was hesitant.

"What are you two doing?"

"He just got here and I'm on my way into work. I left him with Ursa."

"Well, when do you think you can come out? I can help buy the airplane ticket."

"I'm not sure. I have to talk to the boss, see when I can get off."

"I'd love it if you came here. We could do the things we did this summer. Well, not so much sailing and that, but going for hikes and hanging out in the mountains, you know."

"I'm not so sure, though, Peter. I mean—"

"You should at least come to visit. It is beautiful here. I don't want to pressure you, Rebecca. Do what you want to do. But come check it out. I'd love to see you, and once you get here, you'll love it. You can always go back."

The voice came onto the phone and said that time was running out. She needed to deposit more coins and she told Peter.

"What's the number? I'll call you back."

She gave him the number and hung up, eagerly awaiting the phone to ring and she picked it up before the first ring was done.

"Hi," she said.

"Hey. So let me tell you about this hike. We drove up to this mesa in the middle of the desert. It was so beautiful. It's completely different here. The colors are different and there are cacti. We hiked up to the top of the mesa. The trail was really steep and coming down was tough, but it was worth it. When we got to the top, there were hawks flying over us and the view was awesome. You must come at least to visit so I can take you there. Once you see it you'll want to stay."

He continued with stories of other places he had been and the places he wanted to go, where he wanted her to go with him. The Painted Desert at sunrise. Canyon Lands up in Utah. The Grand Canyon and Lake Mead. Sunset Crater and the Petrified Forest. Down to Mexico. Over to Vegas.

"What about school?" she asked cynically. "Work?"

"We can work around that. The weather out here is so incredible all the time that you can plan your day weeks in advance. And when it gets too hot, we'll go back to Wianno for the summer. Or we can go up to Oregon or Washington State. The country is so incredible, Rebecca. We can go everywhere and anywhere we want."

Then she realized that she was ten minutes late for work and standing right outside it. She had to go and with the shortest goodbye that could be mustered, they hung up. Rebecca walked into the Dog, ready to quit if anyone questioned her, but everything was normal. Nobody cared that she was late. There was nobody in the place, just a few people at the bar and one table. Melissa was sitting at the big table reserved for large groups and used most frequently by the staff, especially in the days when crowds dwindled.

She wanted to talk to Melissa about it, but she didn't know where to start. She put her purse in the back and sat down at the table. She just asked her right out: "Do you think Will will let me take some time off?"

"Of course. We'll be lucky if there are enough shifts for all of us. How much time off are you thinking?"

"Like, all winter."

"Really?" Melissa said, her voice growing excited. "What are you thinking about? Tell me the plan!"

"I'm not sure, but you're probably right. I shouldn't stay here for too long."

"You're too young to spend the winter here, Rebecca. But where will you go?"

Willy heard the excitement in Melissa's voice and sat down.

"What's going on?" he asked.

"Rebecca wants to get some time off. Maybe the whole winter."

Rebecca looked at Melissa as though she betrayed her confidence, but Melissa knew the place well.

"Sure," Will said. "I've kept you on because you worked out so well this summer. You can come back next year if you'd like."

"Really?" Rebecca said.

"Of course. Just don't wait too long to tell me what's going on."

"So," Melissa asked again. "Where are you going?"

Back in the sitting room at Ursa's house, Richard had built a fire and they sat in rocking chairs beside it. Richard had an unopened book in his hand. They just gazed at the fire as it came to life.

"I owe you something, Ursa," Richard said. "Rebecca told me what you did."

"You owe me nothing, Richard. She is a friend of mine and I would have stopped that for anybody. I hope she never sees him again."

"I don't think she will. I hope not at least. She's had a rough time the last few years. You probably know that her mother died in a car wreck."

"No, actually, she never mentioned it. I tried to ask about her parents, but I got the feeling I shouldn't."

"It was a few years ago."

"That explains a lot. When she came here, she was doing black and white drawings of the graveyard, of all things. Now that's changed and she has some magnificent paintings. It's as though she's come alive."

"Her pictures are great."

"A friend of mine is sure she can sell them."

"I would rather keep them," he said and paused. "We were having trouble. You know how it is when you're a teenager. It's tough figuring it all out and I was pretty demanding. I insisted that she go to college. I should have encouraged her to do whatever she felt the drive to do."

"College is an opportunity that shouldn't be missed," Ursa said.

"I agree, but when the accident happened, the two of us split apart when we should have gotten closer. I feel bad about that. I tried to help, but I had dug myself into a deep hole with her. When my wife died, it seemed like there was nothing I could do to make her happy. I wasn't happy. Then she left without a trace. I was worried sick. Then to think her boyfriend turned out to be a son of a bitch... Pardon my language."

"That's all right. I had worse words for him," Ursa smiled.

"I should have known."

"You can't blame yourself, Richard," Ursa said as the fire warmed the room. "When my husband died, I was depressed for a while, but then picked myself up. He'd have hated me if I just gave up. Fortunately for you, you're both still alive. It's certainly not too late to patch things up. It's never too late."

The fire crackled and an ember popped out past the hearth. Richard swept it back quickly with his hand and moved the fire screen back into place.

"You know, Richard, I've never flown a plane before. Can you teach me?"

"You want to? Of course I can teach you. I'm an instructor. It's one of the things you pick up as you progress as a pilot."

"I would really love to try it."

"It's a lot of fun. We can go tomorrow, if it's nice out."

"That would be great, Richard."

Chapter 19

Stepping Down

The boat seemed secure and Dave paused before leaving, staring over the Caper's last detail to see if there was anything left to do, anything he forgot to do. Standing too long, he thought, might cause suspicion in the minds of the eyes watching from the Dog, so he moved up the docks toward the bike, glancing back to make sure nothing seemed out of the ordinary.

Barney followed but stopped at every garbage can along the way. Standing up on her hind legs she was just over two feet tall and could never reach into one of the heavy barrels, but she checked the odor of each can just in case it was worth knocking over.

Dave pulled his bicycle from the bushes and climbed on it, pushing with one foot and then with the pedal. The gears ground lower as he shifted for the ride uphill and he whistled once so Barney would follow. It was risky letting Barney run unleashed, but she had been fairly good since they let Thomas go, so it was a chance he would take. Once they were clear of the town, Dave doubted they'd see anything anyway, but Barney followed on heel the whole way.

The bike pushed hard up the hill as the house loomed closer, high on the dune and dark against the night sky. It wasn't fun coming home without the boys here, he agreed with himself. *This is a strange affair I am in now.* Maybe he should have tried harder to break open the box he found behind the wall of the root cellar. He should have found out what was inside, but what if it was drugs? It was probably money. That box could hold a small fortune. It didn't matter. He didn't want it. It was just a tool to play this game with, a bargaining chip with Eddie, and he wondered how many buried treasures there were on the island.

He climbed the hill and onto the porch and looked out at the water. The sea was as calm as the air and a thin fog stuck to everything. Dave opened the door and walked into the house. It was cold; everything was cold. He thought of the boys and Aimee, how he missed them. Aimee is probably worried. I should call just to check in and let her know I am all right, he thought. The phone connected slowly and started to ring. Aimee answered.

"Hi," he said in a low voice as if not to wake someone on the other side. "How's it going?"

"How are *you*?"

"Fine. There's nothing going on," he lied, not wanting to tell her that Thomas had made it ashore.

"The boys are asleep."

"I thought so. I would have called sooner, but I wanted to get something done."

"What was that?"

"Nothing. Let's not talk about it," he said and silently counted to seven before she said something more.

"When should we come back?"

"Probably tomorrow. Are the kids being good?"

"They've been great."

"That's good. You should come back tomorrow night. I miss you all."

"We miss you, too."

After a short while more with nothing to say, they said good night. Dave hung up the phone feeling empty, hating to keep things from her, but he'd rather not have her worry. She might call the police and he simply couldn't have that. She was so strong-willed and often she was right, but he did not have the time to discuss it. He thought back to how she had changed the plans with Eddie the other day, how she had Eddie give him a ride instead of her.

"Now what am I going to do?" he asked himself aloud as he sat on the couch.

"Talking to yourself, Perfessor?" a man's voice asked from the kitchen and Dave turned to see Eddie Vanson standing outside the screen door. Dave jumped from his seat as Eddie took a hit from a cigarette. Barney growled and went under the table.

"Just came to return your quilt," he said and lifted the blanket in one hand. "Mind if I come in?"

"Sure, Eddie. How are you doing?"

"OK. Do you want a hit of this?" he asked and Dave realized from the smell that it wasn't tobacco he was smoking. "Grew it myself. Best time of year. Harvest time!"

"N-N-No, thanks," Dave stuttered.

"Go on, have some. It won't be what kills you."

"What do you mean?"

"You don't smoke too often, do you? So you won't die from smokin'."

"I suppose not. But no thanks, just the same."

"Suit yourself," Eddie said and tipped the ash on the handrail to extinguish the joint. "Hope you don't mind me stoppin' by," he said as he opened the door and exhaled outside. He took out a boat key and broke it in half, put the roach in it and sealed it again.

"You shouldn't sneak up on people like that, Eddie, " Dave said. "My heart nearly stopped."

Eddie said, "There's nothing like a good scare, huh?"

"Listen, Eddie. I don't know what you want, but—"

"I'd take a beer if you have one."

"Looks like you've been drinking for a while now."

"I have, Dave. I've been drinking since I heard about Thomas."

"Maybe I'll join you for one, then," Dave said, remembering that before all of this he and Eddie had some semblance of a friendship. Certainly they had nothing against each other directly, perhaps a common disdain for the other's type. If he could work that and just tell him the truth, maybe Eddie could help him. He went to the refrigerator and took out two bottles, tossed the caps one by one to the garbage can. "Have a seat, Eddie. You want a glass?"

"No thanks. It's in one."

Walking cautiously past him, Dave placed a bottle just within his reach. The stench of his unwashed body overtook the scent of weed on his breath and fumes of alcohol rolled upward every time he spoke.

"Listen, Eddie, I—"

"You're not still milking that concussion, are you, Dave?"

"No, but I know too much and I'm just trying to figure out what to do."

"I saw Thomas today," Eddie said with a long exhale. "Did you?"

Dave's slow response, "I did."

"I figured that's why you seem all freaked out. That's some hole you put in his head."

"He did it himself."

"Did he now? Why'd he go and do that, per-fessor?"

"You should know. You were his friend."

"That's right," Eddie said as he sat up and moved his face closer. "I was his friend and I don't believe he just up and killed himself out there on that island with you standing by. You did it and I came here to find out why. Just what do you mean 'you know too much'?"

"If you were really his friend, then you'd be able to guess why he did it himself."

"What are you talkin' about? Thomas and me were friends since we were kids."

"Yeah, but maybe he stopped being your friend that night," Dave said. Eddie answered with nothing and stared toward Dave at an angle. "You know, the night you let that girl drown or freeze on Stage Island or however it was that she died. You know how that affected him."

"He told you about that, huh? Never thought he'd tell anyone."

"He went crazy over it. And he killed himself for it, as anyone with a conscience might."

"Conscience, huh?"

"Yeah, you know, feelings of guilt, remorse."

"I know what it is, but it's too late to do anything about it! By the time we found out it was too late. She had maybe fifteen minutes in that water. It was foggy and rough. We'd never have found her."

"Didn't try either."

"You weren't there. You don't know what really happened."

"I suppose not. You weren't at Stage Island, either. He shot himself and whipped me with that .45 when I tried to stop him. I just wish I could have talked to him. Talked him out of it. There's no evidence to convict him. He could have done something to atone if it bothered him so much, don't you think? I mean, he could have done charity work or something. Gone to find her folks. Adopted a child from that country. Anything."

"You don't have a tape recorder going, do ya?"

Dave looked over his shoulder toward the stereo. "No. Thing's busted. I've got nothing going on but what I know."

"Yeah? Well, what else do you know?"

"Just that you guys were running boxes into the country and it turned to illegal immigrants. When that girl died, Thomas wanted out. He used his business as a front. I guess that's all I know."

"Mind if I smoke, Dave?"

"Go ahead. Aimee and the boys are away for the weekend," he said, then realized that maybe he shouldn't have told him.

"I know. I saw them get on the ferry." Eddie took the joint out of a boat-key float and re-lit it, bowing his head back so his hair wouldn't catch fire. The lines on his face took on a different appearance, dancing in the glow of the match. Dave smiled and sort of laughed. Eddie asked, "What's funny?"

"I don't know, I guess I thought you meant cigarettes. It's OK, though. But be careful. You never know when the cops might show up. They've got it in for me for some reason," Dave said. That reassured him and he reached over to crank open a window.

A pause betook them as Eddie sucked a few long drags then stubbed out the roach on the beer bottle, wiped it on his pants. He swigged his beer a bit. "Don't worry about it. Times are tough right now for everyone. Hope you weren't planning on gettin' involved."

"I am involved."

"What do you think you're gonna do? Tell the sheriff? There's bigger people than me in this, Dave. Leave it."

"I don't know what I'm going to do. I'm in a pretty bad spot," Dave said as the conversation's tone shifted more trusting. "Nobody here will believe me, but Thomas shot himself. I'm guilty of nothing. I should just ride it out, but if they find his body on the beach…I'm not sure what to do. Christ, I didn't want to know any of this!"

"At first," Eddie said and sipped his beer, "at first, I wanted it. I wanted to play the game, to be important somehow. I looked at all

275

these rich people coming here for the summer, grew up with their kids who went on to be rich, too. I saw all that money and people with power and I just wanted some of it. Those kids all went to college, got jobs, never even came back, most of 'em. They grew up knowing how to make money 'cause their fathers did. I loved my dad, but when he went... Shit! What am I talkin' about? He died and left me with Mom and then she died when I was in prison and I was nowhere but here."

He sipped his beer again. "What the fuck can you do around here?

"Summer comes around, people show up. People with money. They want things. They want pot. I could get it, be their friend and take their money. I was in demand! I had the balls to do it, too. What could I lose? My dad was gone and Mom, she couldn't stop me. All winter long, I'd work out in the gym. Come summer, I'd be so ripped nobody would fuck with me. Back then, at that age, I mean, intimidation worked pretty well. I'd sell only to people I knew. Got to be known. Started growing the stuff just because it's so damn easy and pure profit. Grew some killer shit. Got a reputation as a guy who grew killer weed. I got busted.

"Man, let me tell you one thing about jail: you do not want to go there. I saw this big guy beat the shit out of this little guy until he finally broke down and gave him head, right in front of us. I'll never forget that kid's bleeding face down there sucking things up like spaghetti. Fortunately for me, I been working out my whole life. Somebody tried to fuck with me and I hurt him bad. Then I got a reputation there, too. I fucked up a big guy. Nobody messed with me because there's no point when you might lose. I got in tight with some of the guys there. Not that I liked 'em or anything, but better to be on the good side of some people, you know?

"When I got out, I had no place to go but here. I still can't believe they locked me up that long over pot. Some fuckin' liberty. I ain't makin' excuses, but I came back here and had absolutely nothin'. Thomas came out and met me. Took me to Europe to give me a taste of the world. Best damn guy! Knew I was down and that he should have taken the fall with me. Funny how the world works like that, don't you think, Professor? I mean, kid with money and power behind him gets off and the poor one goes to jail to be taught a lesson. Tell you what I learned. I learned how to know when someone is full of shit and I learned that I was never gonna get out of the hole that those guys were in. Most of them go back to jail if they ever get out. Or they get killed. Me, I'm not going back if I can help it. I'm not as bright as you, Professor, but I ain't as stupid as most of those guys.

"I had nothing. Absolutely nothing. No parents, no money. I started working as a mason and the money was OK, but those kids that did come back, they still wanted pot. One of 'em wanted to do some stuff on the mainland. The money started to flow again. It wasn't like the guys I knew who dealt coke. That was big time money, but I was clearing a couple hundred bucks a day, tax free. That's good money and it got bigger. I bought a boat and went out to meet bigger boats. It's nothing new. Been going on like that forever.

"Thomas got into it, too. He was trapped here same as me. He had some cash behind him, but he was spending it fast. That whole thing with his daughter and his wife really threw him. He felt lost, wanted something exciting. It was running drugs. Nothing more exciting than that 'til you get busted. This one time we went out with a bag of money, well, I shouldn't talk about it. It was scary stuff, though. Glad I brought the shotgun. Didn't use it 'cept to clear their deck while we ran away.

"Then, a better deal came along. We started runnin' paper. It was clean. But everything ends sometime. We started running people, too. I didn't tell Thomas about that and I'm sorry. If he had known, he wouldn't have gone out and I needed him. If I had told him sooner, maybe we could have figured out how to deal with it better. As it was, there was a lot of confusion.

"Course it was stupid to carry both the boxes and the live cargo. If they got caught, they'd sure as hell talk about some boxes that we had. We made them go below. Should have done that in the first place. That's what I do now, anyway. That girl wouldn't a fallen over if we'd done that.

"When we met the boat that took them to the island, the guy was kinda surprised to find only four of 'em. I said she fell over and he didn't even blink. He just got the last one to sit down and without more than a look around he just put the outboard into gear and tore off. Talkin' to those guys later it became clear that it was just part of the deal.

"'These people are desperate,' they told me. 'They're fleeing a place where anything is better. They take a risk, they know it, and if they die, they died trying to escape. They know it. They know the risk.'

"I tried to tell that to Thomas, but he wouldn't listen. He didn't care. He blamed me, I guess, and he's probably right. If I had told him what was goin' on, he would have known what to expect and how to act, what to do. We'd have thought it out together. But I was afraid he'd put up a stink and the gears were already moving. We were into it and these guys weren't gonna stop. They needed us and they were big, bigger than I'd thought. Maybe it just grew that way, you know, kinda snowballed, or whatever. You get that much money goin', you're gonna have to turn to someone and the only one prepared for that shit is big shit, you know. I should've expected it to get this way, but, hey, that's just how it is now.

"I'd talked a bunch with Tom about our organization—call it that I suppose—as it grew. We didn't meet the guys on the mainland for about a year. Didn't want to, but we did a good enough job that they came to us. It was kinda scary. The height of the season and these goons came up to us at the Dog, said they wanted to talk. These guys stuck out like you could only imagine. They were obviously not tourists. Tom and I were scared that someone would see us with these guys. It was stupid of them to get us like that. City folks don't know what a small town is like. Even a tourist town like this, the locals still know each other and see what's goin' on. I mean, come on.

"We got in a big car and drove up to a house they'd rented for a week. We met this guy, I won't say his name. He was a low man, but higher than us. He had these guys with him that, man, we couldn't tell where they were from. But they laid it down, said we were doing a great job and they were happy and wanted to meet us. Then we realized where we'd gotten and it didn't matter. We told them we were happy to do what we were doing but we didn't want to get any more involved than we already were. That was fine with them.

"But it did grow, for me at least. Thomas kept out of it as best he could. He became sort of my right-hand man, as they say. That's kind of funny itself 'cause Thomas was so much smarter than me, but he wanted to do the runs for the excitement as well as the cash and I knew the details. That's how it happened that he didn't know about the people.

"I'll tell you, though. The guys I'm dealing with can scare the shit out of me, things they do. I met this guy from the South. He'd come up to get away 'cause he covered some guy's ass in moss. You ever hear that one? 'I'm gonna cover yer ass in moss.' Think about it. Those fuckin' hillbillies talk about coverin' yer ass in moss, you better get moving, brother. They take you out in the swamp, shoot you and put you underneath a big piece of moss and you're gone, man. Gone. The dogs can't even find you. You think the mob is vicious? You hear about drive-by shootings and hit men taking you out in a restaurant. Hillbillies don't care about that. If there's a problem, just get rid of it and put it out in the swamp as fertilizer for moss. It's that simple.

"It's nothing. It's gone on the same forever. The only thing new is the equipment, and that hasn't changed in a while. It's getting better, but it's still just boats and planes, new types of navigation. There's always been war and people have always wanted to get out of it. Is that my fault? You want out? I'll come get you out. What's that you say? For free? Hell no! Give me somethin' and I'll take a risk. What you got? Chickens? A pony? A sheep? Not worth it. I want good money to take a risk to help out a stranger and if you sign on, you got to realize that you're taking a risk, too. You fall off the fuckin' boat because you're sick, you're weak—what's that you guys call it, Professor? Natural selection?"

He sipped his beer and made a popping sound with the bottle. "She took the risk, she fell overboard and my agreement was to go from point A to point B, not to go searching around for her 'cause she couldn't hold on. I do that and I risk myself and the others who came all that way and didn't fall over."

His face was contorted and Dave wondered where they were headed. He empathized and saw the reasoning. He wondered at the whole thing. The trip from wherever, the whole journey, the start, the middle—how many middles?—and the end, but not the end for the others. He didn't know her. What had happened he couldn't even say, couldn't put into words. Was it just a dream? He felt again the confusion of the days past and for the first time questioned his sanity. The circumstances happened, he silently assured himself. *Weren't they just circumstances?*

He looked at Eddie, who studied the walls with a face of self-righteous indignation, holding back a tear, though the tattoo on his cheek cried for him. Dave wondered what he was going to do. He couldn't trust him.

Then Eddie said, "It's a problem when someone who's not involved gets involved. If you're into it, playing the game, living it, you got to expect to go down by the same rules. It's just business. Most folks don't have a problem because they play a different game. Sometimes the two worlds get caught up with each other. Sometimes there's a fuckin' guy who wants to screw everyone's life up 'cause his is so bad or he thinks he's so tough, but the guys I hang out with, they at least got some reasoning for what they do. They only go for players. If you're not in it or your wife's not in it, then they won't bother you. They won't go after your family like some of those bastards who do that for intimidation. 'Fuck with me and I'll fuck up your whole family,' this one guy said to us. You know what they did? They covered his ass in moss." A smile crept up on his face.

"You ever kill a man, per-fessor?" he said as he stood. Dave stood, too, and said nothing. "Me either. There's always a first time, I suppose."

"Is that a threat?"

"You might call it that."

"You kill me and you'll be the prime suspect, don't you think, Eddie?"

"Prime suspect for what? There won't be no murder. If there was, they'd never find your body. They'd just assume you ran away. They'll find Thomas' body down by the shore, as soon as I call them, and I'll say I saw you leave the island."

"That's a lot of info coming from the prime suspect."

"Yeah. You're right. I won't say a word."

"Well, neither will I."

"We're not so sure you can be trusted."

"We? I guess you're just following orders, but believe me, Eddie, I have no intentions of getting any more involved than I already am. Thomas killed himself."

"Why, Dave? You gotta figure that the cops are gonna want to know why. Let's go."

"Where?"

"For a walk on the beach. Let's go get rid of Thomas' body. We do that and this whole thing is over, right?"

"No. I don't want to go anywhere right now."

"I don't care what you want."

Dave didn't want to let Eddie know he had already sent Thomas' body to sea. "It's still too early. There might be people around."

"It's already too late. Tide's goin' out and he might have moved already."

"No, I'm not going to do it. His head wound was self-inflicted. Any coroner will be able to tell."

"Then we'd better go now so the rest of us are in the clear. Come on!"

"You think I'm just gonna go wherever you say, no fight?"

"You fight me? You are crazy, per-fessor. I figure all I gotta do is hit you once if you don't come along easy. You look like a one punch kinda guy. You ever been in a fight?" he said, moving closer.

"There's something you ought to know, Eddie," Dave said as he picked up a lamp and broke it to make sure that a struggle seemed to have taken place. He broke another lamp on the floor and knocked some books from a shelf.

"What the fuck are you doing? Stop it."

"Looks like a struggle took place here. You gonna clean this up? Hope you brought gloves. How many things have you touched here, huh, Eddie?" Dave paused, confident that enough mess had been made. "When's the last time you were at Krupsky's?" he asked.

"What?"

"You know…the root cellar. Pretty good patch job on the bricks, Eddie. You use some kind of dye or something to match the mortar?"

"Oh, Dave. Now you've gone and made me mad. I'm real mad now."

"Doesn't matter. What's in the box? I didn't look."

"Well, you'll never know. Where is it?" He lunged for Dave, but he ducked and slipped away to the other side of the table.

"Now, Eddie. Be friendly or you'll never get it back."

"Friendly. You want me to be friendly." From the back of his trousers he drew a pistol that was hidden under his shirt. "Friendly? I'll shoot you right in the fuckin' knee, Dave. Right here. Tell me where you put my money!"

"Money, huh? That's a twist. How many treasures you got buried on this island, Eddie?"

"Where is it?"

"It's safe, don't worry."

"Oh, I ain't worried. I just hope I don't have to hurt you too bad before you tell me where it is."

"I'll tell you right now. It's in a storage locker."

"Where's the key?"

"My lawyer has it."

"Your lawyer? Goddamn, per-fessor, that's pretty smart. Pretty fuckin' smart. Not too smart, though. You forget I live here. I know everybody. I even know the guy who has the keys to all those storage lockers."

"It's on the mainland."

"Bullshit! You didn't have time to get to the mainland and back."

"My wife took it yesterday."

"Oh, you bastard. I'm really gonna like killin' you. Now, let's go."

"You don't care about the money anymore?"

"No. I'll get it from your wife. I'll get it sooner or later. Let's go."

He walked slowly in the direction that Eddie waved the gun. It was then that Dave noticed Barney roaming near the edge of the couch. She stared up at Dave and he realized that she was aware of the danger. She loved it. She was ready to fight and let Dave know it through something he could not begin to describe.

When dogs pack together, they hunt instinctively as a team. They know each has a job to do. When dogs chase a prey that is bigger than them, one dog grabs at the ankle. It's one of the most painful things that can happen to any animal and when the victim turns to defend himself against this hurtful attack, another dog jumps on his neck. This was Dave's job. Barney would go for the ankle and Dave would have a split second to strike a fatal blow.

His eyes slowly passed over the table and the room. There was a candlestick there, but it wasn't very heavy. By the wood stove was a fire poker, but all the way across the room. The few lamps left unbroken were not easy to hold and even harder to swing. There must be something, he thought, with only a few seconds before they were out of the house. What can I use? My fists? He has a gun. I need something heavy, something heavy and hard.

They passed the cellar doorway and the wine rack. A wine bottle. That will have to do. Barney had moved quickly toward the door as if she was going with them. Dave wondered how he was supposed to signal the dog, so he looked at her and perhaps through nothing more than Dave's facial expression she understood and lunged for Eddie's ankle. In slow motion, Dave watched as she clamped onto the tendon of Eddie's heel and he screamed, moving to point his gun at Barney. In a sweeping, turning dance, Dave grabbed the bottle and with all his momentum smashed it across Eddie's temple and forehead. The gun fired as Eddie fell backward into a sitting position. Through the deafening ring, Barney still tore at his bloody foot. Red wine seeped down Eddie's face, mixed with blood from a cut above his eye, but he wasn't unconscious. He would be stunned for only a moment.

Dave's fear turned to flight. He must get away from him and bolted for the basement door, faltering as he opened it. Barney, nearly tripping Dave, followed down the stairs as the door closed. A shot fired and hit the door. Dave turned on the light, looked around and then broke the bulb. Eddie was moving upstairs. He called out. Dave opened the door to outside, but didn't run. He knew if he could get to the bike he could ride it downhill and get away, but Eddie would catch him before he could get to the road. Dave went back and hid by the staircase as the door opened. The light silhouetted Eddie and his shadow stepped down the stairway.

Dave thought he would go right out the door to give chase and in the last of the light from upstairs as the door closed automatically, he saw the gaff. It was big enough to use as a club, and heavy. Dave could hook it around his ankle, the injured ankle —which one was it, the left?—and cause him to tumble down the stairs and then beat him senseless. Slowly, silently he lifted the gaff from the nail where it hung. He moved so slowly that not a sound was made, desperately forcing himself to move more imperceptibly than he possibly could as Eddie's eyes adjusted to the darkness. The blue-steel gun, though, shined in the slit of light coming under the bottom of the door as Eddie stepped deliberately down the stairs. Dave saw his belt, then the white of his shirt. With no hesitation, Dave swiped at him with the hook of the gaff.

Dave caught him just in the left side and pulled hard. He turned as Dave pulled. The gaff ripped through him, tearing away a swath of flesh and dragging some of his entrails out and he screamed. He raised his pistol and fired. Dave saw his face in the flash and was deafened again, but he heard him say, "Oh, Jesus Christ!" as he grabbed at his side. Dave swiped again, catching him in the back below the right shoulder. He screamed in pain as Dave pulled hard and he fell down the stairway. Dave heard the metal pistol on the basement floor. Eddie was disarmed. Dave thrust the gaff away from him, clearing it from Eddie's flesh and muscle. He pushed himself up but Dave hit him with the gaff. Then again he hooked him and again. *Paralyze him!* His rage flooded. *Make him suffer worse!*

285

Dave hooked him again and again, the gaff piercing cleanly until he ripped it out or sometimes it scraped just below the layers of skin. *Kill him!* Dave heard in his head, then he heard a sucking chest wound. He had pierced one of his lungs. He stopped.

As Dave wiped his forehead with his sleeve and stumbled, his foot kicked the pistol a short way across the floor. He reached down and felt for it along the dusty cement, found it and took its oiled heaviness into his hand as the gaff dropped. He was safe. The gun smelled of powder and Eddie smelled worse than before. Dave looked at him in the dim light cast from under the door but couldn't stand the sight of the man he just killed. He was breathing, but he would not live for Dave had no urge to do anything for him. His sucking chest wound would collapse a lung. The blood all around showed that he was bleeding badly, probably from the wound in his left side, the first one when Dave ripped him open. An artery was probably torn. He will die all right. *It's better just to let him die.*

Dave walked out the door and onto the sand where he sat and cried. Killing is not for me, he thought. I want no part of it. I never wanted it; never wanted to see this; never wanted to kill a man. He is a bad man, evil. Dave tried to convince himself of this, but it was no comfort. He had avenged a fallen angel, a woman who did not deserve to die. Of all these things he reassured himself, but it didn't make any difference to him. How evil was he? Two men are dead, one by my own hand. *One by my own hand.* I can never change that; I can never forget that. He settled his head deeper into his hand.

Barney came and rubbed up against him. She deserved petting. Dave wondered how he connected with her so that she knew just when to attack. Dave mocked himself. *Maybe she's here right now!* He was about to call for her when the dog barked at something behind him. He turned in the start and there at the door was Eddie, barely standing. Dave pointed the gun at him.

"Gotta get out…gotta get out of here," Eddie said and stumbled forward. Dave was ready to shoot, but Eddie turned and walked around the house. Dave followed him, still with the pistol aimed somewhat toward him, but he was no threat. He walked toward the ocean and came to the edge of the dune, to the steep cliff, and tumbled on his first step downward, stepping down from his life. Peering from the top, Dave saw him on his back with one leg crossing over the other, an arm outstretched, his neck broken. He went inside and called the police.

"I need an ambulance," he said into the phone.

"What's your location?"

"At the end of Last Road, the house on the left."

"What's the number?"

"I don't know. It doesn't have a number. I'll wait down by the road."

"And what is your name?"

"Dave Wyman."

"OK, Mr. Wyman," she said as if she knew him and became a little more excited. "What's the trouble?"

"There's been a fight. A man is injured with stab wounds."

"OK, Mr. Wyman, I have a police vehicle rolling to your location now. An ambulance is on its way there also. How badly is the man injured?"

"He's pretty bad. He attacked me in the house and I fought with him and I thought I knocked him out, but he walked away and last I saw he was lying on the beach."

"You say he attacked you in the house?"

"That's right."

"And now he's on the beach?"

"Yes."

"Do you know who he is?"

"Yes. It's Eddie Vanson."

"OK. Hold on please. Don't hang up."

"All right." In the background, Dave heard her talking to someone and then there was a commotion and someone was talking into another phone to Chief Prence. Dave hung up the phone and went to the door, then returned to the table and placed down the gun. He saw the lights of a patrol car climbing up the road and walked toward the parking area where the car would stop.

"Is there a problem here?" the patrolman asked as he stepped from the car and put his nightstick into a ring on his gun belt. Dave told him about the fight, that there was a gun on the table and that Eddie was on the beach, badly wounded. He called into the microphone to check that an ambulance was coming and said, "Where's the gun?"

"It's on the kitchen table."

"There's no one else in the house?"

"No."

"Take me to the gun, then show me where he is," he said, then spoke into his radio. "Mike Three, ten-thirty-two, gun." A siren wailed.

Dave led him to the house, unaware that the officer had his hand on the gun at his waist, the polished leather holster unclipped for a quick draw, his eyes focused narrowly in heightened alert, watching Dave's hands, friendly and polite and willing to kill him if he made the wrong move. When they stepped into the kitchen and saw the gun on the table, the officer stopped Dave with his left hand and quickly glanced around the room. When he was confident no one else was there, he picked up the gun, checked its safety and put it in his belt. He put the heel of his hand back on his own gun to keep it in the holster.

"Where is the other man?" he asked and Dave pointed toward the dune, aware now that the officer was doing a job. "Show me," the officer said and motioned with his hand for Dave to lead the way. Then they went to the top of the dune and looked down. Eddie was still there, not moving. The officer held his flashlight over his head and shined the light down. There was blood on the sand.

"Is he dead?" asked the officer.

"He might be by now. We fought in the house and I thought he was unconscious, so I came out to get air and calm down. He came out saying 'I gotta get out of here' and tried to walk away but fell down the hill."

They looked back down toward the road as the ambulance and two more police cars drove up. The whole police force is here, Dave thought.

"Let's wait here for the others," the officer said and shined the circle of light toward the ground, halfway up Dave's body to watch his hands. More flashlights lit down below and shined up at them. The officer waved for the others to come up. His radio crackled.

Prence's voice asked, "What's up?"

"Better come up here, Chief," the officer radioed back. "Have a seat, Mr. Wyman," he said. Dave obeyed him and sat in the circle of light on the ground. Chief Prence struggled up the hill towards him.

"What the hell's goin' on, Wyman?" he said.

"Eddie came over with a gun and we fought. I think he may be dead."

"You son of a bitch, I should have put you in jail."

"I might have been safer there. Why don't you chase the real criminals? Guys live here on the island and you don't know what the hell is going on. Some cops."

"What *is* going on?" Prence asked. "Huh?" He turned to the other officer. "What's going on?"

"Looks like Eddie fell down the hill and he may be dead. We just got to this point when you pulled up. These two fought. I didn't want to leave him alone."

"All right. Good job. Go on down there and let me know what's happening." The chief thought about this for a moment. "No, I'll go down there. Transport him back to the station."

"I think I need medical attention," Dave said.

The chief looked at him. "Right," he said and called a name into the radio.

"Yes, Chief."

"You two better get up here with a trauma kit. Have someone back at the station roll a fire truck out here. We're gonna need some guys to help get a man back up the hill," the chief said and shined his light back down the hill. "Wait here with him."

Dave sat again. He watched the ambulance attendants struggle up the hill with a stretcher and bid them hello as they walked past.

"Are you all right?" the leader asked.

"I think so. The other guy's not so good." They went past and stopped at the top of the dune and talked to the first patrolman to arrive. After a moment, the officer walked over to Dave.

"Can you stand, sir?"

"Yes, I think I can manage." He helped Dave to his feet.

"Can you walk?"

"Yes."

"Come with me down to the car, please." He led Dave back to the road with his flashlight. They got to the cars, the bright, flashing lights causing them to squint for a moment. Another officer was standing there. "Could you place your hands on the car, put your feet back and spread them apart, please?"

"Yes, but why?"

"Sir, you are under arrest," he said as he searched Dave for weapons. "You have the right to remain silent—"

"You're arresting me? A stoned, crazy local comes to my house with a gun and you're arresting me?"

"Sir, this is standard procedure. It's the court's job to determine if you are innocent. My job is to contain the situation. If I were you, I'd come along nicely and not say a single word until your lawyer is present. Now let me read you your rights and we'll go to the station."

"I think I might need medical attention," Dave said.

"All right," he said as he placed the handcuffs around Dave's wrists. "We'll sit you over here until the EMTs come back." He walked Dave to the back of the ambulance and sat him on the bumper. "Do you have pain anywhere, sir?"

"No," he replied and noticed that some of the neighbors were walking up the road. "Forget it. Let's get out of here."

In the station, Dave was photographed, swabbed again for powder traces, fingerprinted, left for an eternity with one wrist cuffed to the wall near a bench and finally led, handcuff free, into a tiny cell with bars covered by Plexiglas except for small areas where air came through. In this room with a one-piece toilet and sink and a metal bed with no blanket or pillow, the fluorescent lights shined so bright no one could sleep anyway. The room and its translucent doorway echoed the sounds from outside. A man accused of drunk and disorderly conduct hollered obscenities at no one from the cell next door. Dave watched the clock on the wall silently spin its second hand round the dial each minute, each hour.

After rinsing his face in the washroom near his office, Chief Prence looked in the mirror and saw the face of his father. He closed his eyes but the image remained. The lines in his face shaded the same, his teeth were crooked in the same way, his nose, now larger than when he was a boy, matched his father's exactly. He let out a sigh and stood straight, opening his eyes as he turned around and the image of his father floated before him. Beside and behind the image were faces he remembered—townsmen, friends and family— appearing like setting sunlight falling on the side of a forest by the sea, the trees at the edge shining brightly, yet farther back the trees were darker, some looming with only their trunks seen, others not seen at all but the darkness they filled continued forever. He closed his eyes, feeling their dryness was surely the cause for this apparition, and he blinked erratically, but the image remained.

"You only have a short time." He heard the words of his father that were said over the years of his life, the words his grandfather also spoke. "Feel with your heart. Think with your head. Do what is right." And the images disappeared.

The chief sat alone in his office, the small clock on his desk ticking away the only sound that he heard. It was the golden silence, he knew, and he felt detached and present at the same time as he breathed more lightly than he ever had. He barely moved.

He heard the front door of the station open and close, but remained transfixed on the ticks of the clock. Footsteps up the stairs and slowly down the hall approached. He recognized them as the steps of an elderly man with a cane and soon around the corner of his doorway appeared the face of Stuart Ashton, a man of ninety-five, the oldest man on the island.

"You all right, Chief?" his voice rasped rusty.

"Yeah," Prence said. "Come in and sit down, Stu."

"I saw the light in your office and figured you might want to talk."

"What light is that?"

"I dunno. I guess it was the desk lamp. Why?"

"Oh. It doesn't matter."

"I heard about Eddie. Can't say how sorry I am, but I figured he'd die violently, though I figured a wreck or something."

"What do you think is goin' on?"

"Something tells me that Dave Wyman got caught up in something. You know Eddie. He was trouble. Don't wanna blame him or anything, but he went over to Wyman's house with a gun. You find more than one gun at Wyman's?"

"How did you know there was a gun there?"

"Listened to the scanner. Your boys talked less about it than the state cops. They were much more informative over the radio."

Prence smiled, but his face returned to the look he had had for minutes. "No, we only found one gun. So far."

"I don't believe Wyman has a gun. If he was mixed up in it by his own choice, he would have had a gun of his own. Anyway, Thomas and Eddie have always been into the drugs, at least pot, and it wouldn't surprise me if they kept up with it. Maybe just for the thrill."

"Something in your gut tell you he's innocent?"

"Yeah. You have the same feeling."

"I do. I don't know how I can justify letting him go."

"Let him go and follow him. If he's guilty, he'll probably do something right away that will tell you. Tell him not to leave. Watch the docks and the harbor."

"It might be hard to follow him around the island. I'm not real good at it."

"I can't do it," the old man said and tapped his cane on the floor.

"I suppose not." The chief stared at him a moment, strangely peaceful, and smiled. He put his foot up on the desk and his pajama bottoms showed from under his trouser cuffs.

"You ever see anything, hear anything odd around here?" he asked.

"Well, there's all sorts of rumors goin' round all the time."

"No. I mean like…like…like from beyond or somethin'."

"You mean like ghosts? I never seen a ghost. I hear things, things come to me like it wasn't me thinkin'. One time I was in the living room by the fire with the dogs and a cat when suddenly all of us looked up and over at the same place like something was present, though there was nothing there. The hair on all our backs rose up and I felt something brushin' by. Just the wind, maybe. Not that there can't be spirits in the wind, the trees. Ya know?" His face grew expressionless. "Why?"

"Never mind."

After a long pause, the old guy continued. "Wyman's just killed a man. I hear that killing someone is a hard experience, even if it is self defense. I'll bet he's innocent. Let him out. Let's give him a drink."

"Let him out?"

"Sure. Why not? He's not dangerous. Where's he gonna go? Let him out, watch the docks. Unless he steals a boat, he has to go down to the pier. I say let him out and go easy on him. He's got a family. This ain't his lifestyle. Eddie was up to no good and Thomas was probably in on it, too."

When Dave was led into the office, the three of them sat in calm detachment and Dave asked, "Why is he here?"

"He gives good advice sometimes," the chief said.

"Is that so?"

"He says I should let you out."

"That would be good advice."

"A man's now dead and killed by you. A man who was close to me and maybe that's got me jumping to conclusions."

"I won't say anything about this, now," Dave said. "That cop from the mainland seems pretty intent."

"He's got a lot of crime to deal with."

"Just the same, I won't talk to you without a lawyer. People in this town seem pretty convinced that there's more to this than an accident. People...well, like I say, there's nothing to talk about just now."

"I suppose you won't have a drink then?"

Dave paused and then said, "Just one. I could use it. I'm still shaking. That was the first fight I've been in since high school."

The chief poured Scotch into three glasses and handed them out to the other men. "What are you gonna do if I let you out of here? You got anyplace to go? Your house is a crime scene."

"You can stay at my place," Stu said, and it was agreed.

Then a wave of recognition fell over the chief's face and he said aloud, "You stumbled on something, didn't you? Those two were up to something and you found out what it was."

Dave said, "I'm not saying anything without a lawyer," but maybe his staid face told the chief something and the chief's head nodded.

As they walked from the police station, the clock on town hall chimed and Dave knew he had about a day and a half until a time release on one of his traps would send its buoy to the surface. He just hoped the contents of the box inside the trap would cause him no more trouble.

Chapter 20

Lives Entwined

*If the tides affect fish
and we come from the sea,
and the moon affects tides,
then the moon affects me.*

Beneath the creaking timbers of this weathered footbridge dribble the waters of Barrow's Brook. The water is part of the brook for only a short time, since the run is not long and the tide controls its direction. For six hours and some minutes the water flows in and then out for six more. The marsh is flushed each time, becoming a puddle in the grass and a hummock of mud twice a day.

Standing atop the bridge, looking down at the trickle flow, it's easy to see the tide change. The water flows out until most of the marsh is exposed, living matter, dying with an invisible cloud of organic stench hanging low. When the tide goes slack, as it is now, the flow nearly ceases, though some water still tumbles slowly down the incline carved in the grass and peat, and sweeps out in an intricate fan onto the sand flat. Now the brook does not reach the edge of the bay, instead its water sinks into the sand to rejoin the bay below. It is here at the edge that one notices the change.

There is nothing apparently different in the bulk of the bay, though unseen from here the buoys at the inlet strain in a new direction and cast their wake inland, traveling through the tide yet going nowhere. Deep below them, the tide still flows out, for the momentum that the bay water achieved as a body cannot be turned immediately. So the flows oppose each other, the outgoing tide running as it had and the incoming flooding over top, and somewhere in the middle the two swirl together.

Here at the shore, the waves begin to throw farther up the flats. The wind fights them back. At times, the waves stretch far and thin over the sand before being forced back by the wind in a tug of war fought by pushing. Certainly, the tide wins and the bay builds to a wall that pounds against the ledge where the marsh grass stands in muddy peat a foot above the flat.

The water in the brook, however, still trickles out as the bay did at first, affected not by the pull of the moon, but by the gravity of Earth. Nevertheless, the incoming water reaches a point where it rises so fast that it nearly falls into the brook, flowing farther inland in waves steepened to ridges by the water still flowing out. Wave after wave turns the flow back, flooding the marsh once again with fresh seawater, and here, on the bridge, seeing this display, one must wonder at the celestial control of such an earthly occurrence.

The pull of the moon is what does it. Because the ocean waters are so massive, they bulge out on either side of the earth like an egg, with one side pulled toward the moon and the other forced away from it. The egg follows the moon as it orbits the earth, moving through the sea as a wave that crashes ashore causing the flood tides. When the moon passes far enough past the edge of the land, its effect on the water is diminished, the egg is cracked and the sea falls back to itself from the force of Earth's gravity.

As the water grows higher, here below the footbridge, where sea weeds sway and whip in the current, the effect of a bend in the canal became apparent. The brook bends to the left and the water swirls around in a circle split in half by a curl. From this vantage, the scene was at one time a marvel, for images appeared in the whirling seawater. Like clouds in the sky, resemblances were struck by the incoming tide. People came here to stare at the water for the few hours that the swirl was apparent. They watched and saw pictures, the image of Christ, the Blessed Virgin, the Buddha, Elvis (who knows what they saw?) They tossed coins and watched them shine on the bottom and bury in time, hoping that somehow the mere thought of a wish might cause it to happen.

Then one day, a man, whose ancestors have been associated with evil since written history came to the land, got an early start. At four in the morning, with the island asleep and himself quite drunk, he came to the bridge with a bottle of Scotch and an eel rake. Sand eels, a slimy six inches long and scratched with a rake from the flats at low tide, are a popular fish bait, but he used his rake to take in about eight thousand coins before someone found him passed out by his boat in the morning. His greed kept him there long enough to be caught and long enough to pull out rocks and damage the brook so that the swirl no longer appeared.

The sights from this place are still an attraction, though. The bay backed by dunes and the ocean beyond and the sounds of the water rushing below and lapping the bayside and roaring ashore on the ocean beach over yonder, it all kept people here listening and tasting the salt air. And staring down at creek as the tide reaches its crest, the flow slows and the whole hulk of the water stills and stops for a few brief moments and then it turns and everything moves in the other direction.

Dave remembered a study where oysters were shipped alive from the coast to the middle of the continent. Oysters open their shells in synch with the moon. These oysters were shipped inland and left in the dark so daylight would not affect them. Their shells continued to open and close as if they were still on the coast, but after a week, they were in synch with the moon at their new location.

At the eclipse of the moon one realizes the value of pearls, for there in the shadow of Earth, on a sparkling curtain of starlight, hangs without strings a sphere so close you can feel it. No longer shining brightly and flat, its full roundness apparent, the moon seems lighted by a house across the bay and shaded so delicately that the detail of its surface appears like that of the spheres created on Earth by oysters.

The high tide passed once again and oysters appeared clinging to the rocks below the bridge. The air filled with the stench of muck so rich with unseen life, and from this mud, where the tide washes over marine life left exposed to the air for half the time, perhaps is where some forms of life came from the ocean to the land. If so, then the moon could be given partial credit for life's migration.

Yet he came here again not to ponder the tidal flats that his spirit left those years ago, nor to find some piece of the time he had lost, that time when his mind was in tune to another, when he sat alone on the hills and breathed with the trees as the wind rushed through with a hush. He came not to find other buried treasures. He came for a celebration.

Whenever he returned to a place where he once spent some time, his mind filled with elation at how little had changed, that roads once traveled still led to the same valleys or vistas. It is the same feeling as when he first realized that there is a man in the moon, he had seen him with his own eyes, picked him out like another way of seeing an Escher drawing.

Many years passed before Dave went back to the island. He sailed there alone on the same wooden boat he left the island on—a boat that took much of his life over those years. As he closed on the harbor, his soul with an osprey circled the marsh, but soon dropped like a kite with its wind cut out. So much had changed here in time, so much that it was hard to know where to start. Perhaps he would have known of all this had he read the local paper, but there is so much to read and no need to keep up with the events of such a small land.

The most striking change was the break in the beach. During a storm one winter, the ocean had broken the island in two, sweeping away a few houses and increasing the rate at which the sand disappeared. Practically a quarter of the beach as he knew it was underwater. He had heard about the storm and its effects, but his imagination could not have envisaged the difference.

In that storm, a ship nearly five hundred feet long lost control. The boat was a freighter with no cargo and the ballast pumps had failed. The crew couldn't control the ship's weight and she was so light that her rudder and prop came out of the waves and could not get a hold of the water. She hit the north point of the island, then pinwheeled down the beach. People on land watched the crewmen in fear for their lives as the whole length of her spun end over end and then out to sea, where she sank halfway to the mainland. Even in a hurricane, the Coast Guard came through with helicopters and picked each man alive from the deck.

One of the rescue pilots told that his worst fear was just getting the chopper started. Once the rotors got to speed, they were fine, but in that period when the blades got to spinning fast—not fast enough to fly, but fast enough to cut the tail off if blown by a wind gust—he was scared. Even the tower controller's voice sounded nervous when he said, "Tell me when you're ready and you will be cleared for immediate takeoff." They lifted from the helipad and into pure black. Soon, they left the adrenaline and tunnel vision and concentrated on flying. There was no fear, but now and then he noticed a slight cramp in his hand.

They never saw the ship until they were right on it. They relayed the coordinates to the second chopper coming from another port and moved into position. The second chopper had to fly in small circles until the first finished lifting the injured crewmen to take back to the mainland.

The second copter hovered over the deck, lifted six more and took them to the island, then circled back again and again to get the rest. Each time they got back to the ship, it became clearer how soon she would sink. The wind forced the chopper to fly off and quickly return to the ship, but the pilot wasn't going to let the captain, whose courage held him there, wait a minute alone on deck without a helicopter in sight.

When the captain was aboard, the pilot radioed the base and finally landed safely on the island. The locals came through as well, making a home for the rescued and treating the flight crews like royalty. The next morning, they prepared them all breakfast before the choppers took off. Then they showed the ship's crew around the island since they'd probably never return.

For strangers, the helicopter crews risked their lives and when Dave read about that story, he wondered what they would have thought about Thomas and Eddie leaving someone to drown.

That rescue made international television, but another story also made the news around the world. The candle maker and his candles had become immensely popular, the candles so intricate and beautiful, that he had made a significant fortune. He expanded the operation and hired a dozen people to work in a new building. To the dismay of some, candle making had become one of the island's most lucrative industries.

The problem was that he used so much sand that the town made him stop mining it. He sued, insisting that the sand of this island was so sacred that he could use no other, although he imported the paraffin. The town sued back, claiming all mineral rights and that the industry was leading to the ultimate demise of the island. The town prevailed and he imported sand as well as wax, and you could see the barge tied to a pier by the public dock.

It was not over, however. The man was an artist and was cherished by many who took his words as correct. Many people believed him when he said that the sand was sacred and they began taking grains home with them. More people than ever came to the island, many simply to get some of the sand, and the town had to pass a law against sand removal.

A new sign greeted people when they walked off the ferry. It listed the rules of the island and the number one rule:

REMOVAL OF SAND PROHIBITED - $100 FINE

Dave chuckled at some people who tapped their shoes out before boarding the ferry so as not to be mistaken for thieves.

Under the sign with the rules was a small poster seeking donations to the lighthouse committee. The lighthouse was being undermined by the ocean and threatened to tumble at any moment. "We have to act fast," said the poster, "because we did not think before." It was a beautiful lighthouse and Dave wondered what they would do with it when the island disappeared. They would probably take it brick by brick to the mainland as an historic reminder.

As he walked through the town and strings of sunlight, he saw a notice tacked to a tree. There were many such notices along the road, all tacked to trees, so he read one. It said, "This tree has been cited as a hindrance to traffic and will be removed." Apparently, a man came to the island with a tractor to shore up the dunes with imported stones. As he drove along the road with the tractor on a trailer, the cab of the tractor hit a branch and the tractor fell to the road causing several thousands of dollars in damage. The man sued the island and won. In reaction, the town sent out a team to uncover trees that might block the road and condemn them. It is the wording of the notice that first seemed so strange, "This tree has been cited," but it had to be put up to give people a chance to present an argument as to why each tree should be spared. Of course, the town was thinking of banning cars altogether, as was driving on the beach, but the trees would have to go first.

The island adopted a law requiring cars to drive with headlights on at all times, even during the day. Motorcyclists have known forever that headlights make it easier to be seen by someone else, so you drive with them on and your chances of being hit are lessened. On the narrow streets of Wianno, something had do be done because tourists were colliding two or three times in an afternoon. Dave could not help but notice, however, that as the cars drove around all bunched up behind the slowest car leading, the island seemed like a never-ending funeral procession.

He went back to the House of Time and found the door locked. The House of Time is what they called the place where Thomas lived, for as an hourglass the sands slowly filled it. A padlock and hasp had been fastened to the doors, probably by Chief Prence, Dave thought, since Thomas had no one remaining. Thomas was the last of his line, so there was no one to take any of his memories. Dave wished he could have taken something to remember Thomas, but he had the cross he found when they dived together. He told himself that is all he needed to remember.

Through the dusty, etched windows he could see some of the valueless treasures, remembered the stories that belonged to them and never doubted the truth. Yet how much more complex a man's life is than the simple appearance he wants to project, the pentimento of the past showing through only when you know him so well that you cannot ignore it.

He slipped through the sand around the house, peering through each of the windows, even stepping from the dune to the porch roof to look in the second floor windows. Still he found no comfort, no peace, and reluctantly left the House of Time, looking back as he walked down the beach. He wanted to stop, to go back and look again, but there was nothing there for him, so he walked.

Dave went to Thomas' shop and found the place more abustle with life than ever. He recognized at once the old man in a corner with model ships all around him. It was Ross, the model maker he dismissed years ago as a coot. He was answering the questions of a teenage boy who held in his hand some pieces of joinery to be fastened to one of the boats under construction.

Then he was greeted by Richard Foster, a man who said he never thought he would stay on the island, but fell for the boat business and wanted to have a go at it. A few days later, he would be giving away his daughter, Rebecca, to Dave's son, Peter, at a wedding Dave thought would be extravagant.

Dave's wife and other son came on a ferry later that day and the two men went to meet them, their paces matching step for step as they strode down Main Street past the Dog. The rehearsal dinner was at the Dog, and friends and family made their way in afterwards. The wedding was held under cherry blossoms, a simple service and a small reception back at the Taylor house. In island fashion, though, the beach party lasted well into the night. It might have drawn complaints if it wasn't under the auspices of the former chief of police.

And Dave, there near a bell buoy that was wrecked on the shore, he found himself. Having followed the guidelines of civilization, he came to realize that society had led him off course and aground. Now, with his bare toes planted deep in the sand, he was content to have the stars above, because for him there was no other sign needed from heaven.

He knew that one day as he swam in raindrops, alone among them as they fell to the only pond on the island, the only collector of fresh raindrops. Focusing on the blue needle dragonfly nearing the fringe of the shoreline, he closed his eyes, the beach framed in the hold of his mind, his head sinking back to listen underneath as the rain tapped the surface.

Breaking the surface slowly with open eyes, he watched the million raindrops fall and bounce and fall again on the flat pond curving over its horizon, ending at the opposite shore laced with pink Gentian. Looking at the surface close before him, his feet dangled above the black sticks and leaves resting some twenty feet down. He swam down to them and looked up at the mirror reflecting the clouds and the raindrops joining themselves in ripples. Bubbles led back to the surface, back to the air to breathe, kissing the underside of the surface, eyes closed, floating. The only sounds the raindrops and breath and heartbeat. In those moments when the pond breathed for him, when the waves buoyed him up and let him down so gently that just the right amount of air was forced through his lungs, he realized himself in the cradle of a soul.

All he did before was study the atoms of life, not seeing the how they fit together as a whole, and he could not believe that something was there, something beyond him. All of the education, the years of studying different categories of knowledge, came together as one, flashed in his mind as eureka and left him laughing so hard that he nearly drowned. The most important realization of life is something that cannot be trivialized with a label.

And he knew then that some people share the same dream and it binds them together. Others have their own dreams and make them reality. You are what you dream, be it nightmare or heaven. The choice is yours upon waking. All you need is peace.

As a storm gathered, the backs of blown leaves turned tall trees silver as they swayed in the light cast down through mountainous clouds climbing higher. The blackened sea pushed forward beneath the rhythm of raindrops, the sound of the wind coming suddenly, thunderously, followed by the sound of rain falling hard on the water. Then came a wall of rain. Trees like dragons with rearing heads fought the oncoming squall.

Dave stayed in the water past dark, long after his hands became furrowed, and walked through the sand with wet feet, back through the pines and needled path to his bike, wiping the grit from his ankles and toes before riding off. The questions of an owl repeated. He pedaled in and out of streetlights like a dream forgotten, down to the harbor to watch the fishing fleet come in and he stayed there for an hour, pacing on the wharf above the floating dock, watching each boat back into its slip and toss a cleaned catch into barrels.

After some time the crowd splintered and he walked out on a jetty to sit against the light tower at the end. A boat coming in through the dark and light fog shined its spot lamp on the shore, outlining trees in the marsh grass, and then out on a buoy. It appeared like the boat had tunnel vision and saw only through the narrow beam as it reflected off the water and floating objects. Most of the local captains come in without a spotlight, preferring to see everything rather than just what the light shows.

That is how he left the harbor, with only running lights under clear skies and a low cloud of mist kicked up from the crashing waves on the ocean side. He heard the waves over the idling diesel. The stars, bright as flowers with petals yielding to the breeze, guided him through the silhouetted boats, yet he lingered at low throttle.

On the other side of the dunes, a full moon had risen as expected and came into view as the sails filled with the true wind. The moon still rusty, so low in the sky, the boat rounded the last mark of the harbor. The sails pulled as he set to the west, just off the wind. The moon disappeared for a moment below the dune where the lighthouse stood, though the top half shined through the windows. The lighthouse beam swung around and the flashed once, then the moon reappeared on the other side of the hill.

The small number of people who first came to the island had children who knew nowhere else and assumed it was theirs, even though others had been driven away before them. Over the years, they'd refer to themselves as "locals" and they'd prefer to have the place stay the same. Others washed ashore and stayed because of the summer or simply because and eventually considered themselves locals, too. As the island's reputation spread, tourists migrated with the weather and became hated as they intruded on the locals even though seasonal tourism generated enough money to survive on all year.

Whatever the initial reason for people to come to the island, people need people—waitstaff, fishing guides, police. The economic opportunity for migrant workers opened up, whether they were college students or professional seasonal workers. And the parallel of this microcosm and the greater whole of the planet cannot be overlooked. People immigrate to places for the same reason: economic opportunity or just a better place to live.

Dave sailed under moonlight out towards Stage Island. He didn't get close, though. He had enough of being rescued, but he tacked in the shadow of the main land radar and listened quietly as he palmed the cross he found. He thought of the girl that fell overboard, thought of tossing the cross back to the sea, but he couldn't bring himself to part with it. So he listened a while longer to the bell and horn from the buoys, remembering those sounds from the day he was stranded. Then he tacked again to sail home.

He set the sails so the helm held itself straight, turned on the autopilot, opting for a course that gave a wide berth to everything. He stayed up through the night, though occasionally dozing to be waked by the ship's clock at every half-hour. Once he awoke and the moon hid behind clouds, nothing was there around him but dark swells and a luff of the sails. Another time, he opened his eyes and saw everything so clearly in the moonlight, each cresting wave so detailed and perplexing. The clock bells came closer together and he woke to watch the moon set. The spiraling galaxy showed clearest at the darkest point of the night and the sun soon rose again.

Beyond his time, the sea will have swallowed back all of the sand and what once was will be gone. His days there have passed, there where he was, his story but the tides of a mind flowing in flashes seen only to it. With good fortune, he could live for today. Tomorrow does come, and again without us. The rain on our cheek is just spray from the sea, which weeps not for the changing of ages for it too is but a guest in the House of Time.

2488689